The Way We Really Were

The Way We Really Were:
The Golden State in the Second Great War

Edited by Roger W. Lotchin

University of Illinois Press
Urbana and Chicago

© 2000 by the Board of Trustees of the University of Illinois
All rights reserved
Manufactured in the United States of America

∞ This book is printed on acid-free paper.

Library of Congress Cataloging-in-Publication Data
The way we really were : the Golden State in the Second Great War /
edited by Roger W. Lotchin.
p. cm.
Includes bibliographical references (p.) and index.
ISBN 0-252-02505-9 (alk. paper)
ISBN 0-252-06819-x (pbk. : alk. paper)
1. World War, 1939–1945—California. I. Lotchin, Roger W.
D769.85.C2W39   2000
940.53'794—DC21   99–6190
CIP

1 2 3 4 5 C P 5 4 3 2 1

Contents

Foreword

In 1916, Henry Edwards Huntington acquired his first collection relating largely to California, a shipment of 1,500 books from Augustus S. MacDonald. The books were augmented by a collection of manuscripts relating to the vigilante movement. It could be said, of course, that Huntington himself was creating his own first collection of Californiana, as his papers and those of Collis P. Huntington, still at The Huntington, relate in very large part to the building of the railway system in the state and all the politics that went with that. In subsequent years, we have enlarged the California holdings substantially, not just in acquiring rare and not-so-rare books, but in the variety and depth of our manuscript holdings. It would be impossible in this space to describe the numerous collections that illuminate so many aspects of the history of California. We continue to obtain public records, such as the recently acquired records of the Los Angeles County Superior Court, papers relating to the First Negro Classic Ballet, the papers of Los Angeles County Supervisor Ed Edelman, the archive of the Augustin Hale family that trace their history in the state from the days of the Gold Rush, and some very substantial additions to our large collection of Jack London documents. With these and other collections we retain our commitment to be one of the leading repositories of California history.

Every now and then we have the opportunity to share the collection with the public, and such an opportunity arises with the anniversary of the Gold Rush. This will give Peter Blodgett, the curator of the California collection, the opportunity to display the many treasures in the collection that are available for scholars but rarely seen by others. In this way, we can enrich the public's understanding of the history of the state at one of its critical moments.

The individuals who have constant access to the collection are the scholars who journey to The Huntington to consult the collection. A roster of these scholars would begin with Frederick Jackson Turner, the first Americanist to use the collection. Since his day the number of scholars studying California has grown significantly; if anything, at this time there seems to be a renewal of interest in the history of the state, judging by the number of young scholars who work here. These scholars make The Huntington a lively place in which to study California history. Through informal conversation, organized seminars such as those of the Los Angeles History Group, and conferences on such subjects as the "Origins of Citriculture," there are many ways the history of the state is furthered.

When Roger Lotchin proposed a conference on the impact of World War II on California, it was natural for us to organize the meeting. The conference was made possible through the generosity of George and Marylou Boone, who have supported many projects at The Huntington that have added a great deal to its vitality as a research center.

The conference was particularly successful, presenting the very finest contemporary scholarship in California history. It is good to see the results of that conference appear in print as *The Way We Really Were,* which addresses the extremely important issue of the impact of World War II on California. It is a popular conception that the war was the defining moment in the modern history of the state. That assumption is addressed in this volume by a fascinating group of essays that roam across a very broad canvas and draw a picture of the many sides of California in that era.

Robert C. Ritchie
Director of Research
The Huntington Library

Acknowledgments

I wish to thank the contributors of the essays in this volume and especially the Huntington Library, which hosted the conference on World War II in California that led to *The Way We Really Were: The Golden State in the Second Great War.* I also wish to acknowledge the work of Theresa L. Sears, managing editor of the University of Illinois Press, for her excellent advice on the stylistic and grammatical aspects of the manuscript; the Reference Department of the Davis Graduate Library at the University of North Carolina at Chapel Hill, for finding all the obscure references that historians love to put into their work; and the several anonymous readers of the manuscript, who made very good suggestions for improvement. Finally, I would be remiss in not thanking my wife, Phyllis Lotchin, for reading the manuscript, for making shrewd and frank comments, and for sharing my work on the Golden State for nearly four decades.

This volume is dedicated to Millikin University in Decatur, Illinois, which first opened up the world to me.

Roger W. Lotchin

Introduction:
World War II in the Golden State

Roger W. Lotchin

On the ship taking dependents to the West Coast after the Imperial Japanese attack on Pearl Harbor, the passengers were up before dawn. They sat in hallways and on steps, drinking coffee, eating toast, talking, smoking, and looking at their watches. Wilsie Orjas recalled that sometime after 5:00 A.M.

> everyone went on deck to try to see land. Grayness brightened and the day grew lighter . . . blue. Due to clouds in the horizon we saw no sunrise, at least no spectacular one. But as day came we saw mountains and land!! We were travelling due north, and then swung east. Behold! There in the distance was the Golden Gate Bridge. Tears came to my eyes. I covered Jeane [her baby daughter] carefully against the cold and stood there, half frozen myself, but watching the seeming miracle of the Golden Gate.
>
> Things grew much lighter. Day was here. Planes flew back and forth and around us. Our faithful destroyers still plowed on with us. Seagulls squawked and soared over us. I could recognize Seal Rocks, the Cliff House, the residential sections leading to the beach, Parnassus Heights where my hospital training was taken. The long, green strip of Golden Gate Park. We passed in between special buoys in between the towers of the Golden Gate Bridge. Beside me stood Mrs. Mullenberg, the Colonel's wife, who was with us in the [air-raid shelter] tunnel. I pointed out all the spots of interest as we coasted along in the bay now. Coit Tower on Telegraph Hill, the Ferry Building, and finally our docks. 9:30 A.M.—on the last day of 1941. Mrs. Mullenberg and I nodded good-bye and wished each other luck.[1]

The experience of Wilsie Orjas captures much of the character of the California homefront—the mundane burdens of child care amid hope, fear, and radical mobility; the good-byes to people who had shared sacrifice and danger; the return to familiar haunts and departure from others; the bustle of war and the serenity of nature. For nearly everyone, war was a "gray" dawn that gradually "grew lighter." World War II was America's most participatory war, and California was its greatest "arsenal of democracy." The Golden State was the preeminent Garrison State, as military activities proliferated from one corner of California to the other and people from everywhere drifted in to work. Perhaps 750,000, mostly men, served as military personnel while millions more served on the homefront. Many labored fifty-hour weeks and even longer, at dangerous work. Some chauffeured officers; some trained pilots; others patrolled the beaches; some rented rooms to war workers; others covered the arsenal for the newspapers and radio stations; and a number came out of retirement, home, or school to work. Some did police work by day and guarded convoys by night. Some entertained, while others danced. The range of involvement was remarkable.[2] This first single-volume history of World War II in California intends to broaden our understanding of that experience by deepening our comprehension of familiar subjects and by introducing new ones.

The extensive popular participation on the homefront has not been amply represented in history. Although it is not comparable to the wide range of literature on the military aspects of the conflict, there is a topically limited research literature on the homefront. Women, Japanese Americans, prisoners of war, and African Americans have been the most popular topics. Yet within these categories there are considerable gaps. Other matters, such as labor, economics, Hollywood, and a few others have been studied even less fully. A vast range of experience has been largely omitted from a research literature that is now more than fifty years old. So far as I am aware, there is no single-volume history of California during World War II. Crucial individual subjects, such as technology, economics, education, water, state government and politics, city politics, ethnocultural groups, higher and lower education, and many other subjects have been inadequately addressed in articles. I have no satisfactory explanation for this phenomenon. It is completely counterintuitive that such neglect should characterize the work of historians, who, since the 1960s, have been calling for greater inclusion in the historical record.

This imbalance has set the task of this volume. The essays published here were first presented at a Huntington Library conference on the "Impact of World War II on California," held on November 10–11, 1995. They are designed specifically to furnish a book on Second World War subjects that the current literature fails to address. This agenda has led to two kinds of essays. One set seeks to broaden the range of subject and interpretive matter by ploughing new or relatively undeveloped fields; a second set expands upon the precocious literature that already exists, building in a fresh and innovative manner. Thus we have included essays on several of the more popular topics, like women and

African Americans, that handle these subjects in a novel manner. The collection covers many themes, but several stand out: (1) federal economic policy in California, (2) the dimensions of everyday life, (3) group responses to wartime challenges and changes, (4) local and state politics, (5) assimilation, (6) cross-ethnic interaction, and (7) the transformative potential of the war.

Arthur Verge sets the stage for the volume with an impressive general treatment of the day-to-day existence of a people amid total war. He does not ignore traditional topics, but discusses them within a broader context. Thus his ringing denunciation of the internment of California's Japanese Americans is joined by his explanation of the context of the event—Imperial Japanese submarine attacks off the coast, continued losses at the front, and air-raid scares. He does not overlook the female aircraft or shipyard workers, but he expands the coverage of women to include such neglected groups as the mothers and fiancées of servicemen. One of the genuine experts on World War II in California, Verge picks out the little stories that illustrate the large ones that gave life its meaning in Fortress California. The refrigerator light that broke the darkness of a blacked-out street; the resurgence of pedestrianism among a populace that could not buy cars, gas, or tires; the servicemen and girlfriends sleeping in the movie theater aisles after the last show of the morning; and the grief of a Gold Star Mother illustrate how people really lived and felt. He especially evokes the universal novelty of the war experience. His prodigious research even draws on celebrity sources such as Lana Turner, the movie star, and Bob Crawford, a pitcher for the Hollywood Stars professional baseball team. However, he focuses on the unsung heroes and heroines of the home-front. From his own mother to the black migrant war-worker, Verge speaks for the little people. Thus his essay serves as an ideal, broad introduction to *The Way We Really Were.*

As Verge notes, movies were central to the war experience. Whether servicemen were sleeping in the aisles after hours because they could find no better shelter for the night or people were trying to escape the tensions of the relentless pace of shipyard construction, movie houses claimed the presence of millions. Linda Harris Mehr has investigated what these millions experienced on the silver screen. She believes that movies were conservative and traditionalist. The U.S. government tried to enlist the movie industry in the war effort, but Hollywood tended to proceed with business as usual, serving up modest illusions that did not stray too far from the actual lives of the participants.

To the extent that Hollywood did enter the war effort, it quite literally projected a traditionalist image of American life with only slight modifications. It tried to soften the negative representations of African Americans, Hispanics, and women from their 1930s portrayal and to project a melting pot image of shared ethnocultural sacrifice, inclusiveness, acceptance, and camaraderie, though it never succeeded in altering the traditional impressions very much. A motion picture combat scene like that in *Sahara* might contain a representative sampling of American ethnicity, but the movie industry managed to insinuate its own stereotypes and its unreality as well. In other pictures, a black maid might be allowed enough managerial competence to run a white household without the guidance of her mistress, and an African American could be portrayed as patriotic enough to fight alongside other Americans in the movie *Bataan,* but demeaning stereotypes remained. Full equality was preached but seldom attained.

Nor could the Dream Factory seem to get its approach to Latin America right. On the one hand, the Hollywood "moguls," to use Mehr's phrase, wanted to develop the Latin American movie market to make up for the one that was lost in the Nazi conquest of Europe, which excluded American movies from that continent. On the other hand, the movie bosses continued to portray Latins as happy-go-lucky, dancing, rhythmic, sexual figures that many Latins considered absurd and outrageous.

Women fared little better. Wartime movies allowed women's roles to expand into formerly all-male spheres yet made it very clear that these gains were temporary and for the duration of the conflict only. When the war ended, men expected to come home to what they had left: a stable traditionalist world without too many "surprises." The movie industry retailed that prospect to the civilian audiences it served.

Thus, all of the groups made gains far short of revolutionary, but they did record some modest progress. Of course, giving minorities and women some better roles and easing the stereotypes somewhat might have been change enough to keep these two groups loyal to the war effort but traditional enough to avoid alienating the elusive majority. Mehr does not speculate on whether this approach amounted to effective propaganda, which was what the Office of War Information wanted; but she does demonstrate very clearly that Hollywood's portrayal of the war remained a compromise between the liberal aspirations of the Roosevelt administration and the biases and money-making imperatives of the Hollywood managers.

The current academic literature on World War II heavily stresses conflict. Women and blacks fought for white male jobs; Mexicans sought to work next to Americans; and zoot-suiters and sailors brawled over girlfriends, turf, and culture in the streets of Los Angeles. All this was true, yet homefront warriors played as hard as they worked and feuded. The war influenced music just as it affected other aspects of society, but in a contradictory manner. Blackouts hampered nightclubs and ballrooms; rationing curbed the availability of party clothing such as silk stockings; new autos disappeared; transit needed to access the spread-out recreation places of California cities was overwhelmed; and customary pastimes like the Rose Bowl and the racetrack were temporarily banned. Thousands of young men were sequestered in dreary cantonments far from the excitement of Venice Pier, the Ambassador Hotel, the Trianon and Copacabana dance halls, and the blues and jazz clubs on Central Avenue in Bronzeville.

On the other hand, the conflict generated enough prosperity to enable millions of Californians to patronize an increasingly commercialized musical scene. And the war created tension. People worked twelve- and fourteen-hour days, sometimes seven days a week. Everyone stood on the verge of tragedy because all had a loved one, friend, or neighbor in harm's way somewhere in the world. Millions found themselves adrift in alien waters, lonely and far from home. Between the abundance and the tension, a considerable demand for relief, and therefore music, arose. Just as important, the struggle created a perceived need for overtly martial music, which put melody to work for war.

The conflict also stimulated the migration of various ethnic, racial, and social groups to California, each bringing their own style of harmony, rhythm, and melody. Among these, African Americans, southwestern whites (or Okies), and Mexicans were the most important. All congregated in California cities and popularized their own music while replanting their own customs. Musical traditions began to influence each other as the groups massed, mingled, and mixed despite segregation. They borrowed from each other and modified the ways of mainstream music as well. Thus the influence of the war was doubly ambiguous: it simultaneously encouraged and discouraged music while instigating the transplantation of separate musical traditions, almost immediately merging them into new artistic forms.

Ronald D. Cohen discriminatingly captures this lively and diverse musical scene. Latin, hillbilly, swingbilly, blues, jazz, swing, big band, and bebop vied for audiences. Raucous, gender-dissonant western tunes such as "Pistol Packin' Mama" ("Lay that Pistol Down, Babe, Lay that Pistol Down") vied with such poignant war songs as "White Cliffs of Dover," hard-swinging big band tunes like "In the Mood" or "One O'Clock Jump," and popular numbers such as "Route Sixty-Six." They filled the airwaves, echoed through the great dance halls, accompanied the movies, floated through the USO canteens, sang from a million phonographs, and cascaded onto Central Avenue.

Yet all these developments antedated the war. In fact, James Gregory has estimated that perhaps 250,000 to 300,000 southwesterners "slipped unnoticed into California during the 1920s." The "large majority" who came to California from 1900 to 1930 migrated to cities, not to the dreary cotton fields of the

San Joaquin Valley.[3] Mexican migrants established a large colony in East Los Angeles, and blacks began an enclave along Central Avenue. All the accompanying musical styles existed in California before the war, but the conflict enriched the mixture and accelerated the mingling.

Continuity also prevailed in San Francisco politics. Although war is an eminently political activity, its homefront political implications have generally not been fully appreciated. The neglect of city and state politics is perhaps one reason that historians have exaggerated the magnitude of change in California. As I have written elsewhere, the political actors in the state's two metropolitan districts did not turn over much from 1941 to 1945, and even in smaller cities and towns like San Diego the customs of politics did not alter substantially. William Issel addresses the topic of coalition building in San Francisco city politics, stretching back to the 1920s. In this essay, Issel demonstrates that the institutional arrangements of politics did not undergo revolutionary transformation either.

San Francisco politics built toward a New Deal system of compromise between capital and labor even before the New Deal. From the Progressive Era into the twenties, the growth-oriented, organized business community dominated San Francisco politics. However, even in the twenties, when capital and labor locked horns, capital was groping toward a more inclusive system of politics based on Catholic social thought. The revival of labor strife during the Great Depression temporarily derailed this movement. However, from 1934 on, business began, first haltingly and then insistently, to incorporate unions into the governing coalition of the city. Cooperation was a considerable concession for both sides. The greatest achievements of this growing coalition in the 1930s were emerging labor peace, the 1939–40 Golden Gate International Exposition, and the two magnificent and crucial pieces of infrastructure—the Bay Bridge (1936) and the Golden Gate Bridge (1937). This coalition simply broadened during the war, creating the Bay Area Council to implement its new program. The ultimate coalition of Democrats and Republicans, management and labor, radicals and moderates, and Catholics, Jews, and Protestants was dedicated to restoring robust growth rates to the Bay Area and defeating the appeal of militants on the Left and the Right.

Although homefront historians have emphasized the social effects of the war, the economic impacts were more important. Certainly economic change triggered much of the social history that accompanied the war. Thus, Paul Rhode's essay on the economics of the war effort in the Golden State fills a crucial void in the literature of the last twenty years. Rhode probes the influence of the economic boom and the origins of California's ample share of war spending. His answers are surprising.

In the first place, he stresses that continuity was more important than change during the war. California was heavily impacted by the conflict, but not enough to warrant the term "Second Gold Rush." As he notes, the first gold rush radically changed the state, and nothing since compares with the upheaval caused by gold. Second, much of the effect of the war was "transitory." Rhode cites shipbuilding and airframe manufacture as two examples: Kaiser, Bechtel, and the other shipbuilders performed industrial wonders during the conflict, but when the Nazis and Fascists collapsed, so did mass shipbuilding. Aircraft manufacture did not decline as swiftly, but it shrank greatly; the war actually somewhat displaced California aircrafters. To achieve security, new airplane plants were moved to the interior. Thus, World War II pumped up the business, but also provided other areas with the beachhead into the industry they had fought for since the thirties.

The war was counterinuitive in another sense: the state did not gain war contracts by political pull. Rhode demonstrates with various quantitative analyses that productive capacity was the critical factor in the surge of California defense industries. Before the war, California had already acquired a stranglehold on the airframe industry, which large British aircraft orders had solidified even before American entry. When the United States came in, defense contracts tended to go to the geographic areas with an established track record. There was nothing uniquely Californian about this distribution. The state had no such proven record in shipbuilding. However, Henry Kaiser soon gave it one and simultaneously provided the Maritime Commission with a reason to flood so many ship contracts into California that the state was soon awash in them.

Sarah S. Elkind did not find a similar ending to the story of the environment. Wars obviously drain the physical and mental resources of a nation, and World War II was no exception. It drew briskly on natural resources and greatly polluted both natural and artificial ones. It voraciously consumed scrap iron and iron ore for ships, tanks, trucks, and weapons; huge amounts of copper for ammunition and communications wire; agricultural products for food and fiber; and bauxite for aluminum airplane skins. Immense quantities of petroleum were required to fuel a mechanized war, as were rare materials for high-quality steel and lumber to house 16 million servicemen and servicewomen and to use in myriad other war-generated products, including several hundred thousand coffins.

Pollution accompanied this depletion. The production of synthetic rubber supposedly introduced smog to Southern California, and the population swollen by war workers nearly overwhelmed the sewer capacities of several California arsenals. Even cities with new treatment facilities, like San Francisco, strained to meet the demand, while less well served ones, like Los Angeles, simply polluted their ocean beaches. The conflict almost exhausted San Diego's water supply and war everywhere gobbled up land for bases and factories. Waterfronts in San Diego, Long Beach, Vallejo, South San Francisco, Oakland, and Richmond were rapidly commandeered for shipbuilding and military transportation. These areas quickly became the sites for the marvels of ship production, only to be just as rapidly abandoned in 1945 to rust, rot, and desuetude. The war strained the environment to provide materials and to cope with pollution. Yet in an age of sensitivity about natural resources, almost no one has investigated the impact of history's most important war on the environment.

Fortunately, Elkind has begun to solve this historiographical puzzle. The war affected many parts of California's environment, but oil was perhaps most important. Nonetheless, the war did not have an appreciable effect on the management of California oil resources. As Elkind explains in her essay, American energy policy since the 1920s had been dominated by the major oil companies and the states. This arrangement allowed for hasty extraction from sites like Signal Hill, where wooden oil derricks huddled so tightly together that they sometimes overlapped. Harold Ickes, the secretary of the interior during the New Deal, tried to assert more national control in the name of conservation, preventing pollution of Southland beaches, and national defense. The prelude to the war heightened these concerns, as did the actual outbreak.

World War II seemed to suggest the need for greater conservation measures, but in reality it increased the leverage of the oil companies and states over this critical resource. Total war necessitated all-out oil production, especially for the heavily mechanized war fought by the United States. This imperative undermined any attempt to assert national control over petroleum. Oddly enough, unpopular rationing did too. The exceptional record of productivity by the industry during the conflict also hindered change after the conflict. Thus the war accelerated oil production, as did the cold war and the era of suburbanization. Predictably, the great offshore oil controversy left the petroleum industry firmly in charge, as they had been since the 1920s.

The war's impact on the Golden State can also be measured by the changes that were wrought among its ethnic groups, including Italian Americans, who have only recently been added to the ethnic agenda of California history by scholars such as Rose Scherini, Julia Lothrop, Stephen Cox, and now Gary R. Mormino (who collaborated with the late George E. Pozzetta on the essay that appears in this volume). Before the war, some Italians were spectacularly successful in economic life, although many had not climbed above manual labor. The Italian community in California was heavily insular and pro-Fascist. The

Second Great War accentuated the prosperity while destroying the insularity and Fascism. The government designated unnaturalized Italians as enemy aliens, which unjustly put all noncitizen Italians in the position of having to prove themselves. This they did with remarkable precocity. In addition, the war uprooted rural residents, leading them to work in urban war industries, brought newcomers into the community, encouraged outmigration, took military personnel away from familiar neighborhoods, encouraged intermarriage, and divided families. When the war ended, many Italian Americans rode their VA loans from their center-city homes in North Beach to suburbia. Mormino and Pozzetta insist that the war brought prosperity, wider experiences, greater public acceptance, and, ultimately, mainstreaming, on a considerable scale. Thus, the largest European-derived California ethnic group experienced considerable change.

The exclusion of Chinese Americans from the historiography of the homefront is just as inexplicable as the exclusion of the Italians. From 1848 on, they had built railroads, mined for gold, planted viniculture, and cooked in a thousand western ranches and camps. Their presence triggered a bitter struggle with West Coast labor, and they were the victims of savage physical assaults at places like Rock Creek, Wyoming, and Los Angeles. In 1882, they became the first nationality group ever excluded from emigrating to the United States. World War II was an immediate concern for Chinese Americans too; the Pacific War was fought in large part to rescue their homeland from the Imperial Japanese. Yet few established scholars have made the World War II experience of the California Chinese the subject of their research.

As in the case of women, World War II laid the foundations for the ultimate Chinese advance. Because of widespread discrimination, they were ambivalent about America, wondering whether to identify with their ancestors' homeland or their own. The war resolved this quandary by giving the Chinese a chance to affirm both. It also provided them with an entrée. Chinese Americans were accepted into the services, mostly on an integrated basis. At home, the uniform gave Chinese men a legitimacy they had not had in America before and provided them with crucial entitlements like the G.I. Bill and the mortgage benefits of the Veterans Administration. Economically, the war helped the Chinese escape the ghetto economy. No longer as far removed from the mainstream, Chinatown now shared the most crucial events of its time with those beyond the confines of that settlement. As other foreign wars had done for other ethnic groups, the Second World War allowed these ethnics to claim America while also supporting their homeland. Unlike the Irish and Germans in World War I, the Chinese were not forced to choose. In his contribution to this volume, K. Scott Wong is careful not to overtax his evidence. As he puts it, "The war

left Chinese Americans at the threshold of social mobility and increased assimilation." But the threshold was a lot closer than ever before.

Kevin Allen Leonard, in a most original essay, has provided a comparative
look at the war experience of Hispanics, Japanese Americans, and African
Americans. The comparative mode is an unusual and welcome approach both
for World War II ethnic-group history and for all immigration and ethnic-
group history. Leonard also breaks with custom in another way. The few comparative histories of World War II ethnic groups that have been written stress
the conflict between them. Scholars such as John Stack, Ronald Bayor, and
Charles Trout have found tension between Irish, Jews, Italians, Yankees, and
Germans in Boston and New York before and during the war.[4] However, in
California, Leonard has discovered that intergroup cooperation, cross-ethnic
interaction, and amity outweighed the conflict between groups whose rivalry
would seem to have been almost intuitive. Although the war did generate fric-
tions between groups, as in the Zoot Suit Riots in 1943, the conflict also triggered countercurrents.[5] As Leonard demonstrates, the problems of race and
ethnicity were attacked head-on by groups demanding fair play for Japanese
Americans, equal opportunity for African Americans in the workplace, and
equitable treatment for Hispanics. The war also brought to prominence leaders like Leon Washington, Charlotta Bass, and Floyd Covington, who fought
for justice from the majority and cooperation among minorities. Leonard
shows teamwork between Japanese Americans and blacks to offset the tensions
arising from competition for housing stock, stores, and neighborhood turf. He
calls them "brothers under the skin," quoting Carey McWilliams. As Leonard
puts it, "World War II did lead some Americans to realize that all of their nation's 'racial problems' were similar."

The encouraging beginnings described in this volume did not lead to a wholesale transformation of the status of any of these ethnic groups during the war
or anytime soon after. Nonetheless, wartime cooperation laid the foundation
for the advance of each of them and, as Leonard writes, "set the stage for the
civil rights struggles of the 1950s and 1960s."

Jacqueline R. Braitman has found similar coalition building in women's
politics. She points out that women made very little *electoral* progress during
World War II but advanced in other spheres instead. Braitman rejects the
notion that any single decade was crucial. Rather, each decade built on the
advances of the previous one. For example, the campaigns of Upton Sinclair
and Culbert Olsen and the 1937 California fifty-fifty rule that split party offices
by gender greatly energized California's political women. Despite paltry electoral progress during the Second World War, women prospered as precinct
organizers, campaign managers, officers in the two political parties, advisers,

and political speakers. They also participated in organizations like the League of Women Voters and other female groups, where they honed skills that could ultimately be transferred to the wider partisan arena.

In these capacities, women grew progressively more influential in party politics. Women helped make Earl Warren governor in 1942 and helped elect liberal Democrats such as Helen Gahagan Douglas and Chet Holifield to Congress. The groundwork laid during the twenties, the Great Depression, and World War II ultimately led to much greater gains for women in the fifties, sixties, and seventies. Therefore, World War II does not represent a major turning point for women; as in the case of San Francisco's wartime coalition politics, women continued to build upon previous successes.

The essayists in this volume have all tried to present a new discussion of history's most important war in what has come to be America's most important state. Seven of the ten essays represent new directions in scholarship; the others are fresh approaches to traditional topics. Nonetheless, this volume has not covered every topic that could be discussed. We still need more foundation work in fields such as city and state politics; the history of numerous other ethnic groups (Armenians, Scandinavians, Canadians, Jews, Filipinos, Koreans, Irish, Germans, southern whites, and midwesterners, for starters); the impact of the war on the hydraulic society; the implications, many of them fascinating, of the war on higher and lower education; the impact of the war on unions, labor, and work; the influence of the war on children and seniors; and the impact of the war on what was for years the state's leading industry, agriculture. And these are only some of the many areas that remain to be thoroughly investigated.

Still, this volume delves into many new areas and examines several old ones in novel ways. Ronald Cohen provides fresh insights into the popular culture of the era. Several other essays bear on the topic of diversity. Kevin Leonard documents some attempts at ethnocultural accommodation among several minority groups. By contrast, Scott Wong studies the first important steps toward acceptance of the Chinese by the ethnic majority, and Gary Mormino and George Pozzetta document the flight from ethnicity by the Italians. Jacqueline Braitman demonstrates the important advances made by women, and Sarah Elkind and Paul Rhode show how the actions of the nation-state have enriched yet complicated the economic life of the state at the expense of its environment. William Issel demonstrates how the class conflicts of the 1920s and 1930s turned into the class accommodation of the postwar era. And, most important, all of these questions—whether ethnocultural, gender, economic, popular cultural, or political—bear on the issue of transformation. World War II laid the foundations, or built on pre-existing foundations, for extensive change in California, but it did not create revolutionary change. This first single-volume history on World War II in California is a good beginning, refreshed by the insights of younger scholars and tempered by the understanding of senior ones.

Notes

1. Wilsie Orjas, "Where History Was Made," Regional History Office, Bancroft Library, University of California at Berkeley, 174–77.

2. For an introduction to the extent of war participation, see Roger W. Lotchin, ed., *Fortress California at War: San Francisco, Los Angeles, Oakland, and San Diego,* special issue of *Pacific Historical Review* 63:3 (Aug. 1994); Arthur Verge, *Paradise Transformed: Los Angeles during the Second World War* (Dubuque, Iowa, 1993); Marilynn S. Johnson, *The Second Gold Rush: Oakland and the East Bay in World War II* (Berkeley, Calif., 1993).

3. James Gregory, *American Exodus: The Dust Bowl Migration and Okie Culture in California* (New York, 1989), 9–10.

4. Ronald Bayor, *Neighbors in Conflict: The Irish, Germans, Jews, and Italians of New York City, 1929–1941* (Baltimore, 1978); John F. Stack, *International Conflict in an American City: Boston's Irish, Italians, and Jews, 1935–1944* (Westport, Conn., 1979); Charles H. Trout, *Boston, the Great Depression, and the New Deal* (New York, 1977).

5. I have avoided using the customary term "Anglo" to describe the other participants in this riot because it is not specific enough to describe western whites at a time when ethnicity was still much in evidence, both in the West and the rest of the United States. The Okies, for example, were not very much like other whites in the West and were themselves subjected to considerable bigotry (Gregory, *American Exodus,* 78–113). As Gary Mormino and the late George Pozzetta show in this volume, Italians were not categorizable under the heading "Anglo" or "Anglo Saxon." However appropriate these terms may seem to western historians, to categorize all western Caucasians as "Anglo" or "Anglo-Saxon" would seem to ignore a wealth of ethnic scholarship that contends that American ethnic groups retained marked differences well into the twentieth century and by 1941 had not melted down into one homogeneous mass. I think that this process is much farther along by 1999, but in 1941 it still had a long way to go.

1

Daily Life in Wartime California

Arthur Verge

Roses are Red, Violets are blue,
Sugar is sweet, remember?

Walter Winchell

Sometimes it's the simple things that we remember most. That first kiss, that last good-bye. For many Americans, World War II began simply with the ringing of a phone. "Have you heard? Can you believe it?" Others received the devastating news of the Japanese attack on Pearl Harbor over the family radio set: "We interrupt this program . . ."

From the shouts of newsboys on street corners to suddenly disrupted church services, Americans learned in simple fashion that their lives, their families' lives, their neighbors' lives, the life of the kid down the street was forever changed by the events of December 7, 1941.[1]

In the aftermath of Pearl Harbor, as much of the country steeled itself for a two-front war overseas, Americans on both the East and West Coasts braced themselves for possible surprise attacks. Given their state's geographic location and its possession of numerous defense plants and military installations, many Californians felt particularly vulnerable.[2]

Most people in California reacted to the advent of war in a positive manner; many patriotically signed their lives over to "Uncle Sam," donated blood, or spent long, unpaid hours aiding civil defense. Others, frustrated with the attack on Pearl Harbor, took their anxiety out on those of Japanese ancestry. While local and federal law enforcement agencies began large roundups of "leaders" in the Japanese communities, some citizens took it upon themselves to shout at, and sometimes physically confront, individuals who appeared to be Japanese. Stunned by this sudden animosity, many inside and outside the Asian community saw parallels between racial persecutions in Nazi Germany and their own treatment in California. So concerned was California Governor Culbert Olsen, in whose state more than 75 percent of all Japanese Americans resided, that he considered issuing a proclamation asking all Japanese to keep off the streets until their "loyalty" to the United States had been established. Fortunately, not only for the Japanese community but for Asians in general, the governor decided against the proclamation, fearing an increase in the already growing racial tensions and a large drop-off in much-needed vegetable and seafood production.[3]

Regardless, the die of popular suspicion and distrust of those of Japanese ancestry was cast, and slowly but inexorably the Japanese-American community began to be separated from the rest of "loyal" America.

The shock of Pearl Harbor hit Californians particularly hard. The now legendary Pacific fleet, whose capital ships filled Pearl Harbor's "battleship row," had been home-berthed since 1919 within California's three main naval stations (San Diego, Long Beach–San Pedro, and San Francisco–Alameda). Redeployed to Pearl Harbor in May 1940 as a forward defense against growing Japanese aggression in the Pacific, the fleet left behind numerous family members in California. With the fleet now severely damaged by the Japanese surprise attack, those living on the Pacific Coast feared that they might be the next victims.

In the days immediately following the Pearl Harbor attack, newspapers throughout the West Coast fanned the public's fears with graphic maps and details which specifically emphasized that the Hawaiian Islands were only 2,550 miles away from California. As fear mounted, rumors quickly proliferated. The most frequent object of these rumors were Japanese Americans. Japanese gardeners would allegedly be discovered in a nearby California town or city cleverly trimming lawn bushes into directional markers for that soon-to-come Japanese air attack. Of course such rumors could never be verified. Other Japanese Americans were accused of slowly poisoning the state's vegetable and seafood supply. And on and on it went. Rumormongering, a plague in almost any war, continued long after the Japanese Americans were interned. Fed up with such public fearmongering, a popular *San Francisco Chronicle* columnist, Herb Caen, began running "Rumor of the Day" bulletins in his column. Even the most fearful Californian could not help but appreciate the absurdity of such bylines as, "Rumor of the Day: Golden Gate Locked, Convoy Trapped!"[4]

Nonetheless, the fears of enemy attack remained real and somewhat warranted. While the Japanese surface fleet had been stretched to capacity in carrying out the naval and air attacks on Pearl Harbor, its submarine forces were a different matter. Deploying seven of their fifteen new long-range, I-class submarines along the American Pacific Coast, Japanese naval planners initiated a series of attacks on West Coast shipping beginning on December 18, 1941. While these submarine operations remained limited in scope and, from a military standpoint, relatively ineffective, they did serve notice to Californians that the war was real and nearby.[5] In one instance, residents along the central coast of California were awakened on the morning of December 22, 1941, with the sound of a loud explosion followed by the jolting of doors and windows. The first blast, felt as far as thirteen miles inland in San Luis Obispo, was later attributed to the concussion of a Japanese long-lance torpedo that had missed its target. The same submarine, which had failed to sink two American oil tankers in two previous attacks, finally succeeded an hour and half later, sinking the Union Oil Tanker *Montebello*. Witnesses in the central coastal community of Cambria reported seeing the ship "upended like a telephone pole" before quickly disappearing beneath the surface. Fortunately, all thirty-six crew members were able to make it to lifeboats and survived the harrowing ordeal.[6]

Japanese Americans on the West Coast were not as fortunate. The very day of the attack on the *Montebello,* the latest issue of *Life* magazine hit newsstands. Included in the new issue was a "helpful" article, captioned with illustrated photographs, on how to tell "Japs from Chinese."[7]

As sporadic Japanese submarine attacks continued to hinder Allied vessels plying West Coast waters, jitters concerning a Japanese air attack increased among those living inland.[8] Seeking to keep the public calm and fully prepared in the event of an aerial bombing, civil defense planners organized a wide range of civilian volunteer defense programs. The response in California was tremendous, as thousands signed up to serve as plane spotters, air-raid wardens, ambulance drivers, blackout wardens, firefighters, and first aid providers. In Los Angeles it was estimated that nearly one out of ten city residents was involved in some form of civilian volunteer defense by 1943.[9]

Spurred on by such news headlines as "ENEMY WARPLANES SPOTTED OFF SAN FRANCISCO," the transistion to war-readiness throughout California was swift. Factory windows were immediately painted over and around-the-clock work shifts were implemented. Anti-aircraft-gun emplacements quickly sprang up throughout cities and towns, especially around defense plants and military bases. Miles of barbed wire fences were laid along coastal shores to slow any enemy invasion. Large barrage balloons flew overhead, their steel cables designed to entangle any low-flying enemy aircraft. To confuse any high flying bomber overhead, Hollywood set-designers in Southern California carefully camouflaged the region's aircraft plants, going so far as to put fake grass and wooden cows on the roofs where workers below continued busily to assemble the fighters and bombers that were intended to bring the war to the enemy.

As air-raid wardens scanned the skies, lifeguards and civil defense volunteers patrolled the beaches. Everywhere in California there seemed to be trains and trucks full of young troops being hurridly transported to some unknown destination. Unlike World War I, a distant conflict, where parades and cheers sent off the participants, the Second World War was greeted with few illusions. Haunted by the carnage of World War I and hardened by the ten long years of the Great Depression, the American people entered this war without frivolity. Resignation, determination, and an attitude of "we're all in this together" became the prevailing spirit upon entering the Second World War.

Given the possibility of enemy air attacks, military and civilian defense planners along the Pacific Coast began instituting nightly blackouts. The first of these on the West Coast happened unplanned on the evening of December 10, 1941. As air-raid sirens sounded the possible approach of enemy aircraft, Californians up and down the coast found themselves sharing the first of many collective homefront experiences. While an earlier night's siren alert turned out to be a false alarm, the following night's planned blackout proved to be nothing short of disastrous. Throughout California's cities, despite being fore-warned, many store owners and building managers neglected to turn off their lights. Civic authorities fared little better, as numerous streetlights continued to shine. One air-raid warden complained, "The city lights of San Francisco were so bright, you could see the glow in Tokyo."[10] In contrast, large numbers of war workers proved to be too conscientious as they left work, turning off their headlights in compliance with blackout restrictions as they began their evening drive home. The resultant carnage was so bad in Los Angeles that doctors in the city's Central Hospital, operating among dimmed lanterns, handled eighty-six major injuries in the first four hours of the blackout.[11]

With the high number of civilian causalities and the loss of much-needed war production as factories shut down, military and civilian defense planners were compelled to rethink their blackout plans. Since war production was so essential, factories throughout California were immediately allowed to continue around-the-clock production. To reduce the unusually high number of traffic accidents and also to ease already difficult wartime conditions, civil defense officials eventually eased blackout policies and added the "dim-out." Compared to a blackout, which required the complete extinguishing of all lights everywhere, dim-outs covered only areas visible from the ocean, requiring all lights that could be seen from the sea to be dimmed or extinguished to prevent the shoreline silhouetting of American ships.

The dim-outs certainly allowed more freedom of movement. Cars that need-ed to travel in darkness did so with shielded headlights. Even ocean-side amuse-ment parks were allowed to continue operations under dim-out conditions. However, the West Coast remained on constant alert, and the sound of air-raid sirens signaled the immediate change to blackout conditions.

Unfortunately, things didn't always go as planned. Even though the evening of May 3, 1942, marked the Bay Area's eighth blackout since Pearl Harbor, air-raid wardens were forced to break scores of windows to put out lights left unattended. Even a large aerial beacon in East Oakland continued to revolve, brightly lighting up the night sky. Reflecting on the city's performance, San Francisco Civil Defense Chief Jack Helms complained, "It was terrible."[12] Yet some humor was found. In one part of the darkened city of San Francisco, air-raid wardens noticed periodic flashes of light emitting from an otherwise darkened apartment. These flashes would come and go and would last for varying durations. Fearing that the flashes were coded messages being dis-played by enemy agents, police and civil defense officials raided the apartment only to find a stunned group of partygoers. Apparently, the blackout alert went into effect in the midst of the party. With the lights turned out, the celebrants continued to party and the culprit of the periodic flashes turned out to be the apartment's refrigerator, which emitted its bright flash of light every time its door was swung open by someone in search of libation.

In truth, nearly all did their best to comply with blackout procedures. It was difficult to make sure that every lamp, every neon store sign, and every street-light was extinguished in such a large urban area. But most of the public, and certainly all of the blackout wardens, worked diligently to see that lights were out. Herb Caen, the *San Francisco Chronicle* columnist, noted the city's patri-otism: "The day after a blackout here, Bay Area post offices do practically noth-ing from morning to night except sell bonds and stamps."[13]

As people contended with blackouts and a growing array of federal wartime restrictions, the state's besieged Japanese Americans found themselves under increasing public attack. Despite large-scale Japanese-American protestations of loyalty to the United States and the Allied war effort, leading West Coast politicians and military leaders continued to call for their removal in ever more strident rhetoric. Bending to these demands, President Franklin D. Roosevelt on February 19, 1942, ordered the evacuation and internment of all Japanese Americans from the West Coast, claiming it was "for their protection." Un-able to fight the tide of suspicion of complicity with the Japanese war effort, over one hundred thousand, a majority of them American citizens, saw their businesses, homes, and way of life quickly vanish.[14]

While civil libertarians continued to deem President Roosevelt's Executive Order 9066 "unconstitutional," public support swelled following a Japanese submarine shelling attack on an oil storage area in Ellwood, twelve miles north of Santa Barbara. The attack, which took place only six days after the order's announcement, did little physical damage. However, it was seen by many, especially in California, as a vindication of the decision to remove Japanese Americans from the coast.

Despite the ineffectiveness of the shelling attack, fears of an imminent Japanese attack ran rampant in wartime California. Recalling that trepidation, the screenwriter and actor Buck Henry humorously wrote, "We imagined parachutes dropping. We imagined the hills of Hollywood on fire. We imagined hand-to-hand combat on Rodeo Drive."[15]

On the evening of February 25, 1942, two nights after the submarine attack on Ellwood, army officials warned civil defense leaders that Japanese aircraft were seen approaching the Los Angeles area. Shortly thereafter, at 2:25 A.M., the regions's anti-aircraft batteries went into full action, guns ablaze, firing into the searchlit skies against the incoming enemy aircraft. While some plane spotters would later claim that they had indeed seen an enemy plane, others blamed jittery nerves and a wayward weather balloon for the spectacular fireworks show that is remembered today in a humorous vein as "The Battle of Los Angeles." While the raid's authenticity is still debated, no bombs were dropped and no planes were shot down.[16]

As Californians in the early months of the war steeled themselves against possible enemy attacks and a continuing saga of negative news from the war front, a glimmer of sunshine enveloped the state with the increasing infusion of massive amounts of federal defense dollars. This government largesse, which was largely expended in the building and development of defense plants and military bases, lifted California's economy out of a fiscal depression into a full economic "boom." So great were the expenditures that the average personal income of Californians rose dramatically, tripling from just over an aggregate of 5 billion dollars in 1939 to approximately 15 billion dollars in 1945.[17] Thus, with the federal government spending more than one out of every eleven wartime dollars in California, hundreds of thousands of Americans rushed to the state to take advantage of what one historian has aptly called California's "Second Gold Rush."[18]

Sybil Lewis, a black woman from Oklahoma, recalled the message sweeping through her town in the early days of the war. "'Go west,' that was the theme. Everything is great in California, all doors are open, no prejudice, good jobs, plenty of money."[19] In what became the greatest mass migration in American history, millions of Americans uprooted themselves and moved away from small towns in the heartland and farm belts to large urban areas that offered a wide range of employment opportunities.

California proved particularly attractive to wartime migrants. Not only was the state blessed with great weather and natural scenery, high paying jobs were plentiful in California's burgeoning aircraft plants and shipyards. As hundreds of thousands poured into the state's urban areas, municipal authorities throughout California soon found themselves overwhelmed. Adding to such woes as congested streets, overtaxed sewer lines, and overcrowded schools were the additional arrivals of hundreds of thousands of troops. San Diego's population, for example, doubled in the short space of three years.[20]

When asked what the early days of wartime California were like, a common response from those who experienced it was, "It all happened so fast." The rapidity of change in wartime California was indeed stunning. Californians quickly experienced a transition from peace to world war, saw bread lines turn into employment lines, and witnessed vacant fields transformed into enormous aircraft plants and military bases. Sausalito, a once quiet two-mile stretch of marsh and tideland, was transformed seemingly overnight into the Marinship Shipyard. Developers of Marinship, the Bechtel Corporation, worked quickly to create this "instant shipyard." Workers hammered more than 25,000 pilings into the marsh fill and laid down miles of underground pipe that carried water, oxygen, compressed air, and acetylene. In addition, a highway and a railroad line were relocated to aid the shipyard's production. Incredibly, in less than seven months after plans were drawn up, Marinship delivered its first vessel.[21] Just as stunning was Henry Kaiser's new shipyard complex in nearby Richmond. Inauspiciously begun in late December 1940, when a bulldozer disappeared into the new site's boggy marshland, the shipyard would become the world's most productive in World War II. Whereas Richmond had been a small, sleepy community of 23,000 in 1941, the Kaiser Shipyard itself would employ more than 100,000 workers by 1944. So efficient and productive was the yard that it turned out an incredible 747 ships.[22]

The dramatic changes wrought by the war touched every part of California. From as far south as San Diego, site of a large naval base and naval training center, to the internment camp of Tule Lake in the far reaches of Northern California, to Southern California's vast desert region in which more than one million troops were trained in combat maneuvers, the war's impact throughout the state was prolific and permanent. Longtime locals looked often in disbelief at the great changes taking place around them. Orange groves quickly disappeared, giving way to factories and emergency government housing projects. Streets became brightly filled with southerners, cowboys, farm girls, sailors, marines, soldiers, WACs and WAVEs, bureaucrats, and schemers. Everyone, it seemed, had come from somewhere else.

New arrivals often took a quick liking to California. The historian John D. Weaver reflected, "I can still remember the faces of the sailors and the Marines walking into the winter sunshine at [Los Angeles'] Union Station and just peering at the skies in amazement."[23] Also amazing to new arrivals, especially in light of the recent Great Depression, was the tremendous availability of work. Opal Verge Winters recalled that her husband, Paul Verge, was immediately hired by a Bay Area shipyard as a journeyman electrician despite the fact that he didn't know AC from DC.[24] Women and minorities particularly benefited during the war, as previously closed factory doors were swung open to them both by need and by President Franklin Roosevelt's June 25, 1941, Executive Order 8802, which barred discrimination in federal defense industry work.

The change in California's industrial engagement proved equally dramatic. Women and minorities entered the state's workforce in record numbers. Despite the initial resistance on the part of some companies, the necessities of world war forced the change. This development, in turn, afforded all workers the opportunity to earn good wages while fully contributing to the war effort.

So desperate was the need for all-out production that many war workers willingly worked twelve- to fourteen-hour days, seven days a week. To increase production further, defense manufacturers actively sought out and hired retirees and the disabled; they also created programs that provided child care for housewives with children as well as after-school programs that allowed teenage boys to work in the defense plants.

To meet the new demands brought on by the large-scale employment of women, particularly in Southern California, manufacturers took to redesigning their plants to expedite production. The changes proved beneficial not only to the women but to all the workers, as companies introduced such back-saving devices as chain hoists and load lifts. War production was also increased with the incorporation of conveyor belts, streamlined tools, and worker rest stations.

Despite such innovations, most war production work remained dangerous and dirty. Women workers who ignored safety regulations requiring the bundling up of long hair, for example, risked fatal scalping by plant machinery. Women also had to deal with occasionally crude and rude male co-workers. Regardless, women war workers proudly "carried their weight" throughout California's numerous defense plants and shipyards. Years later, these women would be pleased to recount their participation in the assembling, drilling, and riveting of the ships and planes that helped turn the tide of the war. A few women would tell their children and grandchildren of how they met their husbands, as it was not uncommon for female aircraft workers to hide little notes, messages, and phone numbers in the planes they assembled in hopes of hearing from the pilots who flew them.

While war workers earned record wages, they confronted a wide host of problems on the homefront. In the early months of the war, for example, many workers found themselves unable to purchase such necessities as groceries and dry goods, since many stores and banks kept only nine-to-five hours. Defense manufacturers, fearing a loss of valuable worker hours, labored diligently to keep local stores and banks open as long as possible. To meet the recreational needs of defense plant workers, companies created bowling and softball leagues, and to accommodate its swing shift workers, Douglas Aircraft in Santa Monica built a movie theater that played movies twenty-four hours a day.

As more and more migrants and troops poured into wartime California, housing became one of the state's most pressing needs. Often unable to build new housing, given the shortages of metals and lumber needed for the war effort, federal and state authorities encouraged homeowners to rent out any vacant rooms. Houses often came to resemble miniature hotels, with people constantly coming and going. Some newly arriving migrants, short of money, resorted to living in their cars. These workers often preferred the night shift, which allowed them to sleep during the warmth of the day. Other workers took to "hot bedding," which allowed them an eight-hour sleep shift before the next shift member used the same bed for his or her slumber. Still others lived in tents and trailers. The situation had become so bad outside the shipyards of Richmond that federal and state housing authorities had to make repeated raids to remove war workers from makeshift shanties, such as used chicken-shacks. In addition, health authorities had to deal with the possible rapid spread of communicable diseases, given the overcrowded living conditions and adjacent open privies in the migrant ghettoes.[25]

Besides overcrowded housing and streets, municipal authorities had to contend with a rapidly decaying environment. While such exigencies would be expected in all-out industrial mobilization, the growing level of air and water pollution raised concerns that the civilian war-production effort could be completely thwarted by the spread of environmentally linked diseases. The fears were not unwarranted. In Los Angeles, downtown buildings visible from a half mile away completely disappeared in the haze of dark thick smoke that was later traced to a rubber production plant. Air quality in the Los Angeles basin became so bad that in 1943 a new term was coined, "smog," representing the combined words of smoke and fog.[26] Along the Los Angeles coastline, beachgoers watched in stunned disbelief as large bubbling gushers frequently emerged off shore as overtaxed sewer lines broke open and spewed out their contents. The police chief of Hermosa Beach was so upset that he personally drove up to the city's sewage treatment plant and threatened to arrest the plant's chief operator.[27] The sewage problem became so massive that the city was forced to close its popular beaches for more than two and a half years.[28]

Like all other Americans, Californians had to deal with wartime rationing. Such taken-for-granted commodities as meat, butter, sugar, and gasoline all came under strict federal rationing. Under these laws, all facets of daily life were affected. Women could no longer purchase silk stockings, the silk being needed for the production of parachutes. Metal toys, once commonly found under Christmas trees, went the way of Fourth of July fireworks shows. In response, many on the homefront proved colorfully resourceful. Some women, seeking to remain fashionable, used "pancake makeup" and an eyebrow pencil to fake the appearance of silk stockings. A few meat lovers turned to "Victory Meat" (horse meat) as a substitute for their beloved steaks. And almost all in wartime California used vegetables from home-tended "Victory Gardens."

Adding to rationing woes was the fact that even if one had the necessary coupons to qualify for a rationed commodity, the product was often unavailable. While polite buyers understood and left it at that, some angry consumers took to waving their coupons and money, demanding the items. These individuals would be quickly turned away with the rejoinder, "What's the matter? Don't you know there's a war going on?"

While black market activities did exist, illegal trafficking was heavily frowned upon. Wartime newspaper readers seemed to delight in pictures of skiers having their cars ticketed for unnecessary gas use; also popular was reading about the number of physicians' cars that were found by reporters to be parked at local racetracks. Readers smiled at the numbers, knowing that doctors' vehicles were intended for emergency use and therefore were granted unlimited gasoline. Many Californians, however, went beyond the dictates of rationing, proudly going without for the cause of victory.

As Californians sacrificed the familiar taste of sugar and butter, they also took up walking and public transport in record numbers. Municipalities throughout California continually scrambled to put more streetcars and buses on the roads. Faced with the loss of drivers and conductors to the war effort and to higher paying defense industries, public transportation agencies hired a growing number of women and minorities. While a few transit officials fought against their employment, others gladly welcomed the change, arguing that it was both overdue and necessary.[29] Still, when it was announced that women would be hired as conductors in Los Angeles, the *Los Angeles Times* blared in a front-page headline, "Now It's Women Streetcar Conductors!"[30]

Given California's many military bases and the relatively long distances between the urban centers of San Diego, Los Angeles, and San Francisco, the practice of picking up GI hitchhikers became commonplace. War veterans would fondly recall the kindness extended to them, including instances when motorists would go out of their way, often with a nearly empty gas tank, in order to help a soldier get to his destination. Other veterans would remember finding the food or drinks at a restaurant paid for by an anonymous patron.

Wartime California, as a whole, frequently resembled a large, bustling waiting room. Urban areas were crowded as service personnel jammed into the cities in search of fun before shipping out. Patricia Livermore recalled that in wartime San Diego, "Every night, not just weekends, if you went anywhere from Twelfth and Broadway to Sixteenth and Broadway and you looked down to the harbor, you'd see a sea of white hats. From curb to curb, you could see nothing but sailors."[31] So swamped were city centers that even with confirmed reservations, hotel rooms were next to impossible to come by. Military officials, troops on final leave, wives and girlfriends arriving for what was sometimes a truly final good-bye, all commandeered what they could with "orders," money, booze, and tearful stories. When hotels were overbooked, service personnel took to sleeping in hotel lobbies, on park benches, even in the aisles of movie theaters thanks to cooperative theater owners, who allowed them to sleep following the conclusion of the late show.

With the massive crowds, excitement permeated the air. Despite the exigencies of war, fun was not rationed. Clubs up and down the coast were packed. Jitterbugging, later called swing dancing, was the wartime rage. The music of Glenn Miller, Count Basie, Tommy Dorsey, Duke Ellington, and the Andrews Sisters wafted deep into the night. Romance was everywhere. It was often fast and furious, as anxious young people, suddenly thrown together by the calamity of world war, lived for the moment.

For those not interested in wartime romance, there were plentiful opportunities for gambling and prostitution throughout California's large cities. Often when residents complained of the flourishing and open illegalities, military and civic leaders frantically pointed out the severe lack of available police personnel. In fact, prostitution was tacitly tolerated by military and police authorities in San Diego, Los Angeles, and San Francisco, since the local and military police already had their hands full containing brawls, assaults, and other war-related violent activities.[32]

Most GIs on leave preferred the companionship of a "nice gal." Patricia Livermore, who spent much of the war working six nights a week as a club photographer covering San Diego's twenty-one downtown night spots, recalled, "The servicemen were not looking for sex as much as for companionship. Most of them were small-town boys and they were used to the girl-next-door type, and that's what they wanted—someone to talk to, someone to dance with, a companion, a friend."[33] USO clubs, Red Cross dances, tea parties, and movie studio tours all flourished in wartime California. Favorite among GIs was a visit to the Hollywood Canteen, where they could dance with a Hollywood starlet.

Also popular was attending the taping of a radio comedy show. Particularly popular were radio shows hosted by Jack Benny and Bob Hope. If GIs couldn't make the Canteen or the live radio broadcasts, Hollywood stars often brought the shows to them. What began in California, with stars leaving the studios and traveling to nearby bases to entertain, soon expanded to worldwide traveling shows and programs.[34]

War-weary GIs enthusiastically welcomed the entertainers, loudly cheering, laughing, and clapping during the performances. Ironically, what was intended to be a funny little song about a snowless Christmas Day in Beverly Hills, California, became the most moving and cherished song among the troops. Irving Berlin would later remark that his memorable song, "White Christmas," had taken on a meaning that he never intended. In the midst of one of humankind's most horrific wars, it had become the song of peace. The song's vocalist, popular crooner Bing Crosby, recalled, "So many young people were away and they'd heard this song at that time of the year and it would really affect them. I sang it many times in Europe in the field for the soldiers. They'd holler for it; they demanded it and I'd sing it and they'd all cry."[35]

The visiting entertainers frequently carried with them the pain of war. The very popular Marlene Dietrich, who worked so diligently in the effort to defeat the Axis powers, did so while worrying about the safety of her mother and sister, who were still living in Germany. Comedian Joe E. Brown earned special gratitude among the troops for continuing to entertain despite the loss of his son in the war effort. The USO would later report that its troupers, which included the world's biggest name entertainers, put on 428,521 live shows for an estimated 200 million servicemen and servicewomen worldwide.[36]

The pain of the war front extended deeply back into the homefront. Given its weather and wide range of social activities, as well as the fact that the West Coast fronted the Pacific theater, California became an important R&R ("rest and relaxation") center. Not only were war-worn pilots, many with more than fifty missions under their belts, and combat-hardened troops housed in federally expropriated beach clubs and hotels, but so were hundreds of thousands of recovering wounded soldiers. Soldiers who required more extensive hospitalization were placed in one of the state's many convalescent centers. As the war progressed, more and more Californians saw firsthand the terrible, devastating toll the war had wrought. While physical deformities were in growing abundance throughout city streets and stores, everyone, it seemed, knew someone who had been severely changed by the war. Recalling her experiences in wartime San Francisco, Opal Verge Winters wrote, "A neighbor of ours was the son of the Chief of Police. He was a Navy Lieutenant whose ship had been shot up and brought back to San Francisco for repair. His father picked him up each evening in a chauffeur-driven limo—both father and son in full uniform. His nightmare screams wakened us nightly."[37]

Throughout California's suburban neighborhoods were windows filled with Blue Stars denoting a son or daughter in the service. A long walk through the neighborhoods often yielded the painful sight of a window with a Gold Star in it, signifying the death of a family member in the war.

Since literally everyone had someone in the service, radio broadcasts were carefully monitored and newspapers were scoured. Everyone dreaded reports of large battles, knowing that, weeks later, casualty lists would be released. More frightening was the sight of a Western Union man in the neighborhood. People with sons in the service dreaded the possibity that their doorbell would be the next one rung. As the Western Union man made his way from the telegram's address, neighbors would often rush over to help calm the bereaved's tears and screams of grief.

Despite the agony of war, the mood of Californians remained decidedly determined and increasingly upbeat with the changing fortunes of the Allied war effort. Led by its workers and the innovative assembly methods of Henry Kaiser, California shipyards produced world-record numbers of ships. The aircraft plants of San Diego and Los Angeles had become so efficient that by 1943, Los Angeles plane manufacturers alone were producing one new warplane every seven minutes.[38] And throughout the state, thousands upon thousands of small manufacturers turned out much-needed war supplies, such as canned rations, uniforms, machine guns, bullets, parachutes, life preservers, and so forth. California emerged from the war as the nation's new arsenal of democracy.

While California's incredible wartime production numbers can be quantified and classified, the measure of change that the war wrought on its residents remains variable and subjective. However, few who lived during the war would deny that it caused the greatest of changes in the life they would come to live.

"World War II made me grow up," recalled Elliot Johnson, army veteran of combat service in Europe.[39] "I remember my grandmother always listening to the soap operas on the radio. She did it to take her mind off of her two sons that were at the front," remembered Margaret Anne McInnis of Oakland.[40] "'Gas Lips. Gas Lips Randolph,' that's what we called him. He was the best at syphoning gas. He was quick and quiet. He was a little like Robin Hood. Never cars in Santa Monica. Always Beverly Hills—where they always would find a way to replace the stolen gas," recalled Bob Walthour of Santa Monica.[41] "I remember my brother going down to get information on how to enlist and never coming home," stated Clara Gross of Hawthorne.[42] "Money took care of every shortage: train compartments, hotels, or booze. Thus it ever was and is," reminisced San Franciscan Opal Verge Winters.[43] "You always dreaded the ringing of the doorbell—especially in the days following a large battle," recalled Karen Moss of Vacaville.[44] "Almost all the guys playing pro ball were 4F. Hell, our catcher could barely squat down due to his hernias," humorously recalled Bob Crawford, pitcher for the Hollywood Stars.[45] "At every stop, we were greeted by wildly cheering crowds, often mostly women. That sea of female faces— you knew the men had gone to war," remarked Lana Turner following a Victory Bond Tour.[46] "I remember all of us in our grammar school class writing our classmates/friends who were now in internment camps," wrote Shirley Cragin of Bakersfield.[47] "The seemingly perpetual sunshine. The cute bungalow houses. I knew then I was never going back to Colorado," stated Helen Meyer of El Segundo.[48] "I remember the troops being transported on the cattle trucks. They would go crazy when they saw a gal. It didn't matter if you were six months pregnant. They would shout, wave and whistle. I would go home and cry. They were so exuberant but how many were going to come back," sadly recalled Clara Gross of Hawthorne.[49]

Sometimes, even in the midst of the greatest conflict in human history, it is the simple things that we remember most.

Notes

1. Among the best general studies of the American homefront during World War II are Geoffrey Perrett, *Days of Sadness, Years of Triumph: The American People, 1939–1945* (Madison, Wis., 1973); John Morton Blum, *V Was for Victory: Politics and Culture during World War II* (New York, 1976); Richard Polenberg, ed., *America at War: The Home Front, 1941–1945* (Englewood Cliffs, N.J., 1968); Richard Polenberg, *War and Society: The United States, 1941–1945* (Philadelphia, 1972); Richard Lingeman, *Don't You Know There's a War On? The American Homefront, 1941–1946* (New York, 1970); Gerald D. Nash, *The Great Depression and World War II: Organizing America, 1933–1945* (New York, 1979); Donald Rogers, *Since You Went Away* (New York, 1973); Jack Goodman, ed., *While You Were Gone: A Report on Wartime Life in the United States* (Washington, D.C., 1946).

For oral histories of the period, see Archie Satterfield, *The Homefront: An Oral History of the War Years in America, 1941–1945* (Chicago, 1981); Roy Hoppes, *Americans Remember the Homefront: An Oral Narrative* (New York, 1977); Mark Jonathan Harris, Franklin Mitchell, and Steven Schechter, *The Homefront: America during World War II* (New York, 1984); Studs Terkel, *The Good War: An Oral History of World War II* (New York, 1985); Sherna Gluck, *Rosie the Riveter Revisted: Women, the War, and Social Change* (Boston, 1987). An award-winning documentary of the American people during World War II is Mark Jonathan Harris, Franklin Mitchell and Steven Schechter's *The Homefront: America during World War II* (Churchill Films, 1984).

2. The Second World War's impact on California has been the subject of a growing body of scholarship. Among the important studies are Roger W. Lotchin, *Fortress California, 1910–1961: From Warfare to Welfare* (New York, 1992); Roger W. Lotchin, ed., *Fortress California at War: San Francisco, Los Angeles, Oakland, and San Diego,* special issue of *Pacific Historical Review* 63:3 (1994); Gerald D. Nash, *The American West Transformed: The Impact of the Second World War* (Bloomington, Ind., 1985); Gerald D. Nash, *World War II and the West: Reshaping the Economy* (Lincoln, Nebr. 1990); Marilynn S. Johnson, *The Second Gold Rush: Oakland and the East Bay in World War II* (Berkeley, Calif., 1993); Arthur C. Verge, *Paradise Transformed: Los Angeles during the Second World War* (Dubuque, Iowa, 1993); Kevin Allen Leonard, "Years of Hope, Days of Fear: The Impact of the Second World War on Race Relations in Los Angeles" (Ph.D. diss., University of California at Davis, 1992). Smaller local studies include Milton Shriner, *My Town: Santa Maria, California, 1941–1945* (Santa Maria, Calif., 1991); Donald Young, *Wartime Palos Verdes* (Palos Verdes, Calif., 1984); American National Red Cross, *Reminiscences and Reports of the San Mateo County Chapter in World War II* (San Mateo, Calif., 1970).

3. Donald Young, *December 1941: America's First 25 Days at War* (Missoula, Mont., 1992), 9.

4. *San Francisco Chronicle,* 3 May 1942.

5. For information regarding Japanese submarine operations off California in World War II, see Bert Webber, *Silent Siege: Japanese Attacks against North America in World War II* (Fairfield, Wash., 1984).

6. Young, *December 1941,* 105–7.

7. Ibid., 101.

8. The last Japanese submarine shelling attack along the West Coast took place on 21 June 1942 at Fort Stevens, Oregon. See Brian Chin, *Artillery at the Golden Gate: The Harbor Defenses of San Francisco in World War II* (Missoula, Mont., 1994), 98.

9. "Civilian Defense in Los Angeles," *Western City* 18 (Sept. 1942): 20.

10. *San Francisco Chronicle,* 7 May 1942.

11. "Your City Geared to Defense," *Los Angeles Year Book 1941* (Los Angeles, 1941), 27.

12. *San Francisco Chronicle,* 5 May 1942.

13. Ibid., 7 May 1942.

14. The decison to relocate the West Coast's Japanese and Japanese-American population has received substantial study from historians and legal scholars. Some excel-

lent studies of this issue include Morton Grodzins, *Americans Betrayed: Politics and the Japanese Evacuation* (Chicago, 1949); Roger Daniels, *The Decision to Relocate the Japanese* (Malabar, Fla., 1975); Donald Teruo Hata Jr. and Nadine Ishitani Hata, *Japanese Americans and World War II* (St. Charles, Mo., 1974).

15. *Los Angeles Times,* 1 Sept. 1989.

16. Verge, *Paradise Transformed,* 32–33.

17. James J. Rawls and Walter Bean, *California: An Interpretive History* (New York, 1993), 334.

18. Johnson, *Second Gold Rush.*

19. Harris et al., *Homefront,* 38.

20. Ibid., 30.

21. Charles Wollenberg, *Marinship at War: Shipbuilding and Social Change in Wartime Sausalito* (Berkeley, Calif., 1990), 3–4.

22. Mark S. Foster, *Henry J. Kaiser: Builder in the Modern American West* (Austin, Tex., 1989), 71.

23. *Los Angeles Times,* 1 Sept. 1989.

24. Opal Verge Winters, "San Francisco, 1941–1945," ms., 1996, in author's possession.

25. Johnson, *Second Gold Rush,* 84–87.

26. Marvin Brienes, "Smog Comes to Los Angeles," *Southern California Quarterly* 58:4 (1976): 515–32.

27. James Van Norman, Oral History #300/219, p. 25, Special Collections, University of California at Los Angeles.

28. Ibid. See also Elmer Belt, "A Sanitary Survey of Sewage Pollution of the Surf and Beaches of Santa Monica Bay," *Western City* 19 (June 1943): 17–22.

29. For a description of the hiring disputes involved in Los Angeles's wartime public transportation, see Verge, *Paradise Transformed,* 53–54.

30. *Los Angeles Times,* 26 Sept. 1942.

31. Harris et al., *Homefront,* 170.

32. For insights into the wartime problems faced by police agencies in California, refer to U.S. House, Subcommittee of Committee on Naval Affairs, *Hearings on Congested Areas,* pts. 2, 3, and 8, 78th Cong., 2d sess., Washington, D.C. In particular, see the testimonies of Commander T. M. Leovy, district patrol officer, shore patrol, San Diego, pt. 2, pp. 423–30; George Doran, chief of police, Alameda, pt. 3, pp. 817–25; Charles W. Dullea, chief of police, San Francisco, pt. 3, pp. 676–81; and C. B. Horrall, chief of police, Los Angeles, pt. 8, 1770–73.

33. Harris et al., *Homefront,* 171–72.

34. Bob Hope's first military entertainment show took place at Southern California's March Field on 6 May 1941.

35. Roy Hoppes, *When the Stars Went to War: Hollywood and World War II* (New York, 1994), 297.

36. Ibid., 193.

37. Winters, "San Francisco, 1941–1945," 3.

38. *Los Angeles Times,* 1 Sept. 1989.

39. On-camera interview in Harris et al., *Homefront* (film).

40. Interview with the author, 15 Feb. 1996.

41. Ibid., 21 Mar. 1987.

42. Clara Gross, "Women War Workers" (taped oral history), Special Collections, Long Beach State University, Long Beach, Calif.

43. Winters, "San Francisco, 1941–1945," 3.

44. Interview with the author, 18 Feb. 1996.

45. Ibid., 20 Mar. 1987.

46. Hoppes, *When the Stars Went to War,* 132.

47. Interview with the author, 10 Feb. 1996.

48. Ibid., 22 Feb. 1996.

49. Gross, "Women War Workers."

2

The Way We Thought We Were: Images in World War II Films

Linda Harris Mehr

In an oral history recently conducted by the Academy of Motion Picture Arts and Sciences, the art director Robert Boyle recounted the first day he began work with Alfred Hitchcock. It happened to be a Sunday in December 1941. He and Hitchcock were going over some drawings for the film *Saboteur* at the Universal Pictures Studio lot when the door burst open and a very excited Dave Garber, head of studio operations, entered the room. As Boyle tells it:

> [H]e threw open this door and we looked up and he said, "What are you doing here?" And neither Hitch nor I could answer . . . and he said, "Don't you know? The Japs just bombed Pearl Harbor!" And I didn't say anything. . . . then he turned and ran out and slammed the door.
>
> Hitch looked at me and he said, "What was he doing in that funny-looking hat?" And we went right on working. It was just too much to take in, and there wasn't anything we could do about it anyway.[1]

In another oral history, the composer Hans Salter spoke of the effect of Pearl Harbor and the war on Hollywood: "It was a terrible shock and everybody acted very patriotic after that, or felt very, very threatened. But basically everything continued as before. I remember we had some meetings in the commissary and we sang 'God Bless America' and things like that, but the production went on the same way as before. Maybe at a more frantic pace than before."[2]

Clearly there were numerous factors that would affect the making of films in Hollywood during the war, but these anecdotes are instructive, because in many ways things did go on as before. The business of making motion pictures remained uppermost with those who controlled the front office, and that business was to please the public, to continue to make motion pictures that would register well at the box office. At the time of the bombing of Pearl Harbor, motion pictures were clearly established as the most important form of twentieth-century popular culture. By the year 1941, the average weekly attendance at motion picture theaters in the United States was estimated to be 85 million. According to a business survey by the Department of Commerce, the film theater box office amounted to 80 to 85 percent of the amount Americans spent for spectator amusement.[3]

Recognizing the power of films, the government called upon the California motion picture industry to aid the war effort. Eager to assist, the industry provided material and manpower for training and propaganda films; studio art departments even helped create forms of camouflage. As for the content of entertainment films, the Office of War Information (OWI) and its Bureau of Motion Pictures (BMP) issued directives regarding "appropriate" depictions of American life and values required by the war situation. The directives stressed the importance of representing the United States as a democracy at work, a nation of people united behind the war effort no matter what gender, economic strata, or racial and ethnic background, where all were called upon to perform needed work, and all were capable of doing so. This idealized definition of American society contrasted not only with the reality of American history but also with past depictions on the screen. Studios were urged to submit scripts for review, but compliance with government directives was not universal. The desire to please the public and thereby maintain profits remained the driving force with filmmakers. The government message may have appeared in numerous films, often because that message seemed to be in accord with prevailing attitudes, but at times the films strayed from official dogma, revealing contradicting and ambivalent feelings among both filmmakers and audiences.[4]

A closer look at some of these films may provide some unique insights into this subject. The number of films discussed are, of necessity, only a fraction of those shown during the war years, but their popularity with audiences makes them useful as barometers of contemporary thought. Popular films reveal if not the realities of American life then at least the perceptions, hopes, fantasies, and fears commonly held about that life. Though Hollywood can hardly be viewed as a monolithlic enterprise—several studios were not even within the bounds of the Hollywood area, and the heads of production and creative personnel were unique individuals with differing backgrounds and perspectives, hardly interchangeable—similar themes can be found among the wartime films that emerged from the various studios. By examining a sampling of films in light of important contemporary factors —government directives, the aims of the industry, and the realities of American society—we may gain a better understanding of the way we thought we were.[5]

The theme of America as an ethnic and economic melting pot both is occasionally evident in films prior to World War II. In *Hold Back the Dawn* (Paramount, 1941), for example, Emmy (Olivia DeHavilland) tells her Rumanian husband (Charles Boyer) how proud she is to marry a man named Iscovescu: "This is America—for the Rockefellers and the Joneses—for the MacGonigles and the Frankfurters—for the Jeffersons and the Slivinskies. You see? It's—it's like a lake—clear and fresh, and it'll never get stagnant while new streams are flowing in."

Such themes became more obvious during the war years. To help strengthen the impression of national unity, wartime government manuals suggested that filmmakers show individuals from different national backgrounds. For example, one directive stated: "A movie short could be done taking a typical bombardier crew, which probably has a Johnson as pilot, a Calucci as gunner, a Svendsen as navigator, a Levin as bombardier, a McTavish as radio operator, etc."[6]

Multiethnic fighting forces became de rigeur in feature films. The crew in *Air Force* (Warner Bros., 1943) is made up of Quincannon, Williams, White, McMartin, Weinberg, Winocki, and Callahan. *A Walk in the Sun* (20th Century Fox, 1945) includes Tyne, Rivera, Friedman, McWilliams, Archimbeau, Porter, and Tranella. In *The Purple Heart* (20th Century Fox, 1944), Captain Ross heads a group of flyers that includes Canelli, Greenbaum, and Skvoznik; their plane bears the name of Mrs. Murphy. For the ultimate melting pot one must turn to *Bataan* (MGM, 1943), which includes Dane, Bentley, Feingold, Ramirez, Matowski, Yankee Salazar (from the Philippines), and Epps (an African American). The common element among these characters—whether of Anglo, Jewish, Irish, Polish, German, Mexican, Italian, or African descent—is their loyalty to the war effort. However, there was one exception: the gossip columnist Louella Parsons remarked about the Italian-American character Canelli, played by Richard Conte, in *The Purple Heart,* that "you feel strongly this Italian boy's loyalty," though she viewed the Japanese quite differently: "I defy anyone to see this picture and not want to go out and kill, single-handed, every Jap."[7]

During the war years, Americans of Italian and German descent were viewed positively; in contrast, Japanese Americans were largely indistinguishable from evil Japanese, which was clearly linked to a long history of racial discrimination in America. The portrayal on screen of the enemy powers reflected this differentiation. *Watch on the Rhine* (Warner Bros., 1943) was only one of numerous films to suggest that good Germans opposed Hitler, and Italians had to be forced to support Mussolini in the cartoon *The Ducktators* (Warner Bros., 1943), but the Japanese were always shown to share the ideas and goals of their diabolical leaders.

Names were the most distinguishing feature of those in the film versions of the American fighting forces; otherwise, soldiers were equally capable, brave, pragmatic, democratic, and caring, determined to fight to the end to protect the American way of life. Education was admired, especially if it came from a public as opposed to a private institution. When the lawyer in *The Purple Heart*, chosen by the Japanese court to defend the captured American flyers, introduces himself as "Sakai. Princeton—class of '31," Sergeant Greenbaum responds: "City College of New York—class of '39." Nothing specifically ethnic distinguishes these individuals. During preparations for *Objective, Burma!* (Warner Bros., 1945), Jack Warner told the producer and screenwriter Alvah Bessie: "I like the idea of having a Jewish officer in Burma. See that you get a good clean-cut American type for Jacobs." Like the other primarily Jewish moguls in Hollywood, Warner was aware of the lingering anti-Semitism in American society. The moguls craved acceptance by WASP America, and they did their utmost to fit in by changing Jewish performers' names and avoiding distinctively Jewish ethnic portrayals on film.[8]

What really counted was that these men of different backgrounds work together. As the captain informs the aerial gunner in *Air Force*: "We all belong to this airplane. We're a single *team*. Each one of us has got to rely on every other man doing the right thing at the right time. Teamwork is all that counts." And yet, while teamwork was the government's message as well as that of numerous films, often the film's central figure is left on his own, the last man facing an oncoming army of Japanese, as Robert Taylor does in *Bataan*. The image here struck a responsive chord in audiences—the veneration of individualistic Americans willing to stand up single-handedly against all odds. Numerous films came in for government criticism precisely because they followed the tradition of one man doing it all on his own. While the studios were clearly willing to cooperate with certain government wishes, they also did what they thought audiences expected and wanted. But whether as a team or an individual, it was essential that Americans ultimately prevail.

While ethnic minorities were not always viewed as essential parts of American society, greater acceptance of most European ethnics is evident in the films of the thirties. This was particularly true for Irish Americans, who were portrayed most positively in films during the war years. Though the Irish who came to America in the mid-nineteenth century encountered nativist hostility and anti-Catholic sentiment and were considered "wild" in the way Americans had described the "wild Indians," as they advanced economically and politically, their popular image changed. By the end of the century, Irish Americans had almost become a symbol of American nationalism, viewed not as wild, but as tough and democratic—the "fighting Irish," an image perhaps not unrelated to the coverage of their exploits in the Spanish-American War by newspaper-men who also happened to be Irish-American. The two-fisted, freckle-faced, redheaded Irishman who is twice as brave as anyone else became an American image. As Nathan Glazer and Daniel P. Moynihan observe in *Beyond the Melting Pot*, when the movies began to fashion a composite picture of the American people, the New York Irishman was projected to the very center of the national image, often in the form of the actor James Cagney. Otis Ferguson remarked about Cagney: "[T]his half-pint of an East Side Irish [*sic*] somehow managed to be a lot of what a typical American might be, nobody's fool and nobody's clever ape, quick and cocky but not too wise for his own business, frankly vulgar in the best sense, but with the dignity of the genuine worn as easily as his skin."[9]

The image of the New York Irishman—tough, egalitarian, urban—was adopted to redefine the American character, serving a function similar to the earlier symbol of the yeoman. Quite appropriately, that hymn to American heroism and drive, the 1942 film *Yankee Doodle Dandy*, used an Irishman (James Cagney as George M. Cohan) to symbolize American patriotism at its highest. In *Blood on the Sun* (RKO, 1945), Cagney plays Nick Condon ("half Irish and half Norwegian"), a newspaper editor for an American paper in prewar Japan who aims to expose the militarists' efforts to gain power. Able to speak both Chinese and Japanese, skilled at judo and boxing, Condon's Brooklyn origins are evident in his cocky manner and speech. Whether outnumbered or outsized, he displays bravery and courage in combating his opponents. Irish Americans play pivotal roles in numerous films: as "Irish" Quincannon who guides the plane crew in *Air Force*; as "Big Mike" Harrigan, a priest who restores the lead pilot's faith in *God Is My Co-Pilot* (Warner Bros., 1945); and as Danny McGuire, played by Gene Kelly, a "hard-headed" Irishman who owns a small Brooklyn nightclub and who ultimately wins the heart of dancer Rusty Parker (Rita Hayworth) over a richer and more sophisticated rival in *Cover Girl* (Columbia, 1944).

Irish Americans are central figures throughout *Going My Way* (Paramount, 1944), one of the most popular films of the war years, but their ethnicity is only superficial. At heart the film is just an all-American story about how resourcefulness and determination will overcome difficulties, a message not inappropriate for the war years. It also reiterates common themes of old and young working together and the rich ultimately coming to the aid of those less fortunate. Barry Fitzgerald, as Father Fitzgibbon, is getting on in years and having difficulties running the parish. The head of the savings and loan company threatens foreclosure for nonpayment on the mortgage. Bing Crosby, as

Father O'Malley, is sent to straighten things out. His youthful manner, his love of sports, and his use of psychology in dealing with some rather rowdy youngsters incur the displeasure of the elder priest. But eventually Fitzgibbon is won over to O'Malley's ways; the head of the loan company comes to the aid of the church, and his rich son marries a poor girl of the parish; the juvenile delinquents are reformed by playing basketball and singing in the choir; the multiethnic choir, which includes Irish, Italians and blacks, goes on tour performing the young priest's songs to raise money for the church; and the elder priest's ninety-year-old mother is brought over to be reunited with her son. Happy resolutions all around—no generation gaps, no ethnic or class conflict.

The myth of the happy melting pot, where all components are treated equally, was widely shared, evident not only in government manuals, but in popular films as well. The realities of American life were something else, and some films revealed this, particularly with regard to the portrayals of blacks and Hispanics.

The films of the thirties had indicated that blacks could be part of American society, as long as they remembered their place. Aside from troubled mulattos such as Fredi Washington in *Imitation of Life* (Universal, 1934), who were basically outcasts, black servants played by Louise Beavers, Hattie McDaniel, Bill "Bojangles" Robinson, Willie Best, Manton Moreland, and Stepin' Fetchit were always welcome, helping to assure the status of their white employers, while also frequently serving as the butt of humor. Blacks were depicted as simple but loyal, a rhythmic people fond of singing and dancing.

Portrayals of blacks during the 1930s came in for a fair amount of criticism, particularly from the NAACP. And during the war years, in the face of European fascism, the persistence of bigotry and racial discrimination proved troublesome. In part out of fear that negative stereotyping of blacks in American films could be used as propaganda against the United States by its enemies, the OWI urged Hollywood to project a more positive image of blacks during the war years.

To a certain extent there was a fade-out of servant roles in the 1940s. Entertainers appeared much more frequently during these years—Cab Calloway, Lena Horne, Hazel Scott, Louis Armstrong, Count Basie, Lionel Hampton, Duke Ellington—but they were segregated from the cast and the plot of the film, and such scenes could be cut for screening before southern audiences. Two major Hollywood films, *Stormy Weather* (20th Century Fox, 1943) and *Cabin in the Sky* (MGM, 1943), featured all-black casts. Though the performances were outstanding, the images failed to depart much from older stereotypes. This is evident even in a supposedly positive review in the *New York*

Times: "'Cabin in the Sky' is a beautiful entertainment . . . sparkling and completely satisfying . . . by turn an inspiring expression of a simple people's faith in the hereafter and a spicy slice of their zest for earthly pleasures."[10]

African Americans occasionally appeared as part of the fighting forces in *Bataan, Crash Dive* (20th Century Fox, 1943) and *Sahara* (Columbia, 1943). The aim to include the black soldier as an equal, however, was not always achieved. In *Bataan,* the black character, Epps, is the only one of the squad who is shown without his shirt and the only one so depicted in publicity photos. Frequently we hear him humming "St. Louis Blues." Though he is a demolitions expert, he depends on instructions from his white partner, who is entrusted with setting off the explosion. In *Lifeboat* (20th Century Fox, 1944), Canada Lee plays a black steward referred to as "Charcoal" until he rescues a woman and her baby and then is called by his real name, Joe. Yet he still appears as less than equal in the film and is the only featured performer not depicted in the advertising poster for the film. He is revealed to be a former pickpocket, is deferential to those in authority, and clings to a simplistic religious faith. Though Dooley Wilson as Sam is a sympathetic figure in *Casablanca* (Warner Bros., 1942), he is still a marginal one, little more than an updated combination of faithful servant and entertainer.

Hattie McDaniel is a powerful figure in *Gone with the Wind* (MGM, 1939). In fact she represents something white audiences had long ignored or suppressed. According to Donald Bogle, "Here was a black maid who not only was capable of running the Big House but proclaimed in her own contorted way her brand of black power. McDaniel scared her audience. Indeed, in the South there were complaints that she had been too familiar with her white employers." Hattie McDaniel continued to play maids during the war years, in *The Male Animal* (Warner Bros., 1942) and *Since You Went Away* (United Artists, 1944), but her feistiness was toned down. These films implied that maids were normal components of middle-class life, something hardly borne out by American social realities. While the majority of Americans may have defined themselves as middle class, only a minuscule percentage could afford servants.[11]

In *Since You Went Away,* McDaniel plays a maid appropriately named Fidelia who works for the Hilton family. Now that Tim Hilton, an advertising executive, has gone to war, the family can no longer afford her services. Fidelia takes a job in another household, but doesn't like it, telling Anne Hilton: "I ain't gonna be contentment like I been right here all these years." As the ever faithful servant, she returns to the Hilton home evenings and days off to continue to cook and care for the family. She has no life outside of theirs, and the war only seems to touch her in the most impersonal way. The film fails even to hint at the radical changes for black women afforded by the war— for the first time they had work opportunities outside of being servants and could obtain decent paying jobs in aircraft and other manufacturing plants. Though she is clearly a capable woman on whom the Hiltons rely, Fidelia is treated with rather patronizing affection and they seem amused by her misuse of language: "Men don't fancy disorderment"; "I got some troublement"; "I wants my solitude and my privitation." Old stereotypes persisted.

When pushed by various groups and the government to improve the black image on screen, Hollywood's answer was basically to "write out" the characters rather than change them, to eliminate most roles for blacks altogether. The result was decreasing work opportunities for black performers, a situation that persisted into the postwar period.[12]

Hispanics, such as Desi Arnaz in *Bataan,* might occasionally appear as part of the platoon in wartime films, but more often they were associated with Latin America and its music, as interpreted by Hollywood. Latin Americans had often been characterized as musical, but prior to the late thirties the Latin image, which meant primarily an image of Mexicans, was largely negative. Mexicans were viewed as lawless, violent, lazy, deceitful, ignorant, and incapable of assimilation. They appeared in films as bandits and villains, sensual and vicious. Such was the portrayal of Pancho Villa in *Viva Villa!* (MGM, 1934), and the titles of two films starring Lupe Velez—*Hot Pepper* (20th Century Fox, 1933) and *Strictly Dynamite* (RKO, 1934)—revealed the stereotypical image of Latin women as hot-blooded and passionate. Protests from Mexico against these portrayals in the 1930s had little effect. The Production Code Administration of the Motion Picture Producers and Distributors of America, the trade organization that oversaw film censorship and whose prime concern was protecting the film industry and its profits, paid little heed to such complaints, whereas protests from the German and Italian embassies during the same period led the Code office to urge the studios to exercise restraint in their portrayals of Germans and Italians. Greater revenues could be expected from those markets.[13]

Change occurred due to several factors. The growing war in Europe sharply decreased foreign film revenues. Only Latin America remained as a prime market for American film exports. As the threat of war with Germany increased, the U.S. government sought to ease any remaining tensions with South American governments; it was essential to preserve hemispheric unity in the face of possible foreign invasion. The "good neighbor" policy was resurrected by FDR. Both the government, through the Office of Coordinator of Inter-American Affairs (Nelson Rockefeller), and the Production Code Administration office now applied pressure to the studios to improve the Latin image, to avoid blatant errors that might offend the "neighbors to the South."

Mexico appeared in a new light on screen. *Juarez* (Warner Bros., 1939) offered solemn homage to a nineteenth-century Mexican president, portraying
him as an equal to Lincoln. Juarez not only has a picture of Lincoln hanging
in his office, he dresses like him, complete with stovepipe hat. Though seemingly positive, the film portrays Juarez primarily as a symbol, a defender of
democratic principles, appropriate at a time when Americans felt threatened
by European powers.

A wave of musical Latin films appeared, often set in romanticized south-of-
the-border locales with colorful costumes and elaborate musical numbers. This
aspect of the film industry's support for the good neighbor policy was in part
a response to the new popular interest in South American music and dances,
but primarily it reflected the desire to make up for lost European film revenues. The theme of Pan-American unity is obvious in such films as *The Gang's
All Here* (20th Century Fox, 1943), *They Met in Argentina* (RKO, 1941), *Pan-
Americana* (RKO, 1945), and *Springtime in The Rockies* (20th Century Fox,
1942). *Time* magazine observed that the finale in *Springtime*, with dancers in
both North and South American costumes doing the jitterbug and the samba, brought together Latin America (Cesar Romero and Carmen Miranda), the
United States (Betty Grable, John Payne, and Harry James) and Canada (large
Technicolor shots of Lake Louise). "Only the addition of an Eskimo and a
penguin could have made the show still more hemispheric in scope." In the
film, Carmen Miranda plays a character symbolizing hemispheric unity and
the American melting pot. She is Rosita Murphy, whose mother was from
Brazil and whose father was an Irishman named Patrick Murphy. She has six
brothers, including one named Kelly and one named Alphonso.[14]

As a result of the great popularity of the new Latin rhythms, there was a
tendency to identify Latins with their music; they were usually depicted as singing native melodies and dancing. The hip-swaying dances increased the aura
of sensuality of such performers as Carmen Miranda, Desi Arnaz, and Cesar
Romero. Desi Arnaz appears to be just one of the guys at college in *Too Many
Girls* (RKO, 1940) until he performs a number on drums with such intensity
that the nearby flames almost seem tame by comparison. Carmen Miranda,
in her extravagantly decorated, bare-midriff costume in *The Gang's All Here,*
performs a song and dance number which to call "suggestive" would be a gross
understatement: women holding huge oversized bananas dip down among
other women lying on the ground, their legs outstretched with oversized straw-
berries between them. While American audiences seemed to enjoy this, President Vargas of Brazil censored the film. In fact, there were numerous protests
from Latin Americans about what they viewed as misrepresentations of Latin
American cultures, particularly the inability to distinguish one from another.

Carmen Miranda found herself attacked in her native Brazil for her Holly-wood-style performances. Despite these protests Hollywood continued to make similar films because they proved successful within the United States.

Whatever Hollywood's intentions, filmmakers succeeded in reinforcing the old stereotype of the Latin as passionate, hot-blooded, and forever prone to singing and dancing. Despite the effort to show a sense of equality between people of South and North America, the North American still maintains a sexual superiority in these films. Cesar Romero may dance as an equal with Betty Grable, and may for a while be engaged to her, but he will ultimately lose her to the Anglo from North America in *Springtime in the Rockies.* That Lat-ins are not quite equal to Anglos is also evident in the way Carmen Miranda's mangling of English expressions is used for humor in these films: "You don't like my outfits? I think it's a knock down"; "They spoiled the beans"; "I feel absolutely undressed, like a strip squeezer" (from *Springtime in the Rockies*).

If the images of Latins rarely strayed from the stereotypical, some Anglo women did not fare much better. This was particularly true of Betty Grable and Rita Hayworth, who appeared in roles primarily as decorative objects, sex sym-bols, and pin-ups. One of Grable's films was, in fact, entitled *Pin-Up Girl* (20th Century Fox, 1944), and cheesecake photos of Grable and Hayworth were the most common images decorating the interior of wartime barracks as well as the exterior of combat aircraft and vehicles. However glamorous these wom-en might be in their films, the message was always that they were ultimately attainable by the average guy. In *Cover Girl,* Rusty Parker (Rita Hayworth) may have the opportunity to become a Broadway star and marry the richest, most powerful producer in the business, but she rejects him to stay with Danny McGuire (Gene Kelly) in Brooklyn. And pin-up/swim star Esther Williams as Cynthia Glenn, in *Thrill of a Romance* (MGM, 1945), ultimately chooses Ma-jor Thomas Milvaine (Van Johnson), who plans to return to a small midwest-ern town as a newspaper editor, over a man designated as one of New York's wealthiest corporate tycoons.

During the thirties, majority sentiment did not favor women working. While this theme was often reiterated in films of the period, screen images were fre-quently ambivalent. Women characters might ultimately reject careers for romance, but the stars who played them—Katharine Hepburn, Barbara Stan-wyck, Marlene Dietrich, Jean Arthur, Claudette Colbert, Myrna Loy, Irene Dunne—projected images of strength, intelligence, independence, and capa-bility that seemed to contradict the film's purported message.

The eruption of hostilities generated an unprecedented demand for new workers, and while in 1940 and 1941 there had been resistance to having women take jobs that were not considered traditional female work, such opposition was erased after the Pearl Harbor attack. As men left for the service, women were called upon to fill the gaps. Where women had earlier been made to feel guilty for working, they were now made to feel guilty for not working, either for pay in a war job or as a volunteer.

In its directives to the studios, the OWI said that Hollywood should show how women were stepping forward, filling the gaps left by the men who had gone into service, by becoming war workers and by coping without husbands or sweethearts. A March 12, 1943, OWI/BMP special bulletin urged: "Particular efforts should be made to break down all known resistances (among men and women both) attached to the idea of women working. It should be stressed that women should apply for jobs, and not wait to be called."[15]

Hollywood made a number of films that, on the surface, seemed to assert the importance of working women. Such films emphasized that women must cope without men, but they also suggested that though women may have to step out of traditional roles and work at jobs or in situations previously thought appropriate only for men, they were only doing so temporarily, until the men returned.

Tender Comrade (RKO, 1943), starring Ginger Rogers, depicts four women, all married to men away in the service. All four women work in an aircraft factory and are having difficulty coping economically and emotionally with their husbands away. They decide to pool their resources and rent a house together. Finding it difficult to work all day and also care for the house, they hire a housekeeper—a German refugee who proves to be the most patriotic of all the women (again a housekeeper/maid becomes an essential part of a middle-class household). The film only minimally suggests anything about the work the women do. The main focus is on how much they miss their men, and they longingly look at photos of their husbands and talk with each other about their mates. The film suggests that they are working only while their men are away; the way they fuss over one husband on leave indicates how much they long to return to being housewives. The film also emphasizes their clothes and the well-furnished home they share, an indication of what they appear to long for in the future.

So Proudly We Hail (Paramount, 1943) was one of the few films to focus on women serving a role within the armed forces, in this case nurses sent to tend the casualties on Bataan and Corregidor. The story is told in flashback from the troopship on which some of the nurses are returning after being rescued. One of them, played by Claudette Colbert, is in a catatonic state, and as the story unfolds we are told that she lapsed into this state upon learning that her husband, a soldier she married against regulations, may be dead. In this film the women are shown to perform heroically in combat situations, to be reliable and capable. They give up their white nurses' dresses for male soldier attire, but the film also spends considerable time showing them in various states of undress, and one woman appears obsessed about a black nightgown. Their work as nurses calls on traditional nurturing and healing skills; yet when not dealing with men medically, they are involved romantically. And Colbert comes out of her depression only after a letter from her husband is read to her in which he tells her he is leaving her a home to which she must return to "make things grow."

A few films did show women who enjoyed their work as much as men. In both *Flight for Freedom* (RKO, 1943) and *A Guy Named Joe* (MGM, 1943), the women are aviators who had been flying prior to the war. They enjoy this activity as much as men, appear equally capable, and in fact display a give-and-take reciprocity with the men that implies a real sense of equality. But ultimately the films reaffirm that the best role for a woman is as a helpmate to a man. In *A Guy Named Joe*, Dorinda (Irene Dunne) is at first distraught over the death of her love interest, Pete (Spencer Tracy), but then falls for another aviator, Ted (Van Johnson). Pete returns as an angel who must supervise Ted. When Ted is assigned a dangerous mission, Dorinda takes off in his plane because she wants to protect him and because she feels she is still in love with Pete. She makes a successful mission but we are left to believe that this is in part because Pete, as an angel, flies along with her and guides her. In *Flight for Freedom,* Toni Carter (Rosalind Russell), an Amelia Earhart–like character, is killed when she must fly completely on her own.

The representations of women in these films are ambivalent at best. On the one hand, they seem to give support to women willing to work to aid the war effort, yet they indicate this effort is necessary only as long as an emergency situation exists. And maybe women just want to be women. Why else the obsession with the black nightgown in *So Proudly We Hail* or Dorinda's ecstasy over what she excitedly calls "girl clothes," the dress and shoes Pete gives her in *A Guy Named Joe*? Just wanting to be women may be one way to look at it. Another might be that these possessions were treasured not simply as symbols of their womanhood, but of their status as middle class, a concern that appears to be of equal import.

One of the most popular films of the period, *Mrs. Miniver* (MGM, 1942), attempts to present the British, now caught in a fight for their very existence, in a positive light to encourage American support. It is irrelevant that the film presents a false vision of English life; what the film tells us about American dreams and expectations is significant. The film begins by stating: "This story of an average English middle-class family begins with the summer of 1939; when the sun shone down on a happy, careless people, who worked and played;

reared their children and tended their gardens in that happy, easy-going England that was so soon to be fighting desperately for her way of life and for life itself." The "middle-class" life depicted is, of course, sheer fantasy; it is a lifestyle attainable by only the wealthiest in England or America. Nonetheless, it is a way of life most Americans appeared to desire, if not one with which most could identify.

The opening sequence shows Mrs. Miniver boarding a bus, only to get off quickly and run in the opposite direction to a hat shop. Worried that a particular hat is no longer on display, she is reassured by the clerk that it had been put aside for her. She briefly hesitates. "I know it's foolish and extravagant, and I don't know what my husband will say, but I've simply got to have it!" On the train ride home she encounters the minister and confesses her expensive purchase: "I'm afraid I do like nice things . . . things far beyond my means sometimes. Oh pretty clothes and good schools for the children, the car, the garden." In another scene, the husband, an architect, looks over a car that costs more than he had intended to spend, but he decides to purchase it anyway. Their large home is lavishly furnished, the grounds expansive and beautifully landscaped. The household includes both a cook and a maid. The two young children enjoy many comforts, including nice clothes and piano lessons.

The film raises the issue of class divisions only to suggest ultimately that they do not matter or exist. When Lady Beldon protests that people do not know their proper place and that her granddaughter should not marry the Miniver son because he is of a lower class, Mrs. Miniver manages to win her over, and the uniting of the two families implies the removal of those class divisions. The film also resolves the even greater disparity between the stationmaster Ballard and Lady Beldon. Ballard enters into the local contest, which has always been won by Lady Beldon, a rose he has developed. In the end Lady Beldon awards him the top prize, further indicating the rapprochement between different segments of society.

Within this so-called middle-class world, both before and after the outbreak of war, Mrs. Miniver's primary concern is her home and family. She comforts the children in the shelter, acts as intermediary between the Beldons and Minivers, and also helps facilitate the coming together of Ballard the stationmaster and Lady Beldon, since the rose he enters is named Mrs. Miniver. When her husband returns after a mission to rescue men trapped at Dunkirk, he tells her it was quite exciting and that he almost feels sorry for her being at home where everything is so peaceful. "But that's what men are for, isn't it? To go out and do things while you women folk look after the house." Then he learns that she had expanded her role as protector by courageously and single-handedly capturing an armed, downed Nazi pilot who threatened her and her home. But while extraordinary times may call for extraordinary efforts on the part of women, the film does not suggest this will be the case after the war. The war is being fought to restore and retain the idealized middle-class world depicted before the bombs fell, and in that world women and men have clearly defined and distinctive roles to play.

Mrs. Miniver seemed to resonate with audiences not because of what it said about Britain, but because it projected an idealized middle-class family life that seemed to be what Americans hoped for themselves. *Since You Went Away,* starring Claudette Colbert, makes an even stronger case for a particular sort of American life. The opening statement reads: "This is the story of an unconquerable fortress, the American home, 1943." The home depicted is supposed to be middle class, but as in *Mrs. Miniver,* only the wealthiest could afford what is shown here. The home has three bedrooms, one of which has a fireplace and bay window, and is filled with consumer niceties. Though expensive, the styles shown here could be described as homey and comfortable, a departure from the art deco, streamlined moderne apartment and hotel worlds of thirties films— a change perhaps symptomatic of new concerns. Home and family are most important to Anne Hilton, as they were to the film's creator, David O. Selznick, who appeared to recognize Americans' interests as well.

Anne, whose husband has been called to active duty, must now handle home and family on her own. Her goal, which seemed to reflect a popular sentiment, is to "try to keep things as they were. I'll keep the past alive like a warm room for you to come back to." Though she must learn to cope with various difficulties, she does so primarily by using traditional female nurturing skills. She takes in the cantankerous, retired Colonel Smollett as a boarder to help pay the bills, and through great kindness and patience manages to turn him into a loving member of the family. She even facilitates a reconciliation with the grandson he had rejected. She provides support and guidance to her daughters and comfort and encouragement to the elder daughter Jane when she has to inform her of her fiancé's death in battle. Jane also shows her strength in traditional ways. She encourages the rather shy and timid Bill Smollett to go bravely off to war. When she becomes a nurse's aide, she helps heal men who have been wounded physically and emotionally in the war.

Tony Willett, a wealthy friend of the Hiltons and a former suitor of Anne, expresses what appeared to be common concerns about the future after the war. Tony speaks of those going off to fight:

Tony: They expect to come back to something.
Anne: What do you mean?
Tony: I mean something like they left only better. I hope they don't get too many surprises.

The well-appointed home—with abundant food and consumer items such as stockings and automobiles, things in limited supply during the war—was clearly desired and expected in the future. The film also hints at the perhaps common fear that women might not remain faithful, but puts such fear to rest through Anne's resistance to Tony's romantic advances. The theme of woman's infidelity and untrustworthiness evident in *Double Indemnity* (Paramount, 1944) would become much more prevalent after the end of the war.

Near the end of *Since You Went Away,* Anne comes to feel that she has not done enough and decides to train as a welder in an airplane factory. She does so to help protect her home, the reason given by Tony for trading in his top hat and tails for a navy uniform: that "single corny phrase . . . home, sweet home." She tells her husband in a letter how proud she is to be working with dedicated women, many of whom have names "like nothing ever heard at the country club," such as her refugee friend Zofia Koslowska. She tells him she has changed from the pampered woman he knew, but her hope is that such change will make her a better wife, more worthy of his love. One of the final scenes of the film shows a party at the Hilton home where Anne is not only the keeper of the home but also the facilitator, who brings together her daughters, Tony Willett, Colonel Smollett, Lieutenant Solomon, Zofia Koslowska, and even Fidelia (though she remains a bit apart), suggesting a comfortable, harmonious world that bridges gaps between generations and economic and ethnic backgrounds.

The well-appointed middle-class home, complete with happy family where men and women play traditional roles, was the ideal that numerous wartime films suggested Americans could and should expect for themselves in an America of superior strength—a society in which young and old, rich and poor, labor and capital, and a multiplicity of ethnic groups all resided peacefully. The world of the films certainly didn't match the realities of American life with its labor struggles, rising juvenile delinquency, and racial discrimination, nor did it project an accurate picture of the situation for women, who were encouraged to work yet suffered continued wage discrimination, extremely limited opportunities for advancement, and no real provisions for child care. The films themselves often gave unclear signals. While they spouted the message of equality, the films did not treat all ethnic and racial minorities equally. The films encouraged women to work but only for the duration of the war, presenting a mixed message. In attempting to follow government directives while aiming to please the public, the industry produced films containing contradictory elements that may have reflected the somewhat confused and uncertain state of popular thought. Such films thus provide a unique perspective on American life during World War II.

The postwar world, with its rush to suburbia and the explosion of consumer products, saw the fulfillment of some of the film-dreams, but it also revealed what the films had tried to deny. Not all would share equally in the economic benefits; the gap between young and old would increase; many women seemed reluctant to revert to traditional roles; discrimination against ethnic and racial minorities became even more apparent; and American hegemony itself was soon challenged. In contrast to the confident wartime productions, many postwar films began to reflect the increasing anxieties of the period, but that is a story for another time.

Notes

1. "An Oral History with Robert F. Boyle," interviewed by George F. Turner, Oral History Program, Margaret Herrick Library, Academy of Motion Picture Arts and Sciences, Beverly Hills, Calif., 1998, 55.

2. "An Oral History with Hans J. Salter," interviewed by Warren Sherk, Oral History Program, Margaret Herrick Library, Academy of Motion Picture Arts and Sciences, Beverly Hills, Calif., 1994, 94.

3. Attendance figures provided by Motion Pictures Producers and Distributors of America, *International Motion Picture Almanac, 1942–43* (New York, 1942), 825. By 1942 attendance had risen to 90 million. The U.S. Department of Commerce survey, cited in "U.S. Survey Shows Films Get 80 to 85% of Amusement Coin," *Variety,* 19 July 1944, 1, 38, covered the years 1929–42 inclusive.

4. OWI bulletins, vertical file collection, Margaret Herrick Library, Academy of Motion Picture Arts and Sciences, Beverly Hills, Calif. Analysis of OWI and BMP is covered in Clayton R. Koppes and Gregory D. Black, *Hollywood Goes to War: How Politics, Profits, and Propaganda Shaped World War II Movies* (New York, 1987).

5. For an excellent social history of war movies and American culture, see Thomas Doherty, *Projections of War; Hollywood, American Culture, and World War II* (New York, 1993).

6. "Americans All," OWI bulletins, vertical file collection, Margaret Herrick Library, Academy of Motion Picture Arts and Sciences, Beverly Hills, Calif.

7. Louella Parsons, *Los Angeles Examiner,* 10 Mar. 1944, pt. 1, p. 13.

8. Jack Warner quoted in Philip French, *The Movie Moguls: An Informal History of the Hollywood Tycoons* (London, 1969), 109.

9. Nathan Glazer and Daniel P. Moynihan, *Beyond the Melting Pot: The Negroes, Puerto Ricans, Jews, Italians, and Irish of New York City,* 2d ed. (Cambridge, Mass., 1970), 246–47; Otis Ferguson, "Cagney: Great Guy," *New Republic* 92:1193 (13 Oct. 1937): 271–72.

10. *New York Times,* 28 May 1943, sec. 19, p. 3.

11. Donald Bogle, *Toms, Coons, Mulattoes, Mammies, and Bucks: An Interpretive History of Blacks in American Films* (New York, 1973), 92.

12. Daniel J. Leab, *From Sambo to Superspade: The Black Experience in Motion Pictures* (Boston, 1975), 135.

13. See Allen L. Woll, *The Latin Image in American Films* (Los Angeles, 1977), for a historical overview of Hispanics in films and an analysis of the effects of World War II. The correspondence regarding depictions of Latin, Italians, and Germans is in the Production Code Administration files, Margaret Herrick Library, Academy of Motion Picture Arts and Sciences, Beverly Hills, Calif.

14. *Time*, 9 Nov. 1942.

15. "Recruitment of Women," *War Information Program for the Screen*, OWI bulletins, vertical file collection, Margaret Herrick Library, Academy of Motion Picture Arts and Sciences, Beverly Hills, Calif.

3

Music Goes to War:
California, 1940–45

Ronald D. Cohen

"Tin Pan Alley is being very cautious currently about the patriotic fever engendered in the country as the result of the war abroad, and is going off no deep ends in the matter of prolific production of war songs or even harmless flag-wavers," noted *Billboard,* the show-business weekly, in late September 1940. "The general feeling among music publishers is that there is no sense in creating war hysteria thru flooding the country with war or anti-war ditties, and that even too many 'American' numbers may not be the wisest course at the present time." The music industry held back from much flag waving, following the country's general mood, but as the war crept closer feelings shifted. A year later, over two months before Pearl Harbor, *Billboard* editorialized: "The emphasis of our entire national life is now upon defense; defense industries receive the right of way; non-defense industries have faded, for a time at least, into the background. . . . However, it is neither right nor proper to classify the show business, in all of its many manifestations, among the non-defense industries. It is as vital to true national defense as the manufacturing of tanks and airplanes." For the next four years, popular music would indeed add its voice to the pro-war chorus, but its role during the war was not limited to flag-waving, sentimental tunes, or dance numbers. The war years were surely no break from the past, but provided vibrant musical continuity in California as well as nationwide, while underscoring, even sharpening, particular racial, cultural, and stylistic trends.[1]

"The war sent American songwriters into a flurry of activity in the production of militant songs," David Ewen concludes. Charles Tobias and Cliff Friend composed "We Did It Before" on December 8, upon hearing of Pearl Harbor, and thereafter patriotic songs gushed out of Tin Pan Alley, popular music's commercial center in New York City. Patriotic songs took various forms, however, covering the spectrum from virulently anti-German and anti-Japanese, to continually repackaged traditional themes of love, home, and nostalgia for the good old days. Johnny Mercer and Harold Arlen captured the prevailing mood in 1944 with "Ac-cent-tchu-ate the Positive," a best-seller recorded by Bing Crosby and the Andrews Sisters. Along the way, soldiers and civilians whistled through "Marching through Berlin," "Goodbye Mama, I'm Off to Yokohama," "Praise the Lord and Pass the Ammunition," "Boogie Woogie Bugle Boy," and "Oh, How I Hate to Get Up in the Morning," an Irving Berlin tune dusted off from World War I. Most songs were touched more by nostalgia than patriotism, a longing for home and hearth: "You'll Never Know," "Sentimental Journey," "Don't Sit Under the Apple Tree," "I'll Walk Alone," and particularly "White Christmas." The Andrews Sisters, Frank Sinatra, and scores of others lulled audiences with "Bei Mir Bist Du Schoen," "I've Heard That Song Before," "Saturday Night Is the Loneliest Night of the Week," and "Mairzy Doats." Tin Pan Alley tunesmiths cranked out a flood of songs, eagerly greeted by a public hungry for both entertainment and messages.[2]

Perhaps southern country music best exemplified traditional patriotism as it spread rapidly through the nation. The growth of northern war industries pulled black and white workers out of the South, accompanied by their infectious music. Moreover, the rise of Broadcast Music Inc. (BMI) after 1940 offered music publishers an alternative to Tin Pan Alley, particularly during 1941, when the radio networks banned the use of songs controlled by ASCAP (American Society of Composers, Authors, and Publishers). Both BMI and ASCAP collected performance fees for songwriters and publishers. The spread of country songs was furthered by a strike against the major recording companies by the American Federation of Musicians (AFM), stretching from August 1942 into late 1944, which allowed the smaller record companies to secure a foothold in the national markets. The shellac shortage also cut into production. "Country songwriters explored a variety of themes during the forties, but nothing attracted their attention more than the war itself," according to the historian Bill Malone. "Continuing a tradition set by their ballad-making ancestors centuries earlier, the country singers and writers chronicled the war as they talked of the experiences, suffering, and death of their departed soldiers and of the anxieties and sadness of their loved ones. Patriotic songs were among the most popular numbers in the hillbilly repertory from 1941 to 1946." Differing from Tin Pan Alley tunes, country music could approach war topics in a more earthy manner while still dripping with nostalgia and romance, as in "There's a Star-Spangled Banner Waving Somewhere," a hit by Hank Snow.[3]

Besides Tin Pan Alley and hillbilly tunes, other musical styles filled the jukeboxes, record shops, and airwaves, including folk, ethnic, rhythm and blues, comedy, gospel, blues, and particularly jazz from the sweet and swing bands, the latter most often associated with the war years. David Stowe has captured swing's importance well: "Although some people in and out of the military yearned for the shared marching music and martial songs of the Great War, American culture and its music had been irrevocably changed by the ascendancy of swing in the half-decade before 1941. The scandalous music just entering public awareness during the previous conflict had metamorphosed into swing, a music that by 1940 many Americans and foreigners recognized as America's most distinctive contribution to the world's musical culture. Not surprisingly, swing found itself transformed into a galvanizing symbol of national purpose." Bandleaders Benny Goodman, Count Basie, Duke Ellington, and especially Glenn Miller reached new heights of popularity, along with their singers, including Frank Sinatra, Peggy Lee, and Dinah Shore. Indeed, Stowe concludes, "changes set in motion by the war were already elevating the swing vocalists, male and female, at the expense of the big bands in which they had always served as unequal partners."[4]

The Smithsonian Institution has reissued a collection of recordings originally released by RCA during the war, including Sammy Kaye, Dinah Shore, Xavier Cugat, Elton Britt, Vaughn Monroe, Sons of the Pioneers, Ethel Merman, Glenn Miller, Kate Smith, Spike Jones, Jazz Gillum, Fats Waller, Sonny Boy Williamson, and Carson Robison. After surveying this wide range of popular music, David Tarnow concludes: "The songs that were popular during World War II with Americans—both at home and overseas—were not always about war-related issues. Perhaps this says something about the multifarious role of music; it could rally people to their patriotic duty, just as it could be relied on when what was needed was some romance, hope, laughter, and tears." Tarnow focuses on national musical trends and tastes, with no thought to local or regional differences. Perhaps there were no significant differences, but an understanding of popular music in California, particularly Los Angeles, will reveal particular details and variations. Above all, this will allow a more nuanced understanding of the musical scene in a rapidly changing section of the country, home to war industries as well as the Hollywood dream factory, record companies, and a racially, ethnically, and culturally mixed population thirsting for popular diversions and relevant entertainment.[5]

California's culture became somewhat transformed during the war, but more through an extension of previous trends than from significant shifts in form or style. The state gained well over a million citizens, mostly migrants from the South and Midwest looking for economic opportunities. They added to the state's ethnic, racial, and musical mix. Musical tastes were generally uniform throughout the country, with slight regional contrasts; *Billboard* listed best-selling records nationally and also by region—East, Midwest, South, and West Coast (essentially California). In mid-July 1943, for example, the Song Spinners' "Comin' In on a Wing and a Prayer" topped the charts nationally and in California, followed by Benny Goodman, Frank Sinatra with Harry James, and Dinah Shore. Only the Ink Spots' "Don't Get Around Much Anymore," holding the number two spot in California, broke the national mold. By year's end, "Pistol Packin' Mama," by Bing Crosby and the Andrews Sisters, held the region's top spot, while it trailed in second place nationally. A year later, the Crosby/Andrews Sisters' rendition of "Don't Fence Me In" held sway throughout the country. California's musical public generally followed national trends, with minimal variations, creating an eager, lucrative market for traveling bands and singers.

Nightclubs had struggled through the Depression and still found it rough-going as war loomed. "San Fran Niteries Doing Very Poorly" announced a June 1940 article in *Billboard*. Business was slightly better in Los Angeles, with the seventy-six nightclubs "doing business, with the take ranging from peanuts up to four figures." Only eight clubs featured name bands, including the Beverly Wilshire Hotel, Coconut Grove, and Earl Carroll, although two new spots, the Palladium and the Palomar, promised more elaborate acts. The satin-walled, springy-floored Palladium, touted as a technological wonder, opened with Tommy Dorsey's orchestra. Glenn Miller's two-week stay in May 1941 attracted vast throngs, with 5,200 dancers crowding the floor on opening night. As the center of the movie industry, the city attracted musical acts from throughout the country; a headline in early 1941 explained, "Flood of Screen Musicals Sends Vaude, Club, Air Acts to Coast; Dough Is Far from Fabulous, Tho." Outside of Los Angeles, the pickings were slimmer; "there are few bookings of orks in this immediate vicinity," *Billboard* noted in September. "Most of the spots use small combinations, with many of them letting a piano player take care of their dance-minded patrons."[6]

With war approaching, the increase in military spending added to the burgeoning economy, particularly in industrial areas, but this did not immediately translate into increased profits. "In general, the results of defense spending and population concentration have been extremely disappointing to indoor show-men to date," reported *Billboard*, "but there is some optimism as regards the fall. . . . In the Far West, San Francisco indoor amusements are up somewhat, tho not a great deal, a situation that also holds true generally in Los Angeles." Big bands still shared the bill at a few local theaters with first-run films. Jack Teagarden headlined at the Paramount with *Reaching for the Sun*. Bands appeared at other venues, for example the Pasadena Civic Auditorium, charging only twenty-five cents to hear Kay Kyser, Bob Crosby, or Wingy Manone, where "no stunts are pulled, jitterbugging to extreme is taboo, and there are no pass-outs." Into September 1941, Duke Ellington led the show "Jump for Joy" at the Mayan Theater; Woody Herman, Gene Krupa, and Jimmy Dorsey headlined at the Palladium; and Ted Weems followed Ozzie Nelson into the Casa Maña-na in Culver City. This was perhaps a typical month's selection for the city's white dancers and big band fans. Commercial white swing bands dominated the large dance halls and nightclubs, underscoring the city's racial divide.[7]

"Tin Pan Alley Fires Song Salvo at Axis," *Billboard* reported on December 20, less than two weeks after Pearl Harbor. Tunesmiths rushed to fill the void, but the paper warned that hard times perhaps loomed for the music indus-try, for a variety of reasons: news reports crowded out musical shows on the radio, a paper shortage would raise the price of sheet music, the armed forces would draw away personnel, and other cuts would hurt the record industry. At the local level, specific problems quickly emerged. The West Coast black-out hit the night spots, as they scrambled to adjust. "There is no definite esti-mate as to how much the blackouts have cost night clubs, theaters and other amusement centers since the start of hostilities," *Billboard* reported from San Francisco. "Hardest hit are the niteries. . . . Signs and marquees are blacked out nightly in co-operation with defense plans. Officials have announced there will be no restrictions on shows, and are urging everyone to attend their favorite places of amusement." The industry quickly recovered. Because of the black-outs, radio stations added additional broadcasts from area nightclubs and ballrooms. "That show business will boom for American acts is the consen-sus of opinion here," *Billboard* reported from Los Angeles on December 27. "Bookers feel that public morale will have to be boosted and, for this reason, more acts will be employed." Tommy Dorsey was soon packing them in at the Hollywood Palladium, drawing about 18,000 one weekend in January. Quickly, "night club business [was] back to normal, with some spots doing better than ever before." A few venues closed, but most opened to larger crowds.[8]

Throughout the war, the American Federation of Musicians, led by its dom-ineering president, James C. Petrillo, struggled to balance the financial inter-ests of its members, national patriotism, and Petrillo's imperial style. The main struggle would develop between the union and the record companies, but side issues continually erupted, causing various ill feelings. For example, Local 47 in Southern California ruled that its members could not perform in benefit performances for defense-related causes. A "Dance for Victory" at the Shrine Auditorium in early March 1942, running from 7 P.M. to 5 A.M., featured a stellar lineup of bands playing for free: Bob Crosby, Tommy Dorsey, Kay Kyser, and Paul Whiteman. But the union objected that while the crowd of 15,000 raised over $4,000 for the war effort, a rather paltry sum considering the name talent, the Victory committee paid less than union scale for one union band. Bands would continue to play for defense workers and other war-related events, but the segregated union, with all black musicians in Local 767, regularly objected and tried to control the situation.

The record industry boosted sales as the economy mushroomed. Anxious to take advantage of the situation, Glenn Wallichs, owner of Music City, a record store in Hollywood, joined with the film producer and successful lyricist Buddy De Sylva and the songwriter Johnny Mercer to form locally based Capitol Records in April 1942. They quickly released sides by Paul Whiteman, Dennis Day, Martha Tilton, and Gordon Jenkins. Capitol soon joined the industry's leading labels, despite the crippling effects of the musicians' strike; the company made its peace early with the AFM, in October 1943, then signed Stan Kenton and Benny Carter, among others. Their first new recording was "Pistol Packin' Mama" by Jo Stafford and the Pied Pipers. Wallichs used Music City for radio broadcasts and featured "Autograph Days" with Spike Jones, the Dorsey Brothers, and Dinah Shore; his physical proximity to NBC, CBS, and the Palladium guaranteed access to top artists and thus heightened the store's visibility. There was no shortage of bands and performers in the area, with Harry James appearing at the Palladium and Duke Ellington at the Trianon in South Gate in May. James's eight-week attendance topped 230,000. Name bands continued to shuffle in and out of the clubs and dance halls, as the crowds swelled throughout the war years. "Ballroom business has struck a bonanza and business is on the top shelf," crowed *Billboard* in October.[9]

The Hollywood studios increased their output of white and black movie musicals—including *This Is the Army, Stage Door Canteen,* and *Stormy Weather*—drawing additional bands to the area. But soon enough, gas and tire rationing threatened to keep the fans at home, particularly those unable to get to the civic auditoriums in Pasadena and Glendale, the Aragon and Casino Gardens in Ocean Park, or the Trianon in South Gate. Although streetcars were convenient in some sections of the city, they did not run after midnight. The Colored Musicians' Mutual Protective Association, otherwise known as AFM Local 767, raised its after-midnight prices in order to encourage clubs to start earlier. The curfew generally forced midnight closings, with shows often beginning at seven, six days a week; after-hour spots on Central Avenue attracted white musicians and patrons looking for late action. On the other hand, swing-shift dances were held from midnight into the morning hours on Saturdays and Sundays at the Casino Gardens Ballroom in Ocean Park, featuring Bob Crosby, Alvino Ray, Freddie Slack, and Skinny Ennis. Some bandmembers held regular defense industry jobs while performing on the weekends; personnel from Alvino Ray's orchestra worked the graveyard shift at the Vega

Aircraft plant, then played Saturday nights at the Long Beach and Glendale auditoriums. Similar issues affected night spots in San Francisco, which were doing very well into 1943.[10]

The big bands preferred older tunes, recorded before the strike, and tended to ignore newer compositions. According to *Billboard* in July 1943, "[Band]leaders figure they have nothing to gain by going to the expense of making an arrangement on every ballad or novelty tune. . . . The trend is an expedient policy for the leader and besides, is playing [*sic*] off." While a national tendency, these reports come from Los Angeles, where the trend was most visible. A poll conducted in early 1944 by Al Jarvis, host of the popular L.A. radio show "Make-Believe Ballroom," with all recorded music, discovered that Dick Haymes topped the list of male vocalists, followed by Bing Crosby and Frank Sinatra; Helen Forrest ranked first among the "girl" vocalists, then Jo Stafford and Connie Haines. Sammy Kaye led the bandleaders, ahead of Freddie Martin, Jimmy Dorsey, and Spade Cooley. The returns had a few surprises, particularly western swing–master Cooley's high local showing.[11]

The nightclub business continued to prosper into the war's third year, although a few additional problems emerged. The large influx of musicians to Los Angeles threatened to create a glut and potential lowering of wages, despite the AFM's struggle to maintain union scale. Moreover, a new 30 percent nightclub tax would lead to increased prices. "Feeling was expressed that bad biz would be felt right down to the beer and sawdust spots and that even now many of these bistros are canning live music and trusting to the juke box and the customer's nickels." Despite such problems, business remained good, with the entertainment tax remaining in place. Profits from dance halls seemed so enticing that bandleaders began thinking of purchasing them, particularly after Horace Heidt cleared $40,000 from his Trianon Ballroom in South Gate in one year. Tommy Dorsey began eyeing the Palisades Ballroom in Santa Monica, also considering the Pacific Square Ballroom in San Diego. Charlie Barnet became part-owner of the Hollywood Casino in early 1945. According to *Billboard*, "Policy is already being set calling for ballroom to feature colored as well as white bands, with Lionel Hampton possible future booking." While the big bands filled the clubs and ballrooms at night, they also performed at aircraft plants such as Douglas, Lockheed, and North American, as well as various shipyards, during the day. Some continued to entertain swing-shift workers. Most clubs opened six nights, under union pressure, although the largest, those paying an act over $250, could operate through the entire week.[12]

As the war neared an end in Europe, Southern California's nightlife continued at a fevered clip. Jack Teagarden led his band at the Orpheum in Los Angeles in March 1945, along with Mildred Bailey and other acts, sharing the theater with the film *Lights of Old Santa Fe*. Moreover, top names were scheduled for the summer season at the Hollywood Bowl, including Xavier Cugat, Duke Ellington, Carmen Miranda, Tommy Dorsey, and Frank Sinatra. Through the year the big bands remained highly popular statewide. But they did not monopolize the scene, which remained crowded with various acts and performers, catering to a diverse range of musical tastes and styles.

While both black and white bands were able to perform at the larger, more popular venues, fancy nightclubs, and large ballrooms, racial segregation generally remained in Southern California. There were a few exceptions. The Hollywood Canteen, the largest nightclub in the country, initiated by John Garfield and Bette Davis in 1942, hired one hundred black female dance hostesses and vigorously maintained an integrated atmosphere, but not without difficulty. Black and white musicians volunteered their services to entertain up to 25,000 mostly white soldiers a week. Pressure also came from the NAACP, which launched an Interracial Committee to integrate USO clubs and camp dances, a formidable undertaking. "During the war racial tensions increased in the music world over the meaning of American 'home' values," Lewis Erenberg argues, detailing the burdens of racial segregation and discrimination throughout the country. Still, black and white audiences generally preferred different sounds and environments. Indeed, a thriving black community, with a distinctive musical culture, existed in Los Angeles.[13]

"By the mid-1940s, Central Avenue had become *the* jazz thoroughfare of the West," Gary Marmorstein has written. "On Central itself, there were dozens of legitimate nightclubs, including The Brown Bomber, Bird in the Basket, and the lounge at the Dunbar Hotel, where pianist/singer Nellie Lutcher held court. And there were the so-called breakfast clubs—after-hours places where you brought your own booze and danced past sunrise." A vital social and cultural cement of the black community, these spots also attracted whites from throughout the area looking for hot music and adventure. Whites could always legally frequent black clubs, but the opposite seldom occurred; Jim Crow practice controlled attendance, or at least seating, at many night spots throughout the area. Indeed, racial friction heightened during the war years. "Los Angeles in particular was associated with war-generated racial tensions that reflected the increasing importance of Hollywood to the swing industry," according to David Stowe. He notes that the influx of war workers, combined with the presence of radio shows and Hollywood movies that attracted black and white musicians to the area, "created both the need for entertainment on a massive scale and the potential for racial conflict provoked by friction among different cultural mores and competition for housing and other amenities." Some clubs practiced Jim Crow hiring policies, including Horace Heidt's Trianon ballroom.

Near the end of the war, the Los Angeles Chamber of Commerce tried to suspend the licenses of fifteen clubs, supposedly because they allowed racial fraternizing.[14]

Drummer Johnny Otis, a Greek American who strongly identified with the black community, moved to Los Angeles from the Bay Area in 1943 and quickly plunged into Central Avenue's nightlife. While working in Bardu Ali's pit band at the Lincoln Theater, then as leader of the house band at the Club Alabam, he recorded for the local Excelsior and Exclusive labels. Owned by Otis and Leon Rene, the record company also released Nat "King" Cole, Joe Liggins's 1945 rhythm and blues landmark "The Honeydrippers," and Charles Brown. Brown had moved to California from Arkansas in 1943, and the next year appeared with Bardu Ali and also at Ivie Anderson's Chicken Shack, mostly playing piano. Next, along with Johnny Moore's Three Blazers at the Talk of the Town Club in Beverly Hills, he launched his distinguished singing career.

Numerous jazz musicians were homegrown, such as Buddy Collette, Jack Kelson, Chico Hamilton, Dexter Gordon, and Charles Mingus. "I hit Central Avenue when I was a kid, man, because that was the thing in the forties, '44, '45," Cecil "Big Jay" McNeely reflected. "The Avenue was popping then. You had the Club Alabam—Johnny Otis playing there—and they had a full chorus line, just like the Cotton Club in New York. And you had the Downbeat. You had the Last Word. . . . The clubs were grooving, because money was popping; people had plenty of money."[15]

Countless black musicians made Los Angeles their home, including the electrifying pianist Art Tatum. Tatum returned to Los Angeles from New York in 1942 and quickly melded into the vibrant local music scene. "It was very early in '42, he [Tatum] was appearing at a place called The Streets of Paris, on Hollywood Blvd., it was a saloon down in the basement," Joe Bushkin remembered. "And as I recall, it was Coleman Hawkins and a quartet or quintet, and Art Tatum. We used to shoot crap while the band group was on, with the waiters, Tatum, too." The next year he formed the influential Art Tatum Trio. "On Central Avenue, black music history was compacted within a few city blocks," writes Ted Gioia. "The Downbeat, two doors past the Alabam and three doors beyond the Dunbar, boasted an equally rich past. Howard McGhee's pioneering bebop band—the first modern jazz ensemble on the West Coast, predating the more heralded arrival of [Charlie] Parker and [Dizzy] Gillespie by several months—was formed there in early 1945." Coleman Hawkins opened at Billy Berg's on Vine Street, with another pioneering bebop ensemble. Dolphin's of Hollywood, the neighborhood around-the-clock record store owned by Big John Dolphin, served as a center of social and musical life for the Central Avenue community. Out of this swirl of activity, rhythm and blues also began to develop, particularly through the piano playing of Charles Brown, the electric guitar of Aaron "T-Bone" Walker, and the musicianship of Joe Liggins, Wynonie Harris, and Roy Milton.[16]

Countless black musicians attracted loyal followings. The Nat "King" Cole Trio played the Radio Room on Vine for two years. Jimmie Lunceford's orchestra fronted the show "Harlem Revue" at the Orpheum Theater in mid-1941 and "Paul White sang *Honeysuckle Road* and went to town on a Harlem step that included handsprings and splits." *Billboard,* sensitive to race issues, headlined in early 1942, "L.A. Territory A Hot Spot Now For Negro Orks." Cee Pee Johnson headlined at the Club Alabam, Lorenzo Flennoy at the Club Royal, Sanders King at the Recreation Room in Hollywood, and Slim (Gaillard) and Slam (Stewart) at the Club Caprice. A year later the show-business weekly noted, "[T]he hottest sepia attraction in town, at the moment, at least, is Benny Carter." In addition to performing at Joe Zucca's Hollywood Club, MGM signed Carter to join Lena Horne in the musical *As Thousands Cheer.*[17]

Jimmie Lunceford, who was successful with a nightly broadcast over KHJ and the Mutual network, quit the Trianon Ballroom because of racial discrimination during the hot summer of 1943. Two of Count Basie's bandmembers, Snooky Young and Harry Edison, invited by Lunceford, were refused admittance, but the AFM ordered the bandleader to complete his six weeks at the club, which he agreed to do. The Trianon continued to book black bands, with Louis Armstrong appearing the next year. Zutty Singleton, a drummer who had left New Orleans with Louis Armstrong in the early 1920s, settled in Los Angeles in 1943. He opened at the Club Trinidad, "one of the Coast's hottest hangouts for jazz purists and hot record collectors." Erskine Hawkins appeared at the Plantation on Central Avenue, a "new colored night club," *Billboard* reported in August. Small clubs sprouted throughout the city—the Streets of Paris, the Hangover, the Latin Quarter, the Hollywood Café, Billy Berg's—featuring exhilarating jazz night after night. Norman Granz began staging jam sessions at Herb Rose's 331 Club in Hollywood in 1943, featuring Nat "King" Cole and Lester Young; both white and black patrons were welcomed, breaking the usual Hollywood color bar. Indeed, Granz influenced Billy Berg and other club owners to integrate both their stages and seating areas. Musicians and audiences kept some distance between the different jazz styles—Dixieland, traditional, swing, sweet, and bebop—with often heated exchanges among the musicians. Billy Berg's welcomed bebop soon after VJ day, booking the Dizzy Gillespie Sextet featuring Charlie "Bird" Parker.[18]

The AFM also practiced Jim Crow with its separate black and white locals. Barney Bigard challenged the policy in Los Angeles, claiming he could join the white local because he was not black, but a Creole of Spanish and French ancestry. The NAACP backed the challenge and urged complete integration of all musician locals. Petrillo responded that the segregation was voluntary, preferred by all sides, and that the union's national office had no authority to order the locals to integrate. The policy continued until 1953, when the two locals merged. But generally the color line among musicians wavered, with no clear-cut overall policy of segregation. The increasingly popular Louis Jordan performed at the Trocadero in mid-1944, where he staged his "Teen-Time" show for the bobby-sox trade, and appeared on Al Jarvis's "Downbeat Derby" over the Mutual network. In San Francisco, Louis Armstrong led an all-black review, including Buck and Bubbles, at the Golden Gate Theater in August 1944, sharing the bill with the movie *A Night of Adventure*. At the same time, Count Basie appeared with the Delta Rhythm Boys and other acts at the Orpheum in Los Angeles, appearing with *Leave It to the Irish*. Two months later, Earl "Fatha" Hines headlined at the same spot with an "all-sepia show." While *Billboard* believed the "appeal is limited to the hipsters with the squares finding little solace in the hot music," it made no comment on the accompanying movie, *Block Busters*.[19]

Billboard focused attention on the growing market for black music in Los Angeles in early 1945, summarizing the scene as the war ground on: "Growing L.A. Sepia Clubs Offer 15G Weekly Market." "With what was formerly 'Little Tokyo' and psychic joints being taken over by an incoming Negro population, a number of spots have sprung up in what is today 'Little Harlem,'" the piece began. Black nightlife had moved into "Little Toyko" soon after the Japanese residents had been expelled following Pearl Harbor. Night spots on Lennox Avenue and the adjacent Central Avenue were going strong, including She's Playhouse, the Cobra Club, Café Society, the Last Word, Club Plantation, and the Rhythm Club, which opened after one in the morning. Club Plantation featured name bands, including Count Basie and Lucky Milliner, while the smaller clubs starred more local acts, such as the Harris Brothers, Sammy Yates's four-piece group, and Big Six Reeves and his Orchestra. The article concluded: "The Negro clubs are offering booking agents a pretty lucrative field. Talent has to be in the groove to put the agent in the greener groves." But a few weeks later Club Plantation closed, suffering from a lack of business and the enforced midnight curfew. At the same time, nightclubs on the posh Sunset Strip in Hollywood began welcoming black acts. The Nat "King" Cole Trio and Benny Carter's orchestra appeared at the Trocadero. "Booking of an all-colored show at the Troc is a quick follow-up for Duke Ellington's date at Ciro's, which was a first for a name colored band on the Strip, altho the King Cole Trio held forth in the Troc's cocktail room last summer and did terrific biz," *Billboard* reported. The Trio was also featured in the Paramount film *Stork*

Club and had a national broadcast over the Mutual network. Although still centered in the black neighborhoods, black music by war's end had spread throughout the city's night spots, as it did in most northern cities. Moreover, in the spring of 1945, Jules Bihari, who had been operating jukeboxes in the black community, launched Modern Records in order to keep his machines filled. With the whole Bihari family involved, Modern became one of the most influential rhythm and blues companies.[20]

Perhaps Barney Hoskyns has most colorfully depicted the scene through-out the war:

> As this population grew, so Central Avenue became more bustlingly alive. At night it was hard to move for the crowds promenading and filing into clubs like the Plan-tation, the Downbeat, the Savoy, Lovejoy's, the Memo, and sometime Ellington singer Ivie Anderson's celebrated Chicken Shack. Here was the whole gamut of nocturnal life, from the swankiest vaudeville theatres to the dingiest poolhalls. Here was the 'sea of opulence' Art Pepper recalled from his teenage days in Lee Young's Alabam house band; here also were the cheap Chinese diners and chicken-wire dives where vicious-looking men sat around plotting heists and hijackings. Somewhere between the two extremes were the innumerable 'after-hours' joints which littered the Ave-nue like rats' nests: places like Brother's, the Turban Room, Jack's Basket Room, Johnny Cornish's Double V, Stuff Crouch's Backstage.[21]

Music played a vital role in the black community, offering entertainment and comfort for civilians and soldiers alike during a stressful time, although char-acterized by generally plentiful jobs and economic security. The same held true for southern whites who had migrated to the area during the 1930s and through the war years. James Gregory has captured the move of the "Okies" into Cal-ifornia during the Depression, where they reestablished their subculture: "If the growing popularity of country music made it the pathway to fame for a handful of migrants and a career option for others, it meant something almost as important to the thousands of Okies whose relationship to music was that of listener rather than performer. The music's success gave its migrant audi-ence the chance to bask in the reflected glory of musicians from their home states." Indeed, the "market for hillbillies, real or feigned, whether from the Ozarks or the foothills of Ozone Park, is holding up admirably well under the strain of years of heavy radio play," *Billboard* remarked in late 1940. The steady influx from the South and Southwest created a growing market in Southern California for live music as well as the numerous network hillbilly shows, such as the Grand Ole Opry. "Hillbilly music has evoked such a terrific response in this territory that Foreman Phillips, manager of the Venice (Calif.) Ballroom, plans to extend his County Barn Dances to San Diego, Bakersfield, Fresno, and other California towns," noted *Billboard* in mid-1943. The Venice Ballroom now featured Spade Cooley and His Barn Dance Boys, a band organized in 1941, who remained for seventy-four weeks; it had previously booked Roy Rogers, Patsy Montana, Sons of the Pioneers, Eddie and Jimmie Dean, and Tex Ritter—all country stars. Phillips also featured his County Barn Dances over his daily radio show, "Merry-Go-Round," which included a "Western Hit Parade." Cooley's band first recorded for Columbia in late 1944; "Shame on You," released the next January, became a minor hit.[22]

The area's increasing newcomers from the southern and plains states pressured the big bands to include rural music, both black and white, in their repertoires. "Dance bands . . . are being forced to insert in their books hillbilly, mountain music and to some extent race ballads to comply with request of dancers," noted *Billboard*. Woody Herman had numerous requests for "Fort Worth Jail," while Eddie Miller had difficulty meeting the demand, although he began working up arrangements "with a Texas-Oklahoma flavor to please the dancing Oakies here who expect and demand a dance band to play songs of that nature." Even Louis Armstrong, at the Aragon Ballroom in Ocean Park, catered to the crowd, and Matty Malneck, at the posh Hotel Biltmore Bowl, reported he had requests for square dance music. "One maestro here hopes the current appreciation of corny, race, hillbilly and mountain music continues after the war is won," argued the show-business weekly. "Spike Jones and His City Slickers are the top men on the totem pole, all because the Oakies [*sic*] consider him to have the most to offer." The demand continued to increase. Roy Acuff broke the attendance record at the Venice Pier Ballroom in April 1944: "Proximity of war workers, who have treked to California for the shekels and not the sunshine, was believed responsible for the turnout. Most newcomers hail from those States where music dished up by outfits like the Acuff group is standard Saturday night fare."[23]

After his extended stint at the Venice Ballroom, Spade Cooley, one of the most popular bandleaders in the area, moved to the Riverside Breakfast Club, where his version of western swing, a term he popularized, continued to attract attention. "[This] Music is not the true Western type," noted one review, "with its lyrics of woe-begone affairs. Wailing is out, too. Cooley's type is self-dubbed Western swing. Dancers can fox-trot or do a slow jitter to it. The bounce is neat and the music, without brass, is easy on the ears." Country music was not limited to clubs and dance halls with a western motif, however. The Aragon Ballroom alternated swing bands with the "cowboy outfits" of Cooley and Bob Wills, labeled by *Billboard* "sagebrush musickers." About the same time, in mid-1944, the French Casino on Sunset Boulevard was transformed into the Gower Gulch Dance Hall, "a sagebrush spot" catering to those "who go for the Western jive."[24]

While Cooley scored high in local popularity polls, Bob Wills had greater national acclaim. Long based in Tulsa, Oklahoma, Wills appeared in numerous movies starting in 1940, including eight in 1942, and while he loathed Hollywood, he began spending more time in the area, appearing frequently with part of his big band. After a brief army stint in 1943, he moved to the San Fernando Valley and played weekly at the Mission Beach Ballroom in San Diego. He also had a daily radio show over local KMTR. Country music's popularity, particularly among the uprooted country folk, owed much to its dance appeal and catchy tunes, but James Gregory argues that "all through the difficult resettlement years of the 1930s and the more accommodating 1940s, the music seemed to provide the resources for a sense of independence and pride. Like the evangelical churches, it offered possibilities for ingroup social contacts. . . . Standard country-song symbols like nostalgia, plain living, and cowboy courage helped to reinforce the understanding that the migrants were different from and perhaps better than their California neighbors." Western swing drew much of its style and inspiration from big band jazz, yet catered to a quite separate audience.[25]

Because of the movie and record industries, Southern California served as a strong magnet for musicians throughout the war, including country and western performers. Capitol Records early recorded Tex Ritter, soon followed by Jack Guthrie and Wesley Tuttle. Ritter starred in numerous movies, as did legions of cowboy stars and country musicians, including Jimmy Wakely, Roy Rogers, Gene Autry, and Johnny Bond. Indeed, Hollywood proved a mecca for country musicians, who floated in and out and frequently performed in the area. Merle Travis arrived at war's end, after a stint in the marines, and bounced from cowboy films to radio jamborees, western swing bands, and club dates, performing with Cliffie Stone, Tex Ritter, and Wesley Tuttle. Stone had his own radio show on KXLA, beginning in 1942, the "Dinner Bell Roundup" at midday. Stone also served as band contractor, staff musician, and stand-up comic on KNX's Saturday night "Hollywood Barn Dance," a network show. The stage was filled with singing cowboys and cowgirls, including Foy Willing and the Riders of the Purple Sage. When Gene Autry returned to Hollywood from the Army Air Corps in mid-1945, he resurrected his popular radio show, "Melody Ranch."

The term "folk music" at the time designated white music with rural roots, also called "hillbilly music" (later "country and western"). But there was another sort of folk music present in Los Angeles, with similar rustic roots but closely allied with the political Left. Woody Guthrie had lived in Los Angeles for a few years in the late 1930s, then moved to New York in 1940. He left behind a strong musical legacy, partially assumed by his cousin Jack Guthrie, whose recording of Woody's "Oklahoma Hills" for Capitol became a hit in 1945. A core group of Left activists with a strong interest in folk music, including Lewis Allen (Abel Meeropol), Vern Partlow, Bill Wolff, Bill Oliver, Mario Casetta, Earl Robinson, and Ray Glaser, were centered in Los Angeles during the war. Robinson, a composer deeply involved with Left musical and political culture, had arrived in Hollywood from New York in 1943, where he obtained some film work, scoring *A Walk in the Sun,* and performed for war workers and servicemen. In late 1945, Robinson and his folk friends staged a hootenanny, or folk variety show, the first of many to follow.

While Southern California's musical scene remained vibrant throughout the war, similar activities occurred in other parts of the state. In the Bay Area, for example, both black and white musical styles easily coexisted. The large population of uprooted southerners created a ready market for jazz, rhythm and blues, and hillbilly music. "Victory Barn Dances" attracted large crowds of young white shipyard workers, and a number of local groups emerged to meet the increasing demand: Elwin Cross and the Arizona Ramblers, Dave Stogner and the Arkansawyers, Bill Woods and the Texas Stars, Leo Stevens and the Ozark Playboys, Dude Martin and the Round-Up, and Ray Wade and His Rhythm Riders. Wade had his own dance hall and weekly radio show on Oakland's KWBR, which shared the dial with other country music programs—Eddie the Hired Hand's "Hillbilly Hit Parade" (Oakland), Foreman Bill's "Rhythm Rodeo" (San Francisco), and Long Horn Joe's "Cowboy Hit Parade" (Oakland). Oakland's Cactus Jack developed a local taste for Bob Wills, who toured the area, where he attracted 19,000 to the Oakland Civic Auditorium. The city also sported numerous country night spots, including Craby Joe's Big Barn and John's Half Barrel. The popular Maddox Brothers and Rose, based in Modesto, fragmented by the war, still continued to tour the state with their upbeat country sounds.[26]

The black neighborhoods of the East Bay and San Francisco nurtured a lively music scene, including the Swing Club, Harvey's Rex Club, and Slim Jenkins' Place in Oakland. Louis Jordan, Cab Calloway, Duke Ellington, and Count Basie regularly played the white-owned Sweets Ballroom and the Oakland Auditorium, drawing large crowds of black and white swing fans. As the juke joints and nightclubs augmented their business, rural blues players also began appearing, including Lowell Fulson from Tulsa, Oklahoma. Highly influenced by T-Bone Walker and Jimmy Rushing, and adept at the electric guitar, Fulson helped shape the West Coast rhythm and blues sound. Blues pianist Ivory Joe Hunter arrived in Oakland from Houston in 1942 and quickly made his mark in the Bay Area; in 1945 he launched the short-lived Ivory Records.

Blues and after-hours clubs also sprouted in North Richmond—the Savoy Club, Minnie Lue's, Tappers Inn—rather unsavory places, some with female ownership, where blacks felt comfortable listening to Folson and other familiar performers. Few whites were allowed in. Local gospel groups also developed loyal followings, appearing at ship launchings, church programs, and radio shows. Bob Geddins aided the Rising Stars Singers, then in 1946 began recording Fulson and other bluesmen in his West Oakland storefront, on the Big Town and Trilon labels, helping to develop the Oakland blues sound. Blues singer Jimmy Witherspoon, while a dishwasher in the early forties at Lovejoy's, a popular chicken joint in Los Angeles, had sat in with Art Tatum and Slam Stewart; in 1944, after a Merchant Marine stint, he returned to Vallejo, where his mother lived, and began performing at the Waterfront, a local club. Then he joined Jay McShann's band and achieved national fame.[27]

Musical entertainment spanned the range from the glitz of stars and starlets entertaining the GIs at the very popular Hollywood Canteen, to massive ballrooms as well as intimate clubs, to neighborhood joints. Every racial and ethnic group had its own musical entertainment and night spots. The large and growing Mexican-American population, particularly in Southern California, naturally produced a market for Latin music. The racially segregated city of Los Angeles, further divided by the Zoot Suit Riots in 1943, had little official recognition of the social life of the Spanish-speaking population. The all-Latin program at the Orpheum Theater, however, attracted good notice in *Billboard* in early 1945, with Carlos Molina and his Orchestra sharing the bill with Miguelito Valdez, a Cuban singer. The program preceded the showing of *The Cisco Kid Returns*. A few months earlier, Valdez had headlined at the theater, along with Chuy Reyes, the Samba Sirens, Aurora Roche, and the Cuban Diamonds, followed by the film *Shadow of Suspicion*. Molina would play an important role in introducing the tango and rumba to Californians. In *Barrio Rhythm*, Steven Loza captures the richness and variety of music in the community, although his story begins in 1945: "As World War II was coming to an end, musical life in the Mexican community of Los Angeles continued to be active. Performances by local musicians and other entertainers, films, and theatrical presentations from various Latin American countries were an integral part of the musical scene." Among the artists who performed locally in late 1944 and 1945, he mentions Tito Guizar and Celia Martinez, popular Mexican singers. Both local and international stars filled the clubs and theaters.[28]

"The war years brought new forms of musical expression that coincided with a new mode of awareness emerging among many Mexican Americans," Loza writes.

New styles of music, such as the big band sound, heavily influenced the musical culture of young Chicanos, especially within the pachuco cult of Los Angeles. It was during this period that Lalo Guerrero, for example, composed such songs as "Chuco suave" (which incorporated the *Caló* dialect of Spanish popular among pachucos), "Marijuana Boogie," and "Vamos a bailar," in which musical forms fused the rhythmic structures of swing, rumba, and jazz. Hybridization pervaded the culture in language, music, dance, politics, and patriotism.

The mixing of racial and ethnic groups during the war caused various reactions, positive and negative, and in the process cultural forms were duly influenced. With the war's end, new clubs sprang up, including El Sombrero in Central Los Angeles. On the ground floor Don Tosti, formerly with Tommy Dorsey, led his group, while Tily Lopez's orchestra occupied the second floor. Others soon appeared as the Spanish-speaking population swelled. In September 1945, Paul Merabal, owner of the Club Brazil, Club Babalu, and Club Cobra, reserved the giant Shrine Auditorium to celebrate Mexican Independence Day; the eclectic show featured Artie Shaw, Carmen Cavallaro, Miguelito Valdez, Chino Ortiz, and other favorites in the Spanish-speaking community.[29]

With the end of the war approaching, various constraints, such as the established midnight curfew for nightclubs and bars, were lifted. In June many clubs returned to the prewar 2 A.M. closing time. The entertainment industry continued to prosper. Lena Horne with the Jimmie Lunceford Orchestra and the Step Brothers set a new record at the Orpheum Theater in July, topping the Ink Spots with Ella Fitzgerald and Cootie Williams, who had appeared the previous year. Xavier Cugat opened at the Aragon Ballroom, providing stiff competition for the Dorsey Brothers' Casino Gardens, which had recently secured a liquor license and lined up the Jimmy Dorsey and Glen Gray bands. The Casa Mañana Ballroom in Culver City "turned to a Negro name band policy to meet competition, with Count Basie featured thru July," followed by Jimmie Lunceford. Duke Ellington and Charlie Barnet had shared the stage, and the owners hoped to feature Erskine Hawkins, Cootie Williams, as well as the Nat "King" Cole Trio.[30]

There was talk of expanding some of the dance halls, including Horace Heidt's Trianon. Sherrill Corwin, owner of the Orpheum, the only movie theater still featuring name bands, had plans to open a ballroom in East Los Angeles. "Jump addicts got a taste of top jive last week when Count Basie and his 18-man ork moved into the Orpheum," noted *Billboard* in mid-August. "Sock arrangements, solid rhythm and smooth solo work brought the house down after each number with payees stomping and yelling for more." They shared the bill with the Roy Rogers film, *Utah*. Simultaneously, the Floyd Ray Orchestra with Valaida Snow appeared at Shepp's Playhouse, which "depends largely on mixed colored-white trade." Norman Granz also planned to take his legendary "Jazz at the Philharmonic" show on the road, after a dozen concerts in Los Angeles. He had moved from the smaller 331 Club to the spacious Philharmonic Auditorium for the first of his integrated Sunday afternoon jams in July 1944; the initial concert featured the Nat "King" Cole Trio, with Barney Bigard, Buddy Rich, and the showy guitar player Les Paul. The Philharmonic housed the Duke Ellington Orchestra in early January 1945, part of a national broadcast sponsored by *Esquire* magazine, which also featured the Benny Goodman Quintet in New York and Louis Armstrong from New Orleans. Soon enough, however, the big band era would began to fade, a casualty of high expenses and changing popular tastes.[31]

California's burgeoning population, in the midst of the agonies of war, facing social dislocations accompanied by welcomed economic prosperity, eagerly sought musical entertainment and diversion. Music programs filled the airwaves, record stores stocked a rich variety of music, despite the lengthy recording ban, and a plethora of musical venues—juke joints, large and small nightclubs, ballrooms, theaters, auditoriums, and even factories—catered to throngs of dancers and listeners. The large swing bands and their crooners, male and female, perhaps garnered the most attention, but they had plenty of competition from an abundance of singers, bands, and assorted musicians. The increasingly diversified population demanded their own familiar music—black jazz, white jazz, rhythm and blues, pop, blues, hillbilly, folk, polkas, Mexican-American—which was all readily available.

The musical styles of racial, ethnic, and geographical subcultures influenced mainstream Tin Pan Alley sounds, with considerable cross-pollination, as popular music became increasingly heterogeneous, searching for the widest possible audience. Still, discrete musical forms and styles survived and coexisted. For example, black customers appreciated standard pop and swing arrangements, yet patronized black establishments and record stores, preferring a somewhat different sound and ambience. While racial barriers were not absolute, segregation persisted among musicians, in nightclubs, and throughout society, creating obstacles but also opportunities for performers and audiences alike. Little of the music was overtly patriotic, certainly after the war's early years. Most served to supply a suitable dance beat, appeal to longings for romance, stability, and security, tickle the funny bone, and/or connect with vital ethnic, cultural, and racial identities. California's music scene mirrored national trends, notwithstanding certain local influences and variations—the flourishing film industry, the mounting influx of black and white southerners and

Okies, the vibrant presence of Mexican Americans, and the number of professional musicians who settled in the area. The war years served as no musical watershed, no obvious break from preceding decades, but only magnified earlier styles and interests, which readily continued into the immediate postwar years.

Above all, the state's increasingly heterogeneous population created a healthy market for musical subcultures, mirroring society's fractures and stresses, a tame example of covert, and occasionally overt, racial and ethnic slights and tensions. Throughout the war to combat totalitarianism and racism, musical segregation was rife. However, in some sense popular music occupied the vanguard of the integration struggle, with considerable cross-pollination of musical styles, bands, and perhaps even venues. Yet this only went so far. California surely reflected and refracted national social and musical trends, not initiated but accelerated by the war.

Notes

I wish to thank the following for their advice and assistance: Frank Devenport, Lou Gottlieb, Lew Erenberg, Dave Samuelson, Scott Baretta, Eric Gordon, the annonymous readers for the University of Illinois Press, and especially Roger Lotchin for organizing the conference and always providing valuable feedback.

1. "Song Pubs Wait on Flagwavers; Judge Them Like Other Numbers," *Billboard*, 21 Sept. 1940, 1; "Showdom's Part in Defense" (editorial), *Billboard*, 27 Sept. 1941, 2.

2. David Ewen, *All the Years of American Popular Music: A Comprehensive History* (Englewood Cliffs, N.J., 1977), 427; see also ibid., chap. 25.

3. Bill Malone, *Country Music USA*, rev. ed. (Austin, Tex., 1985), 194; see also ibid., chap. 6.

4. David W. Stowe, *Swing Changes: Big-Band Jazz in New Deal America* (Cambridge, Mass., 1994), 142, 178, and chap. 4; Lewis A. Erenberg, "Swing Goes to War: Glenn Miller and the Popular Music of World War II," in *The War in American Culture: Society and Consciousness during World War II*, ed. Lewis A. Erenberg and Susan E. Hirsch (Chicago, 1996), 144–65; Lewis A. Erenberg, *Swingin' the Dream: Big Band Jazz and the Rebirth of American Culture* (Chicago, 1998); Scott DeVeaux, *The Birth of Bebop: A Social and Musical History* (Berkeley, Calif., 1997).

5. David Tarnow, "Introduction" accompanying the three compact discs that comprise *The Victory Collection: The Smithsonian Remembers When America Went to War* (Washington, D.C., 1995), 2.

6. "Music Box Folds: San Fran Niteries Doing Very Poorly," *Billboard*, 15 June 1940, 17; Dean Owen, "76 Night Spots in L.A. Area," *Billboard*, 24 Aug. 1940, 5; "Flood of Screen Musicals Sends Vaude, Club, Air Acts to Coast; Dough Is Far from Fabulous,

Tho," *Billboard,* 22 Mar. 1941, 4; "Bookings in So. Calif. Spots 25 Per Cent over Last Year," *Billboard,* 14 Sept. 1940, 17; Krin Gabbard, *Jammin' at the Margins: Jazz and the American Cinema* (Chicago, 1996).

7. "Indoor Show Biz Picks Up First Drips of Rearmament Dough; Has Hopes for Real Spending in Fall," *Billboard,* 31 May 1941, 3, 16; "Pasadena Civic Aud. Turnstile Turns 250,000 in One Year: Grosses $62,000 on 25¢ Admish," *Billboard,* 9 Aug. 1941.

8. "Tin Pan Alley Fires Song Salvo at Axis," *Billboard,* 20 Dec. 1941, 11; *Billboard,* 27 Dec. 1941, 5; "Los Angeles Clubs Recover from Lull Following War Declaration; Patrons Back, with More Money," *Billboard,* 31 Jan. 1942, 4.

9. "California BR Biz Hot; Palladium Record Smashed by Jimmy Dorsey," *Billboard,* 31 Oct. 1942, 21.

10. Gary Marmorstein, *Hollywood Rhapsody: Movie Music and Its Makers, 1900–1975* (New York, 1997).

11. "Coast Maestri Spurn Pops in Favor of Oldies They've Recorded; Pluggers Go Gray," *Billboard,* 31 July 1943, 16.

12. "Record Influx of Musikers Plus New Nitery Tax Equals Headache for AFM on Coast," *Billboard,* 12 Feb. 1944, 16; "Baton Wavers Buy Hollywood Casino," *Billboard,* 17 Mar. 1945.

13. Erenberg, "Swing Goes to War," 158; Erenberg, *Swingin' the Dream,* 201–8.

14. Gary Marmorstein, "Central Avenue Jazz: Los Angeles Black Music of the Forties," *Southern California Quarterly* 70:4 (1988): 417–18; Stowe, *Swing Changes,* 161. In general, see Keith E. Collins, *Black Los Angeles: The Maturing of the Ghetto, 1940–1950* (Saratoga, Calif., 1980); Tom Reed, *The Black Music History of Los Angeles—Its Roots: A Classical Pictorial History of Black Music in Los Angeles from 1920–1970* (Los Angeles, 1992), loaded with illustrations and information; Jacqueline C. DjeDje and Eddie S. Meadows, eds., *California Soul: Music of African Americans in the West* (Berkeley, Calif., 1998), especially Ralph Eastman's essay "'Pitchin' Up a Boogie': African-American Musicians, Nightlife, and Music Venues in Los Angeles, 1930–1945," 79–103; and Clora Bryant et al., *Central Avenue Sounds: Jazz in Los Angeles* (Berkeley, Calif., 1998).

15. Bryant et al., *Central Avenue Sounds,* 182; Chip Deffaa, *Blue Rhythms: Six Lives in Rhythm and Blues* (Urbana, Ill., 1996), chap. 3 (on Charles Brown).

16. James Lester, *Too Marvelous for Words: The Life and Genius of Art Tatum* (New York, 1994), 146; ibid., chap. 6 for Tatum's previous stay in Los Angeles; Ted Gioia, *West Coast Jazz: Modern Jazz in California, 1945–1960* (New York, 1992), 5 and chap. 1 (although the book starts with 1945); Ralph Eastman, "Central Avenue Blues: The Making of Los Angeles Rhythm and Blues, 1942–1947," *Black Music Research Journal* 9:1 (Spring 1989): 19–33; Willie R. Collins, "California Rhythm and Blues Recordings, 1942–1972," in *California Soul,* ed. DjeDje and Meadows, 213–43.

17. "Orpheum, Los Angeles," *Billboard,* 28 June 1941, 22; "L.A. Territory a Hot Spot Now for Negro Orks," *Billboard,* 21 Feb. 1942, 23; "Benny Carter Now a Click with Pic, Radio, and Location," *Billboard,* 8 May 1943, 23.

18. "Singleton Signed by Morris Agency," *Billboard,* 10 July 1943, 23; "Erskin Hawkins Starts Plantation's Name Policy," *Billboard,* 21 Aug. 1943, 15; James Haskins with

Kathleen Benson, *Nat King Cole* (New York, 1984), 34–42. Nightclub segregation prevailed nationwide, with a few exceptions. See Erenberg, *Swingin' the Dream.*

19. "Orpheum, Los Angeles," *Billboard*, 7 Oct. 1944, 25.

20. "Growing L.A. Sepia Clubs Offer 15G Weekly Market," *Billboard*, 10 Feb. 1945, 23; "Troc to Take Cole, Carter Despite Curfew," *Billboard*, 24 Mar. 1945, 12.

21. Barney Hoskyns, *Waiting for the Sun: Strange Days, Weird Scenes, and the Sound of Los Angeles* (New York, 1996), 7; see also ibid., chap. 1.

22. James Gregory, *American Exodus: The Dust Bowl Migration and Okie Culture in California* (New York, 1989), 230–31; "Hillbillies Like Broadcastin' Better 'n Stayin' on the Farm; One Feller Makin' 35G One Year," *Billboard*, 21 Dec. 1940, 7; "Phillips Looks Like 'King Korn' Tycoon of West Coast; Barnerys Now Ey[e]ing Rural Calif. Circuit," *Billboard*, 24 Apr. 1943, 4. For brief accounts of Cooley's career and relationship to western swing, see Nick Tosches, *Country: The Biggest Music in America* (New York, 1977), 161–66; Jean A. Boyd, *The Jazz of the Southwest: An Oral History of Western Swing* (Austin, Tex., 1998), 25–27.

23. "Khaki and Overalled Oakies Make Metropolitan Maestri Feed 'Em Down Home Tunes," *Billboard*, 29 May 1943, 25; "Mountain Music Heavy B.O. in Filmtown Spots," *Billboard*, 29 Apr. 1944, 12.

24. "Spade Cooley," *Billboard*, 10 June 1944, 18; "Sagebrush OK with Aragon," *Billboard*, 8 July 1944, 16; "Zuccas Converting French Casino into Sagebrush Terpery," *Billboard*, 9 Sept. 1944, 15.

25. Gregory, *American Exodus*, 238. On Bob Wills, see Charles R. Townsend, *San Antonio Rose: The Life and Music of Bob Wills* (Urbana, Ill., 1976), chaps. 15 and 17. Boyd, *Jazz of the Southwest,* makes a strong case for considering western swing part of jazz rather than country music.

26. Jonny Whiteside, *Ramblin' Rose: The Life and Career of Rose Maddox* (Nashville, Tenn., 1997), 46–56.

27. Marilynn S. Johnson, *The Second Gold Rush: Oakland and the East Bay in World War II* (Berkeley, Calif., 1993), 136–40, 148–49; Shirley Ann Wilson Moore, "Traditions from Home: African Americans in Wartime Richmond, California," in *War in American Culture,* ed. Erenberg and Hirsch, 269–76; Shirley Ann Moore, "'Her Husband Didn't Have a Word to Say': Black Women and Blues Clubs in Richmond, California, during World War II," in *American Labor in the Era of World War II,* ed. Sally M. Miller and Daniel A. Cornford (Westport, Conn., 1995), 147–64; Lee Hildebrand, "Oakland Blues," in *California Soul,* ed. DjeDje and Meadows, 104–23.

28. Steven Loza, *Barrio Rhythm: Mexican American Music in Los Angeles* (Urbana, Ill., 1993), 54.

29. Ibid., 70–71.

30. "Name Band Competition Starts Real Pitch for Coast Terp Biz," *Billboard*, 14 July 1945, 15.

31. "Orpheum, Los Angeles," *Billboard*, 18 Aug. 1945, 26, 27; Mary Alice Shaughnessy, *Les Paul: An American Original* (New York, 1993), 117–19.

4

New Deal and Wartime Origins of San Francisco's Postwar Political Culture: The Case of Growth Politics and Policy

William Issel

Historians have paid insufficient attention to the political history of urban economic development in the period from the Great Depression to the current era of the global economy. The subject is beginning to receive attention, however, and two historians in particular have emphasized the politics of urban growth policy in cities of the American West. Roger Lotchin has examined the role of politics in military and defense-related investment as well as in relation to interurban commercial rivalry; Carl Abbott has described several patterns of growth politics involving business leaders, bureaucrats, and elected officials in the years before, during, and after World War II.[1]

Scholars outside the field of history who have addressed the subject recently have joined Lotchin and Abbott in stressing the importance of politics. Robert Beauregard argues that "Restructuring entails attempts by capital to reassert its dominance over labor at the workplace, to penetrate further the state and involve it more deeply in the accumulation process, and to weaken the ties between labor and the state. The relations among these entities are both economic and political; the one reinforces the other [and] the study of economic restructuring cannot occur unmindful of space and time, and in ignorance of its political impetus and manifestations."[2] Manuel Castells calls for attention to "the variation of the cultural and political factors that shape the process of economic restructuring, and ultimately determine its outcome."[3]

Recent scholarship also stresses the importance of both private initiative and public decision making as well as the historical timing of growth politics. Steven Erie argues that Los Angeles experienced an "entrepreneurial" growth regime in the late nineteenth and early twentieth century, followed by a "statist" regime in succeeding years. "The crucial distinction," he writes, "is a relative one, not an absolute. The difference refers to the *relative* influence and autonomy of private sector-versus-public sector actors in shaping urban growth and to the relative importance of private-versus-public development strategies."[4] According to Clarence Stone, in a recent review of urban restructuring scholarship, "The key question is not really public versus private initiative. Clearly initiatives come from both sectors. What is crucial are the terms on which public and private actors cooperate. . . .We need," he concludes, "to understand the ways in which development elites excel in promoting collective action around their aims."[5]

Because growth coalitions must develop and coordinate collective action over time, the historical analysis of their political activities is crucial; structuralist presumptions of elite domination over growth policy and functionalist assumptions about the causal significance of events such as depression and war invite skepticism and deserve scrutiny. John Mollenkopf has criticized structuralist perspectives and argues that "analysis of dominant urban political coalitions" ought to attend to "pressures from below as well as 'preemptive power' from above. . . . Attention must also be paid to the culture, organization, and dynamics of political participation" and "to the dimensions of space, place, and community as the building blocks of political dominance."[6] Roger Lotchin has challenged the functionalist thesis that World War II caused a transformation in California urban politics and policy, and Robert Beauregard questions "the postwar period as a time of conceptual and empirical integrity. The 1920s and 1930s, significant years for comprehending changes that occurred after World War II, are all but forgotten. The premise, often left implicit, is that the Depression and World War II were qualitative discontinuities, wholly restructuring society, and thus establishing the baseline for the postwar focus."[7] Joel Schwartz has made a similar criticism of several recent studies of urban restructuring in New York City, where "for all the attention to history, there is little genuine interest in it before the mid-1950s."[8]

The San Francisco case suggests that while the economic and social dislocations caused by the Depression and World War II cannot be ignored when accounting for the origins of postwar urban growth politics and policy, the most important source of innovation was the political struggle over how to come to terms with the institutions and ideas associated with the New Deal. The San Francisco case also underscores the need to examine business-government cooperation in decision making in relation to organized labor when accounting for the politics of urban growth policy. San Franciscans reformulated the ground rules for urban development policy-making (the political culture of growth liberalism) during the contentious period between the beginning of the New Deal and the end of World War II. Surprisingly, given the dramatic events in the city (some of which have received a great deal of attention, such as the waterfront strike of 1934 and the signing of the United Nations Charter in 1945), the story of the origins of San Francisco's postwar growth liberalism has not yet been told. By the end of the 1950s, San Francisco's growth liberalism was well established as a centrist and moderate discourse and practice: apparently, a pragmatic reformulation of older booster principles generated by the structural and functional dynamics of postwar political economy and the politics of the national political parties.[9] However, San Francisco growth liberalism actually developed incrementally in a contested and conflicted manner during the middle to late thirties and followed a similar pattern during the war years, influenced as it was by local as well as national sources and by wartime sentiment and war-related events.

Prior to the New Deal, politics in San Francisco had been a highly contested affair, and the city's electorate was frequently polarized along class lines. After 1911, however, policy-making became more dominated by business, in the sense that the city's business elite had successfully elected its handpicked mayor in 1911 (James Rolph Jr., who served for twenty years) and its Industrial Association had, in 1921, thoroughly defeated labor union power in the workplace and severely limited labor participation in urban policy deliberations.[10] Business power experienced numerous challenges in the 1910s and 1920s, and municipal politics was never free of contest, but major growth projects such as the Hetch Hetchy water and power system and the Islais Creek reclamation scheme, while not exactly imposed upon passive city officials and voters, were shaped as much or more by private as by public initiative. Both undertakings required voter approval of financing arrangements, and in both cases voter disapproval slowed the process. In neither case, however, did grassroots demands set the projects in motion or stop the proceedings. Such a relatively directive process operated in relation to more routine matters of municipal policy-making as well.[11]

During the early Depression years, initiative in responding to the crisis came largely from the executives of major commercial banks and from the Chamber of Commerce leaders, who established private relief organizations with the cooperation of government officials and labor leaders, lobbied city government to propose city-financed relief funds when private money ran out, and successfully campaigned for voter approval of the local public relief. This business-dominated leadership process allowed San Francisco to cope with rising unemployment in 1930 to 1932 and to do so, according to historian William Mullins, more effectively than Los Angeles, Seattle, and Portland. Mullins credits San Francisco with coming closer than any other West Coast city to "fulfilling, at least for a time, Herbert Hoover's faith in the ability of a local community to survive and take care of its own."[12]

Frederick J. Koster, a proponent of Herbert Hoover's associationalism during the twenties, became one of the principal architects of organized business's response to the New Deal. As president of the Chamber of Commerce during World War I, Koster had organized the city's broad-based quasi-public Law and Order Committee after the Preparedness Day Parade bombing in 1916.[13] In 1933, in his capacity as the director of the California State Chamber of Commerce and member of the national chamber's executive board, Koster urged business leaders to take charge of the reform process in order to maintain control of future urban policy-making. Like City Controller Harold J. Boyd, a friend and coreligionist who joined him in his later wartime work with the Bay Area Council against Discrimination, Koster described his political activity in the language of Roman Catholic moral discourse and Progressive Era social reform.[14] "If the individual is to intelligently care for his own interests, he cannot escape being, in some measure at least, his brother's keeper. . . . [H]is advantage in the long run cannot possibly be at the expense of others' disadvantage. This is no longer academic. The proof of this is all about us." Noting "distress and actual starvation in the midst of plenty," Koster complained that it was "unbelievable that such stupidity, such utter lack of intelligent leadership could have prevailed as to have rendered such a thing possible; all the result of adherence to the doctrine of laissez faire, and evidence of the lack of intelligent organized business leadership."[15] He continued: "How the new deal is to be handled, what the new deal is to be, what success is to be achieved toward obtaining its objectives, will very positively depend on the degree of intelligent cooperation that is developed through organizations of business."[16]

Koster disagreed with many San Francisco businessmen, who were staunch Republicans and refused even to acknowledge the new terrain of politics and policy that the Roosevelt administration was creating. In 1933, shortly after Roosevelt signed the National Industrial Recovery Act, Koster argued that the New Deal policy should be used to facilitate local economic development. Admitting that "it is regrettable that circumstances have forced the necessity of this [NIRA] partnership between industry and government," Koster nonetheless argued that "it is now definitely before us, and the important consideration is what steps to take to gain the best results from that partnership."[17]

R. Earl Fisher, vice president of Pacific Gas and Electric Company and, along with Koster, one of the founders of the California State Chamber of Commerce, had been advocating a regional business-government organization since the mid-1920s, and in the winter of 1944 and the spring of 1945, Fisher witnessed the achievement of his vision when the San Francisco Bay Area Council was founded. The council was organized at the end of World War II, but it was an outgrowth of more than a decade of preparatory activity. During the 1920s, California State Chamber of Commerce officials, in an explicit attempt to practice associationalism, had created six Bay Area regional councils. The Bay Area organizations, made up of representatives from chambers in area counties, met during May and June 1933, before the NIRA legislation was signed, in order to coordinate local government proposal writing in connection with the public works and highway construction funds anticipated in Title II of the Recovery Act, which created the Public Works Administration. The regional councils worked continuously during the middle and late 1930s in a cooperative partnership with city and county governments on urban development issues.[18]

Alexander Heron, a Crown Zellerbach Corporation vice president from San Francisco, was part of Fisher's and Koster's network of New Era boosters, and Heron had served as director of finance in the administration of the progressive Republican C. C. Young. Heron was an industrial relations pioneer renowned for his record of "not one hour lost" due to labor disputes between 1930 and 1938, and he returned to government service under Earl Warren in 1943. He used his new position as director of the state's Reconstruction and Reemployment Commission to establish the greater degree of coordination in business-government cooperation that Koster, Miller, and other advocates of the "cooperative standpoint" supported. In late 1944 and 1945, Heron presided over the process by which the new Bay Area Council replaced the state chamber's regional councils as the vehicle for "unity of action in solving postwar problems of the Bay Area." Heron also initiated, with the assistance of trade associations and the state chamber, the legislation that created the Community Redevelopment Act.[19]

Considered in its historical context, the Bay Area Council can be seen as more than merely a reaction to World War II and part of the nationwide concern over possible postwar recession. The council also represented a successful conclusion to the long campaign to create a particular kind of corporatist approach to the process of local urban economic development.[20] The state Chamber of Commerce regional councils were associationalist initiatives. Koster and his colleagues refashioned the councils to take advantage of opportunities presented by federal subsidies for urban development under the New Deal and to shape New Deal programs into cooperative local endeavors with businessmen and government officials working together in pursuit of economic growth. During World War II, the regional councils were superceded by an organization that was intended to meet the challenges and the opportunities that had been presented by the war. Frank Marsh, the first executive vice president and general manager of the new organization, came to the Bay Area Council after serving as manager of the Washington, D.C., office of the San Francisco Chamber of Commerce.[21]

It is not surprising that the newly named group, in the words of planning historian Mel Scott, "was therefore composed mainly of businessmen." Scott has emphasized the relative absence of professional city planners in the Bay Area Council as a problematic feature of its work from the beginning. However, an even more striking characteristic of the organization, which Scott mentions but does not analyze, was the participation of labor union leaders.[22] Further attention to historical context helps to explain the presence of labor representatives in the Bay Area Council in 1945, as well as change and continuity in the relationships among businessmen, government officials, and labor leaders during the war years generally.

The changes in wartime relationships were partly the product of prewar developments in the city's labor relations during the New Deal years and the strategy for coping with the New Deal enunciated by Frederick Koster and like-minded colleagues. In 1934, dedication to laissez-faire principles and practices persisted among Republican Old Guard business leaders who, following the lead of William H. Crocker and other conservatives, regarded FDR as a traitor to his class. During the bitter waterfront strike of that year, moderate employers lost control of strike strategy to the conservative faction which, in the words of Thomas G. Plant, president of the Waterfront Employers Union, "[had] urged war from the beginning."[23] An attempt to open the port by force led to the deaths of two men on July 5. Most writing on the waterfront strike of 1934 interprets the three weeks following "Bloody Thursday" as a triumph of labor solidarity expressed in a general strike that forced capital to give the striking workers their most important demands. However, that interpretation fails to take into account an equally important development during those July days. Abhorrence of the radicalism attributed to the strikers and their supporters, shock created by the violence and death, and the fear of worse to come, provided moderate business and labor leaders the opportunity to seize control of the bargaining process and to settle the strike.[24]

The nature of the 1934 strike settlement, as much as the strike itself, set in motion significant changes in growth politics and policy-making in the subsequent decades. Settlement of the strike did not put an end to contention between business and labor, and the waterfront employers would not finally relinquish their hope for a return to pre–New Deal conditions until the late 1940s. However, many local business leaders, including some influential shippers, decided to deal with the unions given the new reality of labor union legal legitimacy. Several factors contributed to the change. San Francisco businessmen, like their counterparts elsewhere, were put on the defensive by passage of the National Labor Relations Act of 1935 and by the Supreme Court's upholding of its constitutionality in 1937. Local labor initiatives added to the pressure. In April 1935, leaders of unions active in the 1934 strike founded the Maritime Federation of the Pacific Coast. In January 1937, a reform "New Deal Slate" won election to the San Francisco AFL Labor Council.[25]

The Maritime Federation's one-hundred-day strike in 1936–37 forced the Pacific Coast shipowners to transform what had been a tenuous and informal alliance into a temporary, then a permanent, parallel and formal organization in early 1937. By June 1937, both local and statewide business leaders had become increasingly fearful of the potential damage of continued labor strife to the local and regional economy's future growth potential. Searching for a strategy to limit the economic damage of future strikes, lessen the appeal of radicals, and restore nationwide confidence in local business leadership, the California Chamber of Commerce adopted "A Program for Labor Peace." This program went beyond Frederick Koster's 1933 call for realism in relation to the NIRA. It established a ten-point "formula for labor peace and social progress that, if followed by employers not only in California but elsewhere in the United States, will almost surely bring to an end the period of strife and strikes through which we are passing."[26] In the same month, presidents of the Bank of California, the American Trust Company, the Anglo California National Bank, and the Bank of America met privately with the president of the Chamber of Commerce. They demanded that the chamber take the lead in establishing a new organization to replace the die-hard Industrial Association, whose intransigent support of the hotel owners had kept a strike against them going for three months.[27]

Then, in November, city voters rejected a ballot measure initiated by the Chamber of Commerce that had proposed to reinstate the two-decade-old antipicketing ordinance that the Board of Supervisors had overturned in March.[28] By March 1938, the Industrial Association, a fixture in the city's public life for nearly twenty years, had been replaced by the Committee of Forty-Three. This new group announced its intention both to defend the prerogatives of capital and to acknowledge the rights of labor. Basing its strategy on the belief that business must organize in order to compete effectively with the newly revitalized labor movement, the Committee of Forty-Three called for public cooperation between labor and capital as a necessary means for the restoration of public confidence in business and for the resumption of city and regional economic growth.[29]

In June 1938, the CIO Council convened a town meeting with an audience of some twelve thousand San Franciscans in the Civic Center Auditorium.

Harry Bridges of the ILWU (CIO), who had become a staunch New Dealer when the Communist Party established its Democratic Front line, appeared with Roger D. Lapham of the Waterfront Employers Association. Lapham, a leader of the die-hard faction of shippers during the 1934 strike, along with the new president of the Chamber of Commerce, joined Bridges and other CIO officers in an affirmation of harmonious labor relations and cooperative civic enterprise.[30]

The city's American Federation of Labor Council delegates were suspicious of the CIO and skeptical about Chamber of Commerce declarations of good faith, and AFL representatives did not attend the town meeting. Their official newspaper, the *Labor Clarion,* responded to the event with a mixture of sarcasm and ridicule. Privately, however, John F. Shelley, president of the AFL Council, signed an agreement with the Committee of Forty-Three to establish a Joint Labor Committee that brought the AFL unions into the same new collective bargaining and economic growth policy system as the CIO.[31] In 1939, the Committee of Forty-Three took a new name, the San Francisco Employers' Council. The director of the new organization, dramatizing the degree to which business cooperation with labor was premised on the fear of continued labor conflict and business stagnation, as well as hope for future growth, announced that "Visitors to the Golden Gate Exposition will find San Francisco at labor peace not at war."[32]

By the time the war in Europe began, some of the most intransigent antilabor business leaders—notably William H. Crocker—were dead, and a new set of leaders, chastened by the conflicts of the recent past and determined to cope with if not celebrate New Deal innovations, had emerged. Roger D. Lapham of the Waterfront Employers, Harry Bridges and other CIO leaders, and John F. Shelley of the AFL now set in motion a process that had been suggested by Ira B. Cross, the University of California labor economist who had urged business to take the lead in urban reform in order to "prevent the growth of revolutionary beliefs and movements."[33] By the time the United States entered the war, new institutional relations had been established, premised upon the the need for moderation and cooperation in the pursuit of future economic growth.

One week after Pearl Harbor, Harry Bridges addressed the three hundred members of the executive board of the California State Industrial Union Council, using the language of the resuscitated Democratic Front. This is "a people's war and it is labor's war. This is no time for post mortems." It is important to emphasize "the need for cooperation with employers and proper governmental agencies in carrying out our plans."[34] In early June 1942, delegates from five hundred unions filled Wheeler Auditorium at UC Berkeley for a weekend California Conference on Labor and the War. Jonathan Daniels, from the Office of Civilian Defense, enunciated one of the two most widely discussed themes of the conference when he criticized San Francisco's Junior League and Chamber of Commerce because they "have represented themselves to be the whole town" and urged the union members "to get your community to be a democratic community." Frank P. Fenton, Director of Organizing for the AFL, stressed the other key conference theme: "The American workman is conservative. . . . [L]abor believes in our present system of free enterprise. We want to preserve it. We can preserve it if organized industry and organized labor join hands together."[35]

Throughout the war years, the Employers Council and the AFL and CIO Councils conducted negotiations in a centralized coordinated process that was typically marked by conservatism, civility, and mutual toleration. However, the long-established mutual suspicions between labor and business did not disappear. In June 1940, the AFL Labor Council expressed a general sentiment when it warned each member of the Employers Council against using "this general [national emergency] hysteria as a means for avoiding responsibility to the social problems of his workers."[36]

Several rancorous labor disputes occurred during the war despite the wartime strike-ban endorsed by both AFL and CIO. In 1941 and 1942 retail clerks struck department stores for six months and hotel workers stayed out until ordered back to work by the War Labor Board after eight months; in the spring of 1944, a seniority dispute broke out between two AFL streetcar operator unions after the consolidation of the private and public systems; also in the spring of 1944, AFL machinists—known for their tradition of militancy and radicalism—demanded a wage increase and refused to accept overtime work. When the local machinists did strike immediately after the war in the fall of 1945, the International Association of Machinists, working cooperatively with the Bay Area Employers Organization, placed the local union in receivership and ended the strike.[37]

In the case of relations between waterfront workers and employers, the war years fostered an armistice, but genuine labor peace was not achieved until after settlement of strikes in 1946 and 1948.[38] Nonetheless, in the maritime industry as in the city's labor relations generally, the New Deal and wartime conditions combined to create opportunities for institutional interaction which, in turn, began the process of moderating old resentments and enhancing opportunities for cooperative action on behalf of urban development.

The pre–World War II changes associated with growth liberalism that influenced regional economic planning and labor relations also contributed to changes in the political and policy process by which infrastructure projects were established. Both the continuity and the change that marked wartime years, and the imprint of the prewar changes on the wartime events, can be seen in the cases of the Oakland–San Francisco Bay Bridge Project, the Golden Gate International Exposition, and the Mayor's Postwar Planning Committee.

Leland W. Cutler, three-term president of the Chamber of Commerce, played the leading role in securing financing for the Bay Bridge during the first years of the thirties. Cutler, a close friend of Herbert Hoover and a strong supporter of Hoover's associationalist ideology, was a zealous believer in "the magic of friendship" that could link together "citizens outside the government" with public officials in the service of city-building projects.[39]

Cutler made the transition from the Hoover to the Roosevelt administration relatively easily. FDR, before becoming governor of New York, had been Cutler's counterpart in New York City: vice president and director of the regional office of the Fidelity and Deposit Company of Maryland. In his position as vice president of the Financial Advisory Committee of the transbay bridge project, Cutler relied first on Hoover's and then on Roosevelt's help in convincing the Reconstruction Finance Corporation to purchase revenue bonds for construction of the bridge. A similar process, begun in the Bohemian Grove encampment, involved Cutler's friend, Democrat George Creel. Creel gave the San Franciscan a personal introduction to Harry Hopkins which eventuated in a $3.8 million WPA grant that allowed the city to reclaim the shoals off Yerba Buena Island and begin construction of Treasure Island, site of the Golden Gate Exposition, of which Cutler served as president.[40]

When Cutler wrote his memoirs twenty years after the beginning of the New Deal, he sharply distinguished between friends such as FDR and George Creel, who shared his philosophy about the role of government and business, and New Dealers such as Harry Hopkins. "Hopkins was an idealist, almost a fanatic; I think his philosophy of government was all wrong . . . terrible and dangerous."[41] Philosophy, however, was one thing, business another; Cutler was as willing to use the help of Harry Hopkins to boost San Francisco and Bay Area economic development as he had been to depend upon Franklin Roosevelt.

In 1939, Cutler and the Chamber of Commerce launched a campaign to develop further San Francisco's role as the leading regional metropolis for business services (a "Hub of Western Industry"), bolster the city's tourist industry, and improve its transportation connections to the rest of the nation and the world at the time of the Exposition.[42] The chamber continued its sponsorship of such business-oriented growth initiatives during the war, and, in 1943, with the support of sympathetic members of the Board of Supervisors, began calling for an official city postwar planning committee. In 1945, Mayor Roger D. Lapham established such a committee and appointed as chairman Chamber of Commerce president Adrien J. Falk, one of Lapham's colleagues who had participated in the town meeting with the CIO in 1938. In 1945, the mayor's committee, like the Bay Area Council, contained both labor and business representatives, and its program, beginning with its number one priority—airport expansion—followed the lines laid out in the earlier Chamber of Commerce priorities.[43]

The importance of the new system of growth liberalism, a prewar phenomenon that continued to develop during the war years, can be seen in its impact on municipal government revenue and expenditure patterns from 1933 through the 1940s. During the 1933–39 period, there were appreciable increases in the share of the municipal budget derived from state and federal funds and in the proportion or size of departmental expenditures for general governance, for public safety (i.e., fire and police), or education and hospitals.[44] That kind of expansion did not occur during World War II. However, two of the four bond issues submitted to city voters during World War II were for major improvements to the city's sewer system and the construction of a juvenile court building, and they passed partly because of the solid support of the new growth coalition, with Mayor Lapham making an extensive publicity campaign on behalf of the bonds.[45] The mayor used a similar coalition-based publicity campaign to win voter approval in a special election in 1944 for the city purchase of the Market Street Railway and the merger of the private firm with the Municipal Railway. Between November 1945 and November 1948, the same strategy was used to secure the passage of nine out of twelve infrastructure-construction bonds.[46]

Unlike his predecessor Angelo Rossi (1931–43), who was more of an Old Guard Republican, Mayor Roger D. Lapham (1943–47) had played a key role in setting in motion the city's growth liberalism in 1938 and 1939, and he went on to facilitate liberal growth policies during the last years of the war and in the early postwar period. The differences between Rossi and Lapham were differences in degree not in kind, however, for both rejected labor militancy and social democracy, and both believed that in any partnership between business, government, and labor, businessmen would be able to represent effectively the interests of the city as a whole, whereas labor leaders would find it difficult to conceive of an interest greater than that represented by their members.

In considering San Francisco's electoral politics, one must not draw too sharp a contrast between the prewar, wartime, and postwar years. Franklin Roosevelt's victory in 1932 and Upton Sinclair's defeat in 1934 prefigured the central themes of San Francisco's municipal politics from the mid-thirties to the sixties: the gradual and largely nonpartisan victory of supporters of centrist, growth liberalism over critics from both the Left and the Right.

The growth liberals were Republicans, Democrats, and independents. All pursued centrist, moderate goals. Several key participants were central figures in the revitalization of the Democratic Party during the years of its recovery in the mid-1930s who went on to play important roles in San Francisco politics during World War II: Maurice E. Harrison, Edward Heller, Elinor Heller, William Malone, and Julia Gorman Porter were among the most important of this group. Maurice Harrison, former dean of the Hastings College of Law and president of the Bar Association of San Francisco, served as chairman of the Democratic State Central Committee from 1932 to 1934. Like thousands of San Franciscans of more modest means in 1934, Harrison voted for the Republican candidate for governor, Frank Merriam, rather than for Upton Sinclair.[47] Harrison's law firm, Brobeck, Phleger, and Harrison, had represented the San Francisco Industrial Association against the carpenters union in the bitter strike of 1926, the Bay Area Waterfront Employers and the Hawaiian Planters Association in 1934, and the DiGiorgo Corporation during the Central Valley labor strife of the late 1930s.[48]

During the war years, Harrison, a Catholic, served as chairman of the Bay Area chapter of the National Committee Against Persecution of the Jews. His friend and coreligionist Frederick Koster became chairman of the San Francisco Conference of Christians and Jews. Harrison's belief in a corporate commonwealth along the lines laid out by Koster in 1933 was grounded in similar Roman Catholic principles. In the late thirties, Harrison helped organize the St. Thomas More Society of San Francisco. The society was a small group of the city's leading Roman Catholic lawyers who believed that a study of More's life could provide "the true answer to the problems which confront the world today," because the saint "was the great witness against totalitarianism of his day."[49] In an address to the society two months before the bombing of Pearl Harbor, Harrison emphasized the importance of seeing in Thomas More's life a model of the kind of reform activity that was compatible with "the integrity of the Christian view of life." "In the true sense of the word he *was* a reformer. He had no fear of change as such; he advocated and welcomed whatever changes were called for by the requirements of justice. His life is proof that such sympathy is consistent with fidelity to fundamental truth when prevailing trends of thought go beyond rational bounds and when fundamental error masquerades for a while as legitimate reform."[50]

Maurice Harrison's association with Edward and Elinor Heller began in 1928, when they traveled together to the Democratic Party convention in Houston. In contrast to the Republican affiliations of most of San Francisco's Jewish business elite, Heller was a Democrat, in major part because of his Atlanta, Georgia, family's long-established party loyalties. Among his New York cousins were Herbert Lehman and Henry Morgenthau. Edward Heller's mother was a delegate to the 1932 Democratic convention, and his wife later became a member of the party's National Committee. Like Maurice Harrison, Heller voted for Frank Merriam for governor in 1934, and like Harrison, Heller and a handful of the California delegation to the Democratic Party convention in 1940 voted for Harry Truman rather than Henry Wallace as the vice-presidential nominee because they regarded Wallace as too radical. (In 1939, When Maurice Harrison was put forward as a possible associate justice of the Supreme Court by his friends William McAdoo and George Creel, Roosevelt placed him on the short list, but criticism by John L. Lewis that Harrison was "anti-labor" led Roosevelt to remove him from consideration.) Edward Heller's support for the Republican centrist Merriam in 1934 earned him a place on the California State Emergency Relief Commission, and his support in 1938 for Culbert Olson, the liberal Democrat, was rewarded with an appointment to the Golden Gate International Exposition Commission.[51]

Another of Olson's appointments to the commission was San Franciscan William M. Malone, chairman of the Democratic County Central Committee from 1937 to 1952, and chairman of the State Central Committee in 1940–42 and 1944–46. Malone and Heller met for the first time during their term on the Exposition Commission; they could hardly have been more different. Malone hailed from St. James parish in the heart of the Irish Catholic Mission District, whereas Heller was part of the Pacific Heights Jewish elite. But they agreed on the need to build the Democratic center and limit the appeal of the extremes on both the Left and Right. They shattered decorum in the 1940 convention when, standing on their chairs and shouting to be heard, they and ten other delegates refused to make unanimous the nomination of Henry Wallace for vice president.[52]

The Democratic State Committee, prodded by women active in the party, reformed itself during the New Deal and created the "fifty-fifty" rule, which required equal representation of men and women on the committee. Julia Gorman Porter, president of the San Francisco League of Women Voters in 1939–40, joined the State Central Committee in 1941 and served as chair of the Northern California Democratic Party Women's Division throughout the war years. In San Francisco, Porter worked with Roger D. Lapham, Maurice Harrison, the Hellers, and William Malone in building the wartime liberal growth coalition.[53]

In 1944, Porter served as vice chairperson of the Franck Havenner for Congress Committee. Unlike Porter, a native San Franciscan whose grandfather had arrived even before the gold rush, Havenner was a transplanted easterner twenty years older than Porter who had lived in Arizona before coming to the Bay

Area. Like Porter, who had come to her political party work by way of a network of Progressive-era reformers that included Lincoln Steffens, Havenner
had impeccable progressive credentials: secretary to Senator Hiram Johnson;
California manager of the LaFollette campaign in 1924; a decade of progressive activism on the city Board of Supervisors marked by steady criticism of
the Pacific Gas and Electric corporation and staunch support for public ownership of utilities. Elected to Congress in 1936, on the Progressive and Democratic tickets, Havenner registered Democratic in 1939 after deciding that FDR's
program best "represented my Progressive philosophy."[54]

In 1939, with William Malone as his campaign manager, official backing from
the Democratic county committee, and the promise of support from the mod-
erately liberal *San Francisco News,* Havenner entered the city's mayoral race.
However, the friendly editor at the *News* died before the campaign, and the
paper's promised endorsement never materialized.[55] Havenner's chances probably were hurt even more by the unsolicited endorsement he received from
longshore leader Harry Bridges. Bridges's endorsement of Havenner and his
criticism of incumbent Mayor Angelo Rossi transpired in the weeks following
the signing of the Nazi-Soviet pact and the Communist Party's repudiation of
the Popular Front line. Between September 1939 and July 1941, Bridges and
other CIO organizers and officials whose discourse derived from or coincided
with the party line were outspoken critics of cooperative relations with business organizations or with government officials presumed to be the minions
of capital.[56]

Havenner was no puppet of radical unionism, but he did not aggressively
repudiate the Bridges endorsement and found himself the target of red-baiting
that portrayed him as a tool of international communism. Rossi supporters
scattered billboards throughout the city that showed the city hall, after a Havenner victory, with red paint covering its French Renaissance dome. When a
Havenner campaign march up Market Street was led by a brass band wearing
longshoremen's caps and dockworkers' shirts, pro-Rossi newspapers took it
as proof that Havenner would be the mayor of radical labor rather than—in
the phrase originated by James Rolph Jr. and appropriated by his successor
Angelo Rossi— "the mayor of all of the people." Voters returned Rossi to office
with a plurality of over 20,000 (48 percent to 41 percent in a six-person race).[57]
One year later, when Havenner fought to keep his congressional seat in a campaign against Thomas Rolph, brother of the late mayor and governor, voters
repudiated him again. While Roosevelt was the city voters' choice for president by 60 percent to Willkie's 40 percent, Havenner was the choice for congressman of only 44 percent of the voters in his district.[58]

The appeals to Roman Catholic moral order and national patriotism represented in the red-baiting that Angelo Rossi and Thomas Rolph used to help defeat Franck Havenner in 1939 and 1940 continued to be central to political rhetoric during wartime and in the postwar era. At the same time, however, the concept of civic virtue enjoyed a revival and became an important factor in electoral politics. The idea that longevity in office made officeholders "professional politicians" and automatically rendered them less able to serve the public interest dated from the early days of the republic.[59] This discourse was dusted off and elevated to prominence in 1935, the first election after the dramatic increases in Democratic Party registration stimulated by the Sinclair campaign. In that election, a slate of young aspirants to the Board of Supervisors who called themselves members of "the New Order of Cincinnatus" and "the New Guard" succeeded in winning one seat on the board and repeated their modest success again in 1939, when the slate included Edmund G. "Pat" Brown, who had been one of the organizers of the group, as candidate for district attorney. In 1941, four members of the five "New Guard" slate won seats on the board and, two years later, Brown defeated Matthew Brady to become district attorney.[60]

A bipartisan group that included several labor union activists, the New Guard advertised itself as interested solely in honesty and efficiency in government and its activities were tolerated and even encouraged by William Malone and the Democratic Party regulars. Years later, Malone likened Brown to "a flower that's budding, I never interfered with him."[61] In 1943, Malone drew upon the discourse of the young New Guard challengers when he put the influence of the Democratic Party behind the candidacy of Roger D. Lapham for mayor on the grounds that Lapham would be a "citizen mayor" who would not be influenced by professional politicians and who would limit himself to one term, thereby demonstrating a disinterested public service–oriented desire to benefit all of the people rather than any special interest.[62]

Malone's support for Lapham's candidacy had origins in the factionalism within the California State Democratic Central Committee, as well as in his commitment to the centrist priorities he shared with his coreligionists Maurice Harrison and Frederick Koster. In 1942, Governor Culbert Olson supported Malone's rival in the party election to choose a new committee vice chairman; the rival was San Franciscan George Reilly, who won by a vote of 218 to 182. A year later, when Reilly decided to run against Angelo Rossi in the mayoral election, Malone refused to support him and joined his friends Maurice Harrison and Edward Heller in backing Roger D. Lapham.[63] Harrison's law partner, Herman Phleger, attorney for the Waterfront Employers, broached the idea to Lapham and his wife during a visit by the couple to Phleger's room in the

Hotel Carlton in Washington, D.C., where Lapham was living while he served as a member of the War Labor Board.[64]

Determined to limit the influence of the CIO Political Action Committee, which had recently launched a well-publicized social democratic program that had, in turn, moved the AFL to create a parallel organization, Herman Phleger and Maurice Harrison were also cognizant of the potential appeal of a candidate who would carry FDR's endorsement, who would draw conservative and centrist trade unionist voters, and who would promise to be a citizen-mayor.[65] The backing for Lapham was bipartisan: Harrison and Heller, along with Malone and Julia Gorman Porter, all Democratic Party insiders, joined with leading Republican conservatives Jerd Sullivan of the Crocker Bank, James Lockheed of the American Trust Bank, William S. Maillard Sr., Chamber of Commerce president during the 1934 strike, and Elmer Robinson, a Republican Party insider who had been active in Merriam's gubernatorial campaign.[66]

San Francisco's labor movement, not yet willing to endorse a candidate who had called for bloodshed in order to end the waterfront strike in 1934, officially opposed Lapham and endorsed George Reilly in 1943.[67] Labor took this position despite Lapham's move to the center in his work with the San Francisco Employers' Council between 1938 and 1941, and his work from 1941 to 1943 as FDR's appointee to the National Defense Mediation Board, the Labor Management Conference, and the War Labor Board.[68]

The electorate provided Lapham with a strong plurality, putting him 33,000 votes ahead of George Reilly and 43,000 ahead of incumbent Angelo Rossi (i.e., 42 percent to 26 percent to 22 percent, with the balance, under 10 percent, going to Supervisor Chester McPhee).[69] In a postmortem on the election, CIO strategists admitted that "the CIO made a large number of bad mistakes in the campaign, which must be learned from immediately." Noting that "our literature was too 'labor' in character . . . not beamed in such a way as to appeal to the middle class, showing them a program which the whole community could agree upon," the report went on to describe "a real isolation between the labor movement and the rest of the community." Finally, the report argued, "We attacked Lapham too much on the old labor issues, which he was able to parry by pointing to a change of heart and the War Labor Board."[70]

The Lapham victory, as the confidential CIO report recommended, moved both the AFL and CIO organizations toward the center in order to compete more effectively for greater influence in city governance. During 1944, in response to the national CIO-PAC campaign and the 1943 defeat in San Francisco, both labor federations participated in a voter registration drive cosponsored with the Junior Chamber of Commerce.[71] The successful registration drive coincided with Mayor Lapham's careful co-optation of numerous Democratic Party, AFL, and CIO leaders. Many of the CIO and CIO-PAC activists had come to the Bay Area during the war, and in 1944 they were leaders in the local Communist Political Association that had replaced the party on the orders of Earl Browder.[72] Oleta O'Connor Yates, a Phi Beta Kappa graduate of UC Berkeley who was a local communist leader and its candidate for the Board of Supervisors, served on Lapham's Civic Unity Council, which was chaired by Maurice Harrison. Daniel Del Carlo of the AFL joined the Public Utilities Commission, now chaired by Marshall Dill, a former Chamber of Commerce president. George Miller of the CIO served on the Postwar Planning Committee. Julia Gorman Porter became a planning commissioner.[73]

Shortly after the war, from early to mid-1946, Lapham faced a recall campaign initiated by Henry F. Budde, editor and publisher of the *San Francisco Progress,* a twice-weekly newspaper distributed free in city neighborhoods. Budde's organization, The Recall Lapham Committee of 1100, Inc., accused the mayor of reneging on his promise to serve as a citizen-mayor and attacked Lapham's record in 1944 and 1945 with a crude appeal to "Lunch-bucket Joe" and "Secretary Sue." "We who are fighting for the little fellow's rights earnestly seek your endorsement and active support in recalling a mayor who has NO LOVE for LABOR."[74] Budde's motives, though somewhat obscure to this day, included personal animosity toward Lapham. The *San Francisco Chronicle* accused Budde of being a front for the CIO-PAC "puppet-show masters . . . out to fool the people of San Francisco about Roger Lapham." In February, Paul Schnur, secretary of the CIO Council, had threatened a recall campaign against what he called "the reactionary clique which dominates City Hall." However, by April the PAC leaders had decided on pragmatic grounds to oppose the recall, even though their organization "look[ed] forward to the time when Lapham and his friends can be eliminated from public life." The recall campaign thus lacked the support of both labor federations, most of the city's neighborhood associations, the mainstream press, and both major political parties.[75]

If the recall vote can be seen as a referendum on Roger Lapham and the growth liberalism he represented, then the mayor and his coalition received a solid endorsement. Throughout the city, the mayor did better than he had in his 1943 election. In voting precincts with large numbers of wage earners and union members, where a majority of the electorate had voted against him in 1943 and later supported his recall in 1946, Lapham nevertheless gained nearly twenty percentage points.[76]

Mayor Roger Lapham's defeat of the recall campaign demonstrates that the liberal growth coalition had become a force to be reckoned with in San Francisco political culture even before the cold war began. Two years later, the scope of the liberal center expanded when shipowners and waterfront employers finally accepted the permanence of labor unions in their industry when debilitating strikes and the re-election of Harry Truman convinced them to endorse a "New Look" on the waterfront.[77] Some of the most militant leaders of the CIO left the labor movement at the time of the Red Scare and the purge of the left-wing unions, as in the case of Paul Schnur, executive secretary of the CIO Council from 1942 to 1949.[78] Others, most dramatically Harry Bridges after the negotiation of the "New Look" in 1948, became both militant defenders of "bread and butter" unionism and growth liberals on urban development issues.[79] These and other developments during the early cold-war years foreshadowed the increasingly centrist character of growth politics and policy making during the 1950s that later accounts would mistakenly explain as structural and functional requisites of the postwar era rather than, more correctly, as part of the product of the political history of the thirties and forties.

Notes

Housing and urban renewal politics and policies are omitted from this essay because of space limitations. The political history described here also contributed to the shaping of land-use policy in San Francisco. Wartime housing shortages and demographic changes, particularly the influx of large numbers of African-American residents for the first time in the city's history, also had an important influence on housing and land-use policy. See William Issel, "Liberalism and Urban Policy in San Francisco from the 1930s to the 1960s," *Western Historical Quarterly* 22:4 (Nov. 1991): 441–43; Eric Fure-Slocum, "Emerging Urban Redevelopment Policies: Post–World War II Contests in San Francisco and Los Angeles" (M.A. thesis [history], San Francisco State University, 1990); Max Silverman, "Urban Redevelopment and Community Response: African Americans in San Francisco's Western Addition" (M.A. thesis [history], San Francisco State University, 1994).

I would like to thank Carl Abbott, Robert Cherny, Daniel Cornford, Steven Erie, Roger Lotchin, and Jules Tygiel for their comments and suggestions on earlier versions of this essay. I alone am responsible for all errors or omissions.

1. Roger W. Lotchin, "The Darwinian City: The Politics of Urbanization in San Francisco between the World Wars," *Pacific Historical Review* 58:3 (Aug. 1979): 357–81; idem, *Fortress California, 1910–1961: From Warfare to Welfare* (New York, 1992); Carl Abbott, *The Metropolitan Frontier: Cities in the Modern American West* (Tucson, Ariz., 1993), 31–49; idem, "Regional City and Network City: Portland and Seattle in the Twentieth Century," *Western Historical Quarterly* 23:3 (Aug. 1992): 293–322.

2. Robert A. Beauregard, "Space, Time, and Economic Restructuring," in *Economic Restructuring and Political Response*, ed. Robert A. Beauregard (Newbury Park, Calif., 1989), 236.

3. Manuel Castells, "European Cities, the Informational Society, and the Global Economy," *New Left Review* 204 (1994): 19.

4. Steven P. Erie, "How the Urban West Was Won: The Local State and Economic Growth in Los Angeles, 1880–1932," *Urban Affairs Quarterly* 27:4 (June 1992): 521.

5. Clarence Stone, "The Politics of Urban Restructuring: A Review Essay," *Western Political Quarterly* 43:1 (Mar. 1990): 225, 230.

6. John Mollenkopf, "Who (or What) Runs Cities, and How," *Sociological Forum* 4:1 (1989): 133; John Hull Mollenkopf, *A Phoenix in the Ashes: The Rise and Fall of the Koch Coalition in New York City Politics* (Princeton, N.J., 1992), 23–43.

7. Beauregard, "Space, Time, and Economic Restructuring," 216; Roger W. Lotchin, "World War II and Urban California: City Planning and the Transformation Hypothesis," *Pacific Historical Review* 62:2 (1993): 143–71; idem, "California Cities and the Hurricane of Change: World War II in the San Francisco, Los Angeles, and San Diego Metropolitan Areas," *Pacific Historical Review* 63:3 (Aug. 1994): 393–420; and other essays in *Fortress California at War: San Francisco, Los Angeles, Oakland, and San Diego,* ed. Roger W. Lotchin, special issue of *Pacific Historical Review* 63:3 (Aug. 1994). David Brody also emphasizes the continuity between the thirties and the forties in "The New Deal and World War II," in *The New Deal: The National Level,* vol. 1, ed. John Braeman, Robert H. Bremner, and David Brody (Columbus, Ohio, 1975), 267–309. See also *The Rise and Fall of the New Deal Order,* ed. Steve Fraser and Gary Gerstle (Princeton, N.J., 1989); Joshua Freeman, "Delivering the Goods: Industrial Unionism during World War II," *Labor History* 19:4 (Fall 1978): 570–93.

8. Joel Schwartz, "Postindustrial New York and the End of Urban History," *Journal of Urban History* 21:2 (Jan. 1995): 271.

9. See Chester Hartman, *The Transformation of San Francisco* (Totowa, N.J., 1984); Susan S. Fainstein, Norman I. Fainstein, and P. Jefferson Armistead, "San Francisco: Urban Transformation and the Local State," in *Restructuring the City: The Political Economy of Urban Redevelopment,* rev. ed., ed. Susan S. Fainstein, Norman I. Fainstein, Richard Child Hill, Dennis R. Judd, and Michael Peter Smith (New York, 1986), 202–44; John H. Mollenkopf, *The Contested City* (Princeton, N.J., 1983).

10. William Issel and Robert W. Cherny, *San Francisco, 1865–1932: Politics, Power, and Urban Development* (Berkeley, Calif., 1986).

11. William Issel, "'Citizens Outside the Government': Business and Urban Policy in San Francisco and Los Angeles, 1890–1932," *Pacific Historical Review* 62:2 (May 1988): 117–45; idem, "Business Power and Political Culture in San Francisco, 1900–1940," *Journal of Urban History* 16:1 (Nov. 1989): 52–77. James P. Walsh and Timothy J. O'Keefe demonstrate the role of James D. Phelan in the Hetch Hetchy project in *Legacy of a Native Son: James Duval Phelan and Villa Montalvo* (Los Gatos, Calif., 1993), 119–30. The Islais Creek project stretched over nearly thirty years and has yet to find its historian. Local newspapers, city records, and the minutes of the Board of Directors of the San Francisco Chamber of Commerce contain abundant documentation.

12. William H. Mullins, *The Depression and the Urban West Coast, 1929–1933: Los Angeles, San Francisco, Seattle, and Portland* (Bloomington, Ind., 1991), 36–38, 103–4.

13. See Issel and Cherny, *San Francisco, 1865–1932*, 177–80.

14. The role of the Roman Catholic Church in San Francisco public life during this period is the subject of William Issel and James Collins, "The Catholic Church and Organized Labor in San Francisco, 1932–1958," in *Catholicism in California,* ed. Steven M. Avella, special issue of the American Catholic Historical Society of Philadelphia *Records* (forthcoming). Harold J. Boyd was a native San Franciscan with roots in the Irish Catholic Mission District. He served as president of the San Francisco Federation of Municipal Employees, was a strong supporter of Franklin D. Roosevelt, and earned a reputation as a "Champion of the Underdog." In a speech at the Golden Gate Exposition in 1939, Boyd became one of the first public officials to attack the Nazi government's racist policies, and, when the work of the Bay Area Council against Discrimination was absorbed into the city's Council for Civic Unity, Boyd became its first president. See *San Francisco Chronicle,* 30 Jan. 1936, 16 May 1942, 19, 20, 21, 22 Oct. 1945, 19 Oct. 1946.

15. Frederick J. Koster, "Organization of Business," *California Journal of Development* (Sept. 1933): 6.

16. Ibid., 18.

17. Frederick J. Koster, "National Industrial Recovery Act," *California Journal of Development* (June 1933): 4–5, 14, 24–25.

18. The mobilization of Regional Councils is described in ibid., 24, and A. E. Goddard, "The Whole State Speaks thru the Regional Councils," *California Journal of Development* (June 1935): 4.

19. Alexander Heron announced the formation of the Council in *San Francisco Chronicle,* 1 Sept. 1944. See also Richard A. Sundeen Jr., "The San Francisco Bay Area Council: An Analysis of a Non-Governmental Metropolitan Organization" (M.A. thesis, University of California at Berkeley, 1963), 68–71; *San Francisco Chronicle,* 17 Nov. 1943, 8 Feb. 1965 (Heron obituary).

20. On corporatism and corporate liberalism, see Ellis W. Hawley, "The Corporate Ideal as Liberal Philosophy in the New Deal," in *The Roosevelt New Deal: A Program Assessment Fifty Years After,* ed. Wilbur J. Cohen (Austin, Tex., 1986), 85–103; idem, "A Partnership Formed, Dissolved, and in Renegotiation: Business and Government in the Franklin D. Roosevelt Era," in *Business and Government: Essays in Twentieth Century Cooperation and Confrontation,* ed. Joseph R. Frese, S.J., and Jacob Judd (Tarrytown, N.Y., 1985), 187–219; Colin Gordon, *New Deals: Business, Labor, and Politics in America, 1920–1935* (New York, 1994); Donald R. Brand, *Corporatism and the Rule of Law: A Study of the National Recovery Administration* (Ithaca, N.Y., 1988); Larry G. Gerber, "Corporatism and State Theory: A Review Essay for Historians," *Social Science History* 19:3 (Fall 1995): 313–32.

21. Sundeen, "San Francisco Bay Area Council," 73; F. N. Belgrano to George Wilson, 20 Nov. 1944, San Francisco CIO Council Records (hereafter CIO Records), Bancroft Library (hereafter BL), University of California at Berkeley, carton 1, Committees of SF CIO Council folder; Fred A. Chase to F. J. Connolly, 19 July 1945, CIO Records, carton 18, SF CIO Housing Committee folder; memorandum from Frank N. Belgrano

Jr. to Members of the San Francisco Bay Area Council, 3 Aug. 1945, CIO Records, carton 3, General Correspondence Folder; "Building a Better Bay Area, 1945–1970: A Brief History of the San Francisco Bay Area Council," copy in Institute of Governmental Studies Library, University of California at Berkeley; *San Francisco Chronicle*, 12 Dec. 1944.

22. Mel Scott, *The San Francisco Bay Area: A Metropolis in Perspective* (Berkeley, 1959), 261–63.

23. Telegram from Thomas G. Plant to Frances Perkins, 23 June 1934, Papers of Secretary of Labor Frances Perkins, National Archives, Record Group 174, box 35, Conciliation-Strikes-Longshoremen-1934 file.

24. Letter from W. J. Conboy to Thomas L. Hughes, 28 July 1934, International Brotherhood of Teamsters Collection, State Historical Society of Wisconsin, series 1, box 21, folder 9; letter from John F. Neylan to F. C. Atherton, 16 Aug. 1934, J. F. Neylan Papers, BL, box 56, series 3, folder 218: strike of 1934.

25. Article on the San Francisco Labor Council's "New Deal Slate of Officials," *Voice of the Federation* (newspaper of the Maritime Federation of the Pacific), 28 Jan. 1937, 9. The founding and activities of the Maritime Federation of the Pacific are documented in the organization's records at the Northern California Labor Archives and Research Center, San Francisco State University, San Francisco, California.

26. "Frank J. Taylor, "All Quiet on the Waterfront," *California: Magazine of Pacific Business* (Apr. 1937): 18–21, 36, 38–39; idem, "A Program for Labor Peace," ibid. (June 1937): 34–35.

27. Minutes of the Board of Directors, 24 June 1937, San Francisco Chamber of Commerce Records, California Historical Society, San Francisco.

28. *San Francisco Chronicle*, 3 Nov. 1937, 1

29. Chamber of Commerce minutes, 13 Jan. 1938, 3 Feb. 1938; "Laboratory of Labor Relations," *California: Magazine of the Pacific* (Jan. 1939): 10–11, 23.

30. *San Francisco News*, 4 June 1938, 3, 6; *San Francisco Chronicle*, 4 June 1938, 1; Bruce Nelson, *Workers on the Waterfront: Seamen, Longshoremen, and Unionism in the 1930s* (Urbana, Ill., 1988), 226–66; Harvey Klehr, John Earl Haynes, and Fridrikh Igorevich Firsov, *The Secret World of American Communism* (New Haven, Conn., 1995), 104.

31. "The 'Town Meeting'" (editorial), *Labor Clarion*, 10 June 1938, 4; "The San Francisco Labor Council and the Committee of 43 hereby announce the establishment of THE JOINT LABOR COMMITTEE," memorandum in San Francisco Labor Council Records, BL (hereafter Labor Council Records), carton 117, Committee of 43 file.

32. "Laboratory of Labor Relations," 23.

33. Ira B. Cross, "Why a Dictatorship?" *Organized Labor*, 5 May 1934, 1.

34. Minutes of the meeting of the California State Industrial Union Council, 14 Dec. 1941, in CIO Records, carton 1, Protest letters and replies (national) folder.

35. Mimeographed transcript of the proceedings of the California Conference on Labor and the War, 6–7 June 1942, 75, 24, copy in CIO Records, carton 18, CIO Report on the War folder.

36. San Francisco Labor Council resolution "Resist Trimming Labor Gains," attached

to J. A. O'Connell to Franklin D. Roosevelt, 17 June 1940, Labor Council Records, box 37, U.S. President folder.

37. The events of the hotel and department store strikes can be followed in the extensive newspaper clipping files on the strikes in the San Francisco History Room, San Francisco Main Public Library. See the vertical file collection, S.F. Strikes, Department Store Strike (two folders) and S.F. Strikes, Hotel Strike (one folder). See also *San Francisco Chronicle*, 12 Mar. 1942, 5 June 1942; *Journal of Proceedings* (2 Feb. 1942): 225–26, (11 Feb. 1942): 264–69, (16 Feb. 1942): 278–80. The streetcar controversy is described by Mayor Lapham in "Mayor's Message" (reviewing events of 1944), *Journal of Proceedings* (2 Jan. 1945): 8–11, and discussed by the Board of Supervisors in *Journal of Proceedings* (9 Oct. 1944): 2128–29. The machinists' dispute is analyzed by Richard P. Boyden in "The San Francisco Machinists and the National War Labor Board," in *American Labor in the Era of World War II*, ed. Sally M. Miller and Daniel A. Cornford (Westport, Conn., 1995), 105–19.

38. Howard Kimeldorf, *Reds or Rackets? The Making of Radical and Conservative Unions on the Waterfront* (Berkeley, Calif., 1988), 148–49, 208, and Charles P. Larrowe, *Harry Bridges: The Rise and Fall of Radical Labor in the United States*, rev. ed. (Westport, Conn., 1972), 293–97, provide a generally pro-labor analysis of the 1946 and 1948 strikes. For the employers' point of view, see "White Paper: West Coast Maritime Strike," Oct. 11, 1948, Pacific American Shipowners Association and Waterfront Employers of California, copy in vertical file collection, San Francisco Strikes, Maritime, 1946 folder [*sic*], San Francisco History Room, San Francisco Main Public Library.

39. Issel, "'Citizens outside the Government,'" 142, 144.

40. Leland W. Cutler, *America Is Good to a Country Boy* (Stanford, Calif., 1954), 182–94.

41. Ibid., 184–85.

42. The Chamber of Commerce described its program in *San Francisco: Hub of Western Industry* (1939), copy in BL. See also the chamber's "Annual Report 1939 and Work Program for 1940," mimeograph, copy in Chamber of Commerce Records, California Historical Society Library; *San Francisco Examiner*, 6–7 Nov. 1939.

43. The evolution of this growth policy process can be followed in Wm. L. Montgomery to R. R. Cooley, 8 June 1943, CIO Records, carton 2, Postwar Plan folder; *Journal of Proceedings* (29 Mar. 1943): 718–19, (5 Apr. 1943): 758; San Francisco League for Municipal Research, Inc., vol. 1, no. 1 (April 1943); *Journal of Proceedings* (21 June 1943): 1661–62, (21 Aug. 1944): 1812–13, (18 Sept. 1944): 2019–20. For the committee's report, see "Mayor's Message" (events of 1945), *Journal of Proceedings* (14 Jan. 1946): 58–59, and "Report of the Citizen's Postwar Planning Committee," 20 Aug. 1945, Appendix E, "Mayor's Annual Report to the Board of Supervisors" (1946), 40–76, copy in Labor Council Records, carton 52, Mayor's Office 1946 folder.

44. Theresa Selfa, "Revenue and Expenditure in San Francisco: A Study of the Controller's Annual Reports, 1933–1987" (Independent Study Paper, San Francisco State University History Department, 1989), 4–9.

45. San Francisco Chamber of Commerce, Municipal Affairs Committee, "History

of General Obligation Bond Issues, 1928 through 1948" (5 Nov. 1948), 4, 6–7, ts., Chamber of Commerce Records, California Historical Society Library. For details of the campaigns, see "Mayor's Message," *Journal of Proceedings* (2 Jan. 1945): 9; "Report of the San Francisco Juvenile Court," ibid., 83–86; *San Francisco Examiner,* 11 Nov. 1944; Citizen's Committee for Sewer Bonds to Dear Friends, 15 Sept. 1944, Labor Council Records, box 50, Law and Legislative Committee, 1944–46 folder.

46. "History of General Obligation Bond Issues," 4, 6–7; Edward V. Mills (chairman, San Francisco Airport Bond Committee) to Dear Friends, 27 Sept. 1945, and "United Labor Says Do Your Part for Jobs and Security" campaign flyer, Labor Council Records, box 50, Charter Amendment folder 1945; *San Francisco Examiner,* 4 Nov. 1945.

47. Royce Deems Delmatier, "The Rebirth of the Democratic Party in California, 1928–1938" (Ph.D. diss., University of California at Berkeley, 1955), 236, 239; *San Francisco Chronicle,* 18 and 22 Sept. 1934.

48. See Herman Phleger, "Sixty Years in Law, Public Service and International Affairs," oral history interview by Miriam Feingold Stein, (1979), BL, 65, 75, 87, 88–99; Roger Lapham, "An Interview on Shipping, Labor, City Government, and American Foreign Aid," oral history interview by C. L. Gilb, (1957) BL 140–41.

49. Maurice E. Harrison, *St. Thomas More: An Address before the St. Thomas More Society, Oct. 8, 1941* (privately printed), 7, copy in BL.

50. Ibid., 9.

51. Elinor Raas Heller, "A Vounteer Career in Politics, in Higher Education, and on Governing Boards," two-volume oral history interview conducted by Malca Chall, 1974–80, Regional Oral History Office, Bancroft Library, University of California at Berkeley (hereafter ROHO/UCB), 1984, 33, 48, 91, 115, 197, 254; *Brobeck, Phleger, and Harrison: The Earlier Years* (privately printed, 1973), 59, copy in Herman Phleger Papers, carton 2, BL.

52. William Malone, oral history interview conducted by Malca Chall, 1978, BL, 33, 48, 91, 115; Heller, "Volunteer Career in Politics," 254.

53. The fifty-fifty rule is described in Heller, "Volunteer Career in Politics," 206. The Julia Gorman Porter Papers, BL, contain information about her work. See also "Dedicated Democrat and City Planner, 1941–1975," interview by G. Marin, ROHO/UCB, 1977.

54. "Julia Gorman Porter: Biographical Information," Porter Papers, BL, box 1, folder 1:49; Franck Roberts Havenner, "Reminiscences," oral history interview by Corinne L. Gilb, 1953, BL, 91, 93.

55. Havenner, "Reminiscences," 95; Malone interview, 116.

56. Nelson, *Workers on the Waterfront,* 226–66; Harvey Klehr and John Earl Haynes, *The American Communist Movement: Storming Heaven Itself* (New York, 1992), 92–95.

57. Havenner, "Reminiscences," 97; Malone interview, 117–19; *San Francisco Examiner,* 8 Nov. 1939.

58. Havenner, "Reminiscences," 99–102; *San Francisco Examiner,* 6 Nov. 1940.

59. Norman Elkington, "From Adversary to Appointee: Fifty Years of Friendship with Pat Brown," oral history interview by Julie Shearer, 1978–79, ROHO/UCB, 1982, 8–10,

21; Harold Clinton Brown, "A Lifelong Republican for Edmund G. Brown," oral history interview by Julie Shearer, 1978, ROHO/UCB, 1982, 15–28.

60. *San Francisco Examiner,* 5 Nov. 1941, Nov. 3, 1943; *Journal of Proceedings* (8 Jan. 1942): 21–23.

61. Malone interview, 121.

62. Ibid., 151–55.

63. Ibid., 24; Julia Porter to Helen Gahagan, 2 July 1943, Porter Papers, BL, box 1, folder 1:1.

64. Lapham, "Interview on Shipping," 140–41; Phleger, "Sixty Years in Law," 75–76.

65. Roosevelt's letter of commendation is described in Phleger, "Sixty Years in Law," 75–76. During the campaign, Lapham urged voters to support him with the claim, "I know my way around Washington." The quotation was used in a campaign speech on radio station KFRC by Julia Porter. A copy of the speech is in the Porter Papers, BL, box 1, folder 1:48.

66. Malone interview, 154.

67. Richard Lynden and David Hedley to Dear Brothers and Sisters, 8 Oct. 1943; CIO Political Action Committee to Dear Fellow Union Member, 29 Oct. 1943, both in CIO Records, carton 17, CIO Stuff [*sic*] in Municipal Elections folder; *Labor Herald,* 15 Oct. 1943.

68. Lapham's liberal strategy generated criticism from business defenders of capital's sole right to control economic policy, as well as from labor advocates of social democracy in economic policy-making. Lapham wrote a lengthy and detailed elaboration of his strategy, "Thinking Aloud; or, The Present Thoughts of One Employer," 18 Mar. 1942. The treatise was intended, Lapham wrote, "to provoke discussion among employer members of the War Labor Board," and he sent copies to business and labor leaders all over the country. A copy of the document, along with replies and responses from a wide variety of correspondents, is in the Roger Dearborn Lapham Papers, BL, carton 1, Thinking Aloud folder. See also Nelson Lichtenstein, *Labor's War at Home: The CIO in World War II* (New York, 1982), 216–21; Andrew A. Workman, "Creating the Center: Liberal Intellectuals, the National War Labor Board, and the Stabilization of American Industrial Relations" (Ph.D. diss., University of North Carolina at Chapel Hill, 1993), 41, 135–49, 158–61.

69. *San Francisco Examiner,* 3 Nov. 1943.

70. "Factors Contributing to the Victory of Lapham in the San Francisco Elections," n.d. (but after the Nov. 1943 election), CIO Records, carton 17, Election Campaign Summaries folder. Someone wrote in the top margin of the typewritten report, "Lapham is still bad."

71. "United Labor's Legislative Committee, Executive Board Report on 16 May 1944 Primary Election," Labor Council Records, box 48, Miscellaneous folder 1944; "Report of the Political Action Committee of the SF CIO Council," 21 July 1944, CIO Records, carton 16, PAC 1945–44 folder.

72. See David Jenkins, "The Union Movement, the California Labor School, and San Francisco Politics," oral history interview by Lisa Rubens, 1987 and 1988, ROHO/UCB,

1993, 68, 113, 141; Estolv Ethan Ward, "Organizing and Reporting in the East Bay, California and the West, 1925–1987," oral history interview by Lisa Rubens, 1987 ROHO/ UCB, 1989, 59, 100; Klehr and Haynes, *American Communist Movement*, 68, 113, 141.

73. Lapham, "Interview," 179–80. Porter eventually served under four mayors for a total of nearly twenty-five years (1943–47 and 1956–76).

74. "Can S.F. Endure Two Years More of Lapham and his Downtown Pals?" front page editorial, *San Francisco Progress*, Richmond [district] Edition, 14–15 Feb. 1946. The Recall Lapham Committee of 1100, Inc. to CIO Community Services Committee, nd, in SF CIO Records, carton 6, Roger D. Lapham Mayor folder.

75. Lapham, "Interview on Shipping," 166–75; "Blind-Date Proposal" (editorial), *San Francisco Chronicle*, 14 June 1946; Paul Schnur quoted in "C.I.O. Steps Up Interest in City," *Christian Science Monitor*, 16 Feb. 1946; CIO Political Action Committee Minutes, 2 Apr. 1946, carton 5; CIO Political Action Committee Minutes, 19 July 1946, CIO Records, carton 6, June–Dec. folder; CIO Council recall election statement, 21 June 1946, CIO Records, carton 6, Roger D. Lapham Mayor.

76. Election data was compiled from the San Francisco City and County Registrar of Voters official statement of votes cast, San Francisco History Room, San Francisco Main Public Library. Dennis P. Kelly offers a different interpretation of the recall election in "Mayor Roger D. Lapham, the Recall Election of 1946, and Neighborhood Voting in San Francisco, 1938–1952," *California History* 76:4 (Winter 1997–98): 122–35, 152–55.

77. Norman Leonard, "Life of a Leftist Labor Lawyer," interview by Estolv E. Ward, 1985, ROHO/UCB, 1986, 84–89.

78. Ward, "Organizing and Reporting in the East Bay," 162; *San Francisco Chronicle*, 22 Jan. 1949, 26 Apr. 1949. See also Kimeldorf, *Reds or Rackets*, 162–69.

79. Frederick M. Wirt, *Power in the City: Decision Making in San Francisco* (Berkeley, Calif., 1974), 144, 199.

5

California in the Second World War:
An Analysis of Defense Spending

Paul Rhode

Between 1940 and 1945, California experienced what Milton Silverman of the *San Francisco Chronicle* called its "Second Gold Rush."[1] The state's population increased by 1.6 million persons, or almost one-quarter. Migrants moved west in unprecedented numbers to fill jobs in the state's rapidly expanding war industries. Driven by growth in aircraft production and shipbuilding, California manufacturing employment expanded almost two and one-half times during World War II. The federal government spent over $19 billion on major war supply contracts, new manufacturing facilities, and military installations in the state.

California, in turn, made major contributions to the war effort. The state's airframe plants delivered about one-third of the military planes (measured by weight) built during the war, and its shipyards accounted for a comparable share of the nation's new merchant ships. Military facilities in California were home base for thousands of soldiers and sailors engaged in the Pacific campaign. Finally, the state's university system served as the prime contractor for the Manhattan project to build the atomic bombs that ended the conflict.

This essay examines two key questions concerning California's war experience. First, what were the immediate economic impacts of the boom? After documenting the growth of military spending in the state during the early 1940s, this essay traces how the spending surge affected California's labor market, including its impacts on the real wage, migration, labor force participation rates, and the sectoral allocation of employment. The evidence highlights the remarkable responsiveness of the state's labor market.

Next, the essay asks what military, economic, and political forces caused California to play such a key role in the war effort. Among the factors potentially affecting the regional distribution of military spending were (1) existing expertise, infrastructure, and production facilities in either the production processes or the products required for the war effort; (2) surplus labor pools, including both unemployed workers and underemployed rural residents; (3) national security objectives, such as avoiding enemy attack; and (4) the political influence of members of Congress, the military, and the civilian administration.

Adopting the methodology of those who have explored the political economy of New Deal spending, this essay investigates the relative importance of these forces in determining the regional pattern of military expenditures during World War II. In general, the empirical findings suggest that preexisting production capacity, as measured by 1939 manufacturing employment, best explains the contracting pattern. In the case of California, the prewar development of the aircraft industry was of particular importance. (Strategic and political motivations appear to have had little effect on contracting; instead they mainly influenced the location of new facilities.) By examining the prewar roots of California's defense industries, these findings reinforce the historical interpretation that stresses continuities in the West's wartime experience.[2]

Employment Expansion, Wage Movements, and Population Growth

Without question, military spending was the treasure driving the so-called Second Gold Rush. Between June 1940 and September 1945, California received about $16.4 billion in major war-supply contracts and over $2.5 billion in federal investments in military and industrial facilities. Most of the contracts were for aircraft (over $8.8 billion) and ships (over $4.9 billion). Of the federal investments, about $1.5 billion were used for military installations and over $400 million were used for shipyards.[3] As table 5.1 shows, California was at the top of the list of states in terms of new military facilities, aircraft contracts, and shipbuilding. In terms of total spending, it ranked third overall, behind only New York and Michigan. With the exceptions of ordnance and communications equipment, California's share of military spending in each category exceeded its 1940 share of the nation's population (5.2 percent) and its 1939 share of the nation's manufacturing wage-earners (3.5 percent). The cumulative figures for the entire 1940–45 period do not give a full picture of the effects of wartime expenditures on California's economy because the state's role was relatively greater in the early mobilization period. For example, in the first year of the war program (from June 1940 to June 1941), California received slightly over 10 percent of the nation's defense contracts.[4]

The early and disproportionately high level of spending led the state's labor market to tighten more rapidly than in the nation as a whole. Table 5.2

Table 5.1. Military Spending by Category, June 1940–June 1945

Category	National Spending (in billions)	California's Share	California's Rank
Supply contracts			
Aircraft	$ 59.3	15.6%	1st
Ordnance	49.4	1.1	15th
Ships	29.7	17.3	1st
Communications			
equipment	10.2	1.2	11th
Other	47.3	4.8	8th
	196.0	8.7	3rd
Facility investment			
Industrial	18.1	5.6	7th
Military	13.6	11.1	1st
	31.1	8.0	· 1st
Totals	$227.7	8.6	3rd

Source: Paul H. Anderson, *State, Regional, and Local Market Indicators, 1939–46,* Office of Domestic Commerce, Economic Studies No. 67 (Washington, D.C., 1948), 36–38.

compares the changes in several key labor market variables over the wartime period in California with the rest of the country. The civilian labor force grew about 26 percent in California between 1940 and 1944, compared with a 2 percent fall for the nation as a whole. California's unemployment rate, which had been above 12 percent in 1940, fell below 1 percent at the peak of the boom. (The War Manpower Commission classified all three of the state's major coastal cities as "acute labor shortage areas" by 1943.) Between 1939 and 1944, the real hourly wage in California manufacturing increased by about 25–30 percent, rising roughly 4–5 percent relative to the national average.[5]

Growth in manufacturing and government led the expansion in the state's labor force. Between 1940 and 1944, the government sector's share of the total labor force increased by about one-half, from 9 percent to 14 percent. The manufacturing sector's share virtually doubled, rising from 15 percent to 29 percent.[6] Manufacturing attained a relative importance in the California economy not even closely approached before or since the war. And for a time, the structure of the manufacturing sector was fundamentally altered. As figure 5.1 shows, the wartime boom was associated with two significant changes: (1) an increase in the durable goods share and (2) a dramatic rise in the employment of women.

Driving these trends was the expansion of the aircraft and shipbuilding industries. Between 1939 and 1944, the number of production workers in the state's shipyards soared from 4,000 to 242,000, while the number in its aircraft

Table 5.2. Selected Indicators of California Labor Market Conditions, 1939–46

	Civilian Labor Force (in thousands)		Unemployment Rate		Average Hourly Earnings in California Manufacturing	
	California	United States	California	United States	Nominal	Real
1939		55,218		17.2%	$0.73	$ 98.00
1940	3,083	55,640	12.3%	14.6	0.75	100.00
1941	3,316	55,910	9.0	9.9	0.84	106.80
1942	3,566	56,410	4.5	4.7	1.03	117.00
1943	3,794	55,540	0.7	1.9	1.16	122.90
1944	3,886	54,630	0.8	1.2	1.23	129.80
1945	3,880	53,860	3.1	1.9	1.23	126.30
1946	4,219	57,520	8.8	3.9	1.29	127.30

Sources: U.S. Bureau of the Census, *Historical Statistics of the United States: Colonial Times to 1970,* pt. 1 (Washington, D.C., 1975), 126; California State Economic Development Agency, *California Statistical Abstract, 1961* (Sacramento, Calif., 1961), 61; California Division of Labor Statistics and Research, *Labor in California, 1945–1946* (San Francisco, June 1947), 48–56.

plants climbed from 17,000 to 190,000. During the war, both industries hired unprecedented numbers of women. For example, West Coast shipbuilders led the nation in utilizing women's labor, accounting for well over one-half of the female wage earners employed in the industry nationwide in 1944. About 16–18 percent of the Pacific Coast shipbuilding labor force was women, roughly twice the share in the yards of the Atlantic Coast, Gulf Coast, and Great Lakes. The transformation of the gender composition of aircraft employment was even more extensive.[7]

Table 5.3 illustrates the large shifts within the manufacturing sector, showing the changes in employment and wages over the 1940–43 period by detailed industrial category. (The industries are ranked by the absolute level of growth in employment.) Three points stand out. First, the growth of a handful of war industries dominated the overall expansion; aircraft and shipbuilding made up over four-fifths of the entire increase. Second, many industries, such as textiles and tobacco, experienced little or no growth in employment; others, including automobile production and printing, even declined. Third, these enormous shifts occurred with apparently little effect on the distribution of wages. Indeed, wages in shipbuilding, which experienced the fastest employment expansion, actually grew more slowly than the state average. Undoubtedly this was in part due to the changes within the shipbuilding labor force (e.g., reduced skill levels), to the appeal of the industry's preexisting status as a high-wage employer, and to the wartime wage controls and the resulting substitution into fringe benefits. Nevertheless, one is left with the impression of remarkable flexibility in the labor market. Tidal shifts in sectoral al-

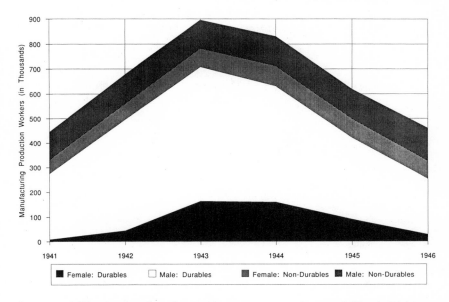

Figure 5.1. California Manufacturing Employment, 1941–45. *Sources:* California Division of Labor Statistics and Research, *Labor in California, 1945–1946* (San Francisco, June 1947), 57, and *Handbook of California Labor Statistics, 1951–1952* (San Francisco, April 1953), 81.

location appear to produce (or require) only ripples in the sectoral wage structure.[8]

A similar picture of quick adjustment and a high degree of responsiveness characterizes the aggregate supply side of the labor market. Rising real wages, increased job opportunities, and patriotic appeals induced an extremely rapid expansion of the force. More specifically, migration soared and labor force participation rates, especially of housewives, students, retirees, and others discouraged from work by a decade of depression, rose dramatically. These forces more than offset the state's losses due to military enlistment and conscription.[9]

According to estimates from the U.S. Bureau of Labor Statistics, the total labor force in California (including the armed forces) increased from about 3,056,000 in April 1940 to 4,207,000 in April 1945. Of the 1,151,000 added workers, natural increase accounted for only 67,000 workers, or about 6 percent; the participation of "extra workers" added 442,000, about 37 percent of the total. Interstate migration made up over one-half (58 percent) of the increase, some 662,000 workers. Of this number, an increase of 336,000 would have been

Table 5.3. Manufacturing Employment and Hourly Wages by Industry, 1940–43

	Number of Production and Related Workers (in thousands)				Average Hourly Earnings		Real Wage Growth
			Change (1940–43)				
Industry	1940	1943	Absolute	Relative	1940	1943	
37 Shipbuilding	7.3	274.3	267.0	37.58	$0.98	$1.37	$1.12
37 Aircraft and parts	41.2	237.4	196.2	5.76	0.73	1.06	1.16
35 General industrial machinery	9.7	31.3	21.6	3.23	0.79	1.21	1.23
36 Electrical machinery	4.2	14.3	10.1	3.40	0.73	1.01	1.11
34 Nonferrous metal products	4.4	13.5	9.1	3.07	0.79	1.09	1.10
33 Miscellaneous iron and steel products	5.6	14.3	8.7	2.55	0.79	1.13	1.16
30 Tires and tubes	3.7	9.3	5.6	2.51	0.97	1.06	0.87
33 Structural steel	4.0	8.9	4.9	2.23	0.88	1.26	1.15
39 Miscellaneous industries	3.9	8.6	4.7	2.21	0.79	1.02	1.03
33 Iron and steel foundries	5.0	9.6	4.6	1.92	0.74	1.13	1.22
35 Construction machinery	2.8	7.1	4.3	2.54	0.84	1.16	1.10
30 Miscellaneous rubber products	1.4	5.0	3.6	3.57	0.63	0.94	1.20
20 Bakery products	12.5	15.7	3.2	1.26	0.78	1.05	1.08
20 Miscellaneous food products	5.9	8.9	3.0	1.51	0.74	0.99	1.08
25 Furniture	9.0	12.0	3.0	1.33	0.71	0.99	1.11
32 Miscellaneous stone, glass, and clay products	5.1	8.1	3.0	1.59	0.73	1.04	1.15
28 Industrial chemicals	4.5	7.1	2.6	1.58	0.83	1.10	1.06
23 Women's outer clothing	9.6	11.9	2.3	1.24	0.57	0.99	1.40
28 Miscellaneous chemical products	4.2	6.4	2.2	1.52	0.72	0.95	1.05
33 Blast furnaces and rolling mills	5.4	7.5	2.1	1.39	0.96	1.23	1.02
20 Beverages	4.5	6.4	1.9	1.42	0.92	1.16	1.01
33 Heating and plumbing supplies	6.6	8.5	1.9	1.29	0.75	1.13	1.21
34 Sheet metal products	1.8	3.6	1.8	2.00	0.84	1.27	1.22
35 Miscellaneous machinery	1.6	3.3	1.7	2.06	0.75	1.03	1.10
29 Petroleum refining	8.3	9.8	1.5	1.18	0.99	1.23	1.00
33 Cutlery, tools, and hardware	1.2	2.6	1.4	2.17	0.74	1.11	1.21
26 Converted paper products	3.2	4.6	1.4	1.44	0.70	0.91	1.05
35 Engines and turbines	0.8	2.1	1.3	2.63	0.81	1.33	1.32
23 Miscellaneous apparel	5.1	6.3	1.2	1.24	0.53	0.77	1.16
32 Glass and glassware	1.9	2.9	1.0	1.53	0.83	1.12	1.09
35 Special industrial machinery	1.5	2.5	1.0	1.67	0.83	1.19	1.14
20 Dairy products	2.7	3.6	0.9	1.33	0.64	0.87	1.09
32 Cement	1.5	2.4	0.9	1.60	0.84	1.09	1.04
25 Finished lumber products	4.2	5.1	0.9	1.21	0.65	0.95	1.16
20 Grain mill products	2.3	3.1	0.8	1.35	0.76	1.03	1.09
31 Miscellaneous leather products	0.8	1.6	0.8	2.00	0.57	0.87	1.21
34 Nonferrous metal foundries	0.8	1.5	0.7	1.88	0.74	1.11	1.21
22 Knit goods	1.5	2.1	0.6	1.40	0.61	0.93	1.22
24 Planing mills	5.4	6.0	0.6	1.11	0.74	1.10	1.19
23 Men's tailored clothing	2.4	2.7	0.3	1.13	0.71	1.01	1.13
28 Paint and varnishes	1.5	1.8	0.3	1.20	0.78	1.03	1.06

Table 5.3. (cont.)

Industry	Number of Production and Related Workers (in thousands)				Average Hourly Earnings		Real Wage Growth
			Change (1940–43)				
	1940	1943	Absolute	Relative	1940	1943	
29 Miscellaneous petroleum products	0.9	1.2	0.3	1.33	0.72	1.06	1.17
31 Boots and shoes	0.9	1.2	0.3	1.33	0.63	0.94	1.19
26 Paper	2.3	2.5	0.2	1.09	0.76	1.04	1.10
33 Tin cans and other tinware	2.9	3.1	0.2	1.07	0.75	0.98	1.04
22 Fabrics	1.2	1.3	0.1	1.08	0.51	0.77	1.21
22 Miscellaneous textile mill products	1.4	1.5	0.1	1.07	0.77	0.94	0.98
21 Tobacco	0.9	1.0	0.1	1.11	0.61	0.82	1.08
32 Pottery	1.6	1.7	0.1	1.06	0.68	0.96	1.13
20 Meat products	6.7	6.7	0.0	1.00	0.75	1.01	1.07
23 Men's work garments	4.5	4.5	0.0	1.00	0.51	0.75	1.18
31 Leather tanning	0.6	0.6	0.0	1.00	0.70	0.98	1.11
20 Confectionery	2.3	2.2	−0.1	0.96	0.54	0.74	1.09
23 Millinery	1.3	1.1	−0.2	0.85	0.59	0.80	1.08
37 Miscellaneous transportation equipment	1.5	1.3	−0.2	0.87	0.79	1.09	1.10
27 Allied printing and publishing	1.1	0.9	−0.2	0.82	1.20	1.44	0.96
20 Beet sugar	2.0	1.6	−0.4	0.80	0.74	1.00	1.08
27 Printing, book and job	7.8	7.3	−0.5	0.94	0.95	1.13	0.95
20 Canning, fruit and vegetable	28.5	27.9	−0.6	0.98	0.52	0.88	1.34
32 Structural clay products	3.0	2.3	−0.7	0.77	0.59	0.88	1.19
27 Newspapers and periodicals	7.4	6.4	−1.0	0.86	1.09	1.26	0.92
20 Canning, fish	5.9	4.8	−1.1	0.81	0.66	1.00	1.22
24 Logging and sawmills	18.1	16.8	−1.3	0.93	0.74	1.11	1.20
37 Automobiles	8.0	5.0	−3.0	0.63	0.93	1.21	1.04
All manufacturing	320.1	896.4	576.3	2.80	$0.75	$1.16	$1.24

Sources: U.S. Bureau of the Census, *Historical Statistics of the United States: Colonial Times to 1970,* pt. 1 (Washington, D.C., 1975), 126; California State Economic Development Agency, *California Statistical Abstract, 1961* (Sacramento, Calif., 1961), 61; California Division of Labor Statistics and Research, *Labor in California, 1945–1946* (San Francisco, June 1947), 48–56.

Note: The numbers at the beginning of each row are Standard Industrial Classifications (SIC) of the U.S. Census, each one depicting a product category (e.g., stone, glass, and clay) and its subcategory (e.g., ceramics, bricks, cement, etc.).

expected if interstate migration over the 1940–45 period had maintained its 1935–40 level. The bureau concluded that "abnormal" migration accounted for 326,000 added workers (or about 28 percent of the labor force growth). Most of the wartime interstate migrants came from the "North Central," "West South Central," and "Mountain" regions, where the expansion of economic opportunities did not keep pace with California.[10]

As a result of this surge in migration, World War II was a period of vigorous population growth in California. Between July 1940 and July 1945, the state's civilian population expanded by almost one-quarter, from 6,899,000 to 8,523,000 residents. Natural increase accounted for only 367,000; net migration contributed 1,987,000 new residents. (These two components exceed the total increase because the losses to the military must also be offset.) At the height of the inflow from 1941 to 1943, more than a half-million people per year moved to California. Figure 5.2, which graphs the rates of migration and population growth in California from 1900 to 1970, helps put the World War II period into perspective.[11] The early 1940s represent a clear acceleration in growth above the levels of the depressed 1930s and the reconversion period of the late 1940s.

Not all regions of the state experienced demographic gains during the war. According to Leisa Bronson, twenty-six of the state's fifty-eight counties lost population during the early 1940s. Most of the increase occurred in the coastal cities, as table 5.4 illustrates. In absolute terms, the Los Angeles area had the greatest expansion, while in relative terms San Diego experienced the most rapid growth—doubling in size between 1940 and 1945. The wartime growth-

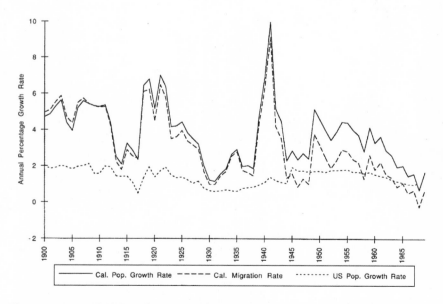

Figure 5.2. Long-Term Population Growth in California. *Source:* California Department of Public Health, *Vital Statistics of California, 1971* (Sacramento, 1971), 1–3.

Table 5.4. Population Growth in California's Coastal Cities

	Resident Population (including Military)			
	1940	1944	Growth	Percentage
Los Angeles				
Metropolitan district	2,882,236	3,383,366	501,130	0.1738
City	1,504,277	1,690,547	186,270	0.1238
San Francisco				
Metropolitan district	1,409,142	1,970,392	561,250	0.3982
City	634,536	786,590	152,954	0.2396
San Diego				
Metropolitan district	256,368	523,062	266,695	1.0402
City	203,341	401,860	198,519	0.9763

Source: Leisa Bronson, *Industrial Economy of the Pacific Coast States,* Public Affairs Bulletin No. 60 (Washington, D.C., 1946), 19.

rate of the San Francisco Bay Area was actually more rapid than that of Los Angeles, its traditional rival.[12]

The rapid growth of California's population, labor force, and war industries has tempted some observers to view World War II as a watershed in the state's development. Such interpretations, which stress discontinuities in the region's development, are complicated by two issues. The first issue, which is largely beyond the scope of this essay, is that many effects of the war boom appear either to have had transitory impacts or to have induced more permanent changes only because other forces intervened.[13] As one example of the short-lived nature of the war's effects, the dramatic shifts in employment structure associated with the boom had largely reversed by the end of the 1940s. The 1950 structure closely resembles that before the war. More generally, assessing the impact of the war requires one to examine the potentially difficult reconversion experience as well as the war itself. The second issue is that the war's impact also depended critically upon prewar conditions. Why did the federal authorities allocate a disproportionate share of military spending to California? I would argue that if it was due to the region's previously developed capacity to produce war material (and not to official favoritism), then the historical interpretations emphasizing continuities in the region's development are considerably strengthened.[14]

The Evolution of Defense Procurement Policy

How then did the federal government make its defense spending decisions during the Second World War? For the decade and a half before 1940, the military spent the predominant share of its relatively small procurement budget according to rigidly specified competitive procedures. After advertising for clearly defined quantities and qualities for a specific item, procurement officers in the army or navy invited bids and awarded the contract to the lowest bidder. Long-term contract relationships, with the provision of development funding, were rare. In addition, the Vinson-Trammel Act (1934) and the Merchant Marine Act (1936) imposed limits, ranging between 8 and 12 percent on the profit margins of government aircraft and shipbuilding contracts.[15]

The combination of unfavorable return-to-risk conditions, the still-fresh experiences of contracting difficulties in the First World War, and the prevailing adverse public opinion toward "merchants of death" led many businessmen in the 1930s to avoid military contracting. Facing the 1940 crisis in Europe and the reluctance of firms to enter the munitions business, the federal government chose to sweeten its terms. The expediting acts of June 28 and July 2, 1940, introduced the use of negotiated, cost-plus-a-fixed-fee contracts and partial payments before delivery (including advances and progress payments).[16] While procurement authorities continued to use advertising and competitive bidding for some small contracts, the bulk of defense business rapidly shifted to a negotiated basis. According to Robert Higgs, between July 1, 1939, and June 30, 1940, 87 percent of the War Department procurement occurred through the advertising/invitation-to-bid procedure; whereas between July 1, 1940, and February 28, 1941, 74 percent of purchasing was under negotiated contracts. In addition, in October 1940, the government eliminated the profit ceilings on aircraft and ship contracts. (Instead, it imposed excess-profit taxes that were partially offset by various loopholes, such as liberalized accelerated depreciation allowances.)

The federal government also began to invest its own funds to expand manufacturing capacity, especially for war material. Between July 1940 and June 1945, roughly $17.2 billion of the total $25.8 billion invested in manufacturing plants and equipment was federally financed. (A small share of privately financed investment benefited from federal loan guarantees under the Emergency Plant Facility program. A notable example is the Douglas Long Beach plant, built with a $211 million EPF advance.) Of the federal total, about $9 billion was spent by the army, navy, and Maritime Commission, primarily for munitions plants and shipyards. (The Maritime Commission funded most of the investment in the new California shipyards operated by Todd and the Kaiser-McCone-Bechtel group.) In addition, the Defense Plant Corporation, a new subsidiary of the Reconstruction Finance Corporation, invested $7 billion, chiefly for plants and equipment in the aircraft, shipbuilding, synthetic rubber, machine tools, and metal industries.[17] Examples of DPC-funded expansion in aircraft capacity in California include Consolidated's new San Diego plant and North American's new Inglewood facility. The largest DPC project was the West's most heralded "war winning," the $2 million steel plant at Geneva, Utah, operated by U.S. Steel under a government-owned, contractor-operated (or GOCO) arrangement.

The administration of the huge flow of defense dollars came to rely substantially on the talents and efforts of the "dollar-a-year" men, executives drawn from America's biggest businesses. Throughout the war, the nation's leading corporations received the great majority of prime contracts and leases for government-financed plants. On the eve of the bombing of Pearl Harbor, the top one hundred contractors accounted for over four-fifths (82 percent) of procurement spending. This concentration of contracts and investment, together with difficulties receiving materials priorities, led many small manufacturers to cry foul. Responding to intense political pressure, Congress established the Smaller War Plants Corporation in 1942 to increase the participation of small firms. Complaints over the distribution of defense business persisted through the wartime period, often with good reason.[18]

Besides the conflicts between big and small business over favoritism, there were numerous, more personal accusations of influence peddling, kickbacks, and conflicts of interest regarding defense spending. With the possible exception of the judiciary, virtually every branch of the federal government was tarred with at least one well-publicized contracting scandal. Among the notable cases capturing the attention of Truman's special Senate committee were those of Thomas Corcoran, a political operative associated with the president; General Bennett Meyers of the Army Air Corps; Representative Andrew May of Kentucky, chair of the House Committee on Military Affairs; and Senator Theodore Bilbo of Mississippi. The allegations in these cases involved charges of personal gain.[19]

Most histories of the agencies and officials involved in contracting note that the spending process, especially plant-location decisions, induced a torrent of lobbying from politicians and business and community leaders. For example, Donald M. Nelson, a former executive at Sears and Roebuck who headed the plant-location efforts of the Office of Production Management in 1941, observed: "We were operating in a democracy which was still at peace and subject to the pressures of politics. Platoons of Senators and Representatives, stimulated by their constituents, descended upon us. Hundreds of briefs were submitted by towns all over the United States, and since we were thinking about defense only, I suppose that our selection of sites pleased nobody."[20]

War administrators responded in their time-honored fashion to the surge of lobbying and to the complaints voiced by the rejected parties, who charged "favoritism" and the need for "the right connections." They bureaucratized the process, enacting contract-review procedures and establishing Plant Site

Boards to conduct systematic location searches. And while most official histories cite isolated instances of the successful application of political pressure or of questionable plant/contract placement, they generally paint a picture of spending decisions that were economically and strategically rational. The "official" view is well captured in the following statement by Donald Davenport, chief of the Employment and Occupational Outlook Branch of the U.S. Bureau of Labor Statistics, in early 1942: "It is obvious that both prime contracts and subcontracts have tended to be distributed in accordance with existing production facilities. Contracts for new industrial facilities, however, have been distributed in such a way as to bring about increased geographical dispersion."[21] Strategic concerns and congestion in the early centers of war production were said to dictate spreading contracting and investment, especially away from the coast regions.

Yet the perception prevails that lobbying played a key role in many contracting and investment decisions, especially for large projects in the West. For example, Gerald Nash has carefully documented Senator Patrick McCarran's application of political pressure to garner $133 million from the DPC to build the world's largest magnesium plant at Henderson, Nevada, near Las Vegas. The wartime record of the Basic Magnesium plant was unsatisfactory, raising serious questions about its economic justification. Henry J. Kaiser, whose Washington lobbying experience dated back to the Hoover administration and whose connections with Interior Secretary Harold Ickes and friend of FDR Tommy Corcoran were close, is commonly viewed as enjoying preferential treatment. Kaiser's success in securing defense dollars for his organization's shipyards, magnesium and aluminum operations, and the modern steel plant (at Fontana, California) added to his reputation as a "New Deal Darling."[22] It is possible to offer numerous other cases of lobbying for contracts and installations. Indeed, I suspect with enough effort one might find examples from every industry and region. Before drawing strong conclusions, however, one must supplement the examination of specific cases with an analysis of the overall pattern of spending.

The Political Economy of Military Spending during World War II

Did lobbying systematically bias spending toward California? Or was the placement of contracts and new investments as divorced from politics and the use of influence as the "official" view suggests? These questions can be more sharply posed because there already exists a large economic history literature on the political economy of New Deal spending. This earlier research offers useful analytical tools to address such questions and, what's more, clearly suggests that during the 1930s the West enjoyed the fruits of political favoritism.[23]

This literature began with Leonard Arrington's studies documenting the highly uneven regional distribution of federal outlays over the 1933 to 1939 period. On a per capita basis, spending was highest in the Mountain states ($716), followed by the Pacific ($536), Great Plains ($424), Midwest ($380), and Southeast ($306), with the Northeast ($301) bringing up the rear. (California ranked tenth among the states, receiving outlays of $538 per capita.) Using regression analysis, Don Reading investigated the relative importance of the two stated goals of the New Deal—"relief" and "reform"—in accounting for this spending pattern. Based on the strong explanatory power of variables reflecting economic decline and the weak power of those associated with long-term poverty, Reading concluded that "relief" motivations dominated "reform" motivations. Otherwise, it is hard to explain why the relatively wealthy West received far more than the impoverished South.

In a reconsideration of Reading's findings, Gavin Wright added presidential election as a potential motivation. He reasoned that intelligent politicians seeking re-election would allocate government spending to woo swing voters as opposed to party loyalists. By including in the regressions political variables capturing the likelihood that a state's presidential contest would be close, Wright explained a substantial share of the regional variation in spending and, moreover, wiped out the explanatory power of Reading's "relief" effects. In Wright's view, the West got money because it was traditionally a "swing region"; the South received little because it was solidly Democratic. Supplementing Wright's analysis, Anderson and Tollison found that the power of a state's congressional delegation, more particularly its role in the leadership structure and tenure on key committees, also mattered significantly.[24]

How important were political motivations compared with economic and strategic considerations in determining contracting and investment decisions during World War II? This essay will apply the econometric framework of the political economy literature to analyze the regional distribution of defense spending during the early 1940s. The state-level data for military spending, covering the period from June 1940 to June 1945, include total funding, defense contracting (in total, and on aircraft and shipbuilding separately), and government investment in facilities (in total, and for industrial plants and for military facilities separately).[25] To enhance comparability, I have converted the spending data into per capita terms by dividing it by the 1940 population. Table 5.5 provides the summary statistics for the key variables used in the analysis; the appendix provides the definitions and sources.

Table 5.5. Summary Statistics of Spending Regression Variables

Variable	Mean	Std. Dev.	Minimum	Maximum
Total spending				
Sppc45	1334.492	1121.635	15.919	4194.071
Contracting				
Contpc45	1087.301	1092.072	7.645412	4749.412
Airpc45	319.7397	527.6272	0.000000	2435.809
Shippc45	219.4796	329.4537	0.000000	1461.66
Ordpc45	240.5269	389.3428	0.000000	2177.864
Investment				
Facpc45	257.1913	310.9838	2.635514	2178.109
Milpc45	112.8646	127.7026	2.448598	800.4545
Indpc45	144.3267	201.536	0.1869159	1377.655
Presidential politics				
Polprod	0.3383123	0.2882734	0.000000	1.433612
Sdev	0.1237706	0.1691939	0.0223877	1.237032
Ecvpc	0.0055064	0.0037187	0.0031852	0.0272727
Congressional politics				
Stenpc	0.1628914	0.1919272	0.0060783	1.181818
Htenpc	0.2537423	0.1600187	0.0206767	0.9545454
Scetpc	0.1109463	0.1769885	0.000000	0.9545454
Hcmtpc	0.0951213	0.1506638	0.000000	0.9727273
Sleadpc	8.07E-06	0.0000399	0.000000	0.0002316
Hleadpc	9.54e006	0.0000661	0.000000	0.0004579
Economic utilization				
Unemp	14195.83	2813.036	9400	21200
Rural	526.875	183.8496	80	800
Production capacity				
Mwepc	49.56807	36.28785	4.057632	148.7924
Airwepc	0.3125281	0.8594178	0.000000	426.7984
Shwepc	0.49262	0.9012133	0.000000	3.146378
Strategy				
Mil40pc	2.345231	3.088026	0.0961538	17.13147
Coast	0.4375	0.501328	0.000000	1.000000

Sources: See the listing for each set of variables in the appendix.

Note: The number of observations for each variable is 48. For a key to the variables, see the appendix to this chapter.

The explanatory variables fall into three categories: (1) economic, (2) political, and (3) strategic. The economic variables themselves fit into two groups: (a) measures of under-utilized resources, including the fraction of the labor force that was unemployed or on relief in 1940 and the fraction of the state's population in rural areas; and (b) measures of the state's prewar (1939) manufacturing activity, including the number of wage-earners in aggregate and in the aircraft and shipbuilding industries.

The political variables also fall into two groups: (a) presidential variables, including Wright's productivity index updated to 1940, the standard deviation of the Democratic share of the vote in presidental elections over the 1896 to 1940 period, and the number of electoral college votes in the state in 1940, and (b) congressional variables, including the tenure of the state's House and Senate delegations (as of December 1941); their tenure of key committees (appropriations, military affairs, naval affairs, maritime); and the role of the state's members in the congressional leadership structure. The strategic variables include the level of military employment in 1940 and the location of the state, on the coast or in the interior. As in the case of the spending variable, the explanatory variables are in per capita terms where relevant.

Tables 5.6 and 5.7 present the results of ordinary least squares regressions of per capita defense spending on the full set of political variables as well as our bevy of economic and strategic variables.[26] It is helpful to consider the results at three levels: (1) total spending, (2) contract spending and its components, and (3) government-financed investment and its components. First, examining total spending, we find that none of the coefficient estimates of the political variables, presidential or congressional, is statistically significantly different from zero (no discernible effect). Most have the wrong signs; sometimes the magnitudes are absurdly negative. In addition, the slack capacity variables do not conform to the stated objectives of utilizing underemployed resources. Spending was negatively related to the percent of a state's population in rural areas and had no significant relationship with the percent of its labor force that was unemployed or on relief in 1940. None of the strategic variables have a significant impact either. But two economic variables—1939 wage-earners in manufacturing in general and in the aircraft industry in particular—had large, statistically significant, positive effects. The estimates imply that an extra manufacturing wage-earner added about $12,741 to a state's per capita defense receipts; if the workers were in the aircraft industry, the take increased an additional $648,807 (for winnings totaling $661,548).

The same general pattern, demonstrating the importance of prewar manufacturing activity, prevails in the regressions analyzing contract spending. In all of the regressions, the slack variables drop out and the political variables remain statistically insignificant, that is, there is no discernible effect. In overall contract spending, only the numbers of manufacturing workers and of aircraft workers have significant effects. In the aircraft spending equation, only aircraft workers matter. In the ordnance regression, the number of manufacturing wage-earners and the coast variables are significant, and in the shipbuilding regression only coast matters. The coast variable obviously captures more than simply strategic effects. It is positively correlated with production

Table 5.6. Locational Determinants of Defense Spending, 1940–45

	Sppc45	Contpc45	Airpc45	Shippc45	Ordpc45
Polprod	−234.81	77.974	65.363	2234.18	−181.12
	(−0.320)	(0.114)	(0.172)	(0.724)	(−0.537)
Sdev	−948.06	−513.88	−129.71	−31.358	−381.66
	(−1.193)	(−0.696)	(−0.315)	(−0.094)	(−1.046)
Ecvpc	85634	8823.4	−83.157	−16216	30676
	(0.856)	(0.095)	(−0.002)	(−0.384)	(0.668)
Stenpc	−40.001	26.583	141.86	364.87	−263.77
	(−0.032)	(0.023)	(0.218)	(0.690)	(−0.458)
Htenpc	1271.5	631.42	1019.6	−293.36	133.22
	(0.884)	(0.473)	(1.367)	(−0.483)	(0.202)
Sleadpc	−18.3E05	−96.2E03	−77.9E04	−65.9E04	−14.2E04
	(−0.637)	(−0.359)	(−0.521)	(−0.542)	(−0.108)
Hleadpc	−71.3E04	−98.5E03	−66.4E03	−11.7E04	22.8E04
	(−0.375)	(−0.056)	(−0.671)	(−0.145)	(0.261)
Scmtpc	−1052.0	−1263.1	−840.94	−453.05	−487.28
	(−0.819)	(−1.058)	(−1.262)	(−0.835)	(−0.826)
Hcstpc	104.87	232.00	−440.08	286.37	17.929
	(0.056)	(0.134)	(−0.456)	(0.364)	(0.021)
Rural	−2.0089	−1.4822	−0.2550	−0.16524	−0.43200
	(−2.021)	(−1.606)	(−0.495)	(−0.394)	(−0.947)
Unemp	−0.01357	−0.0213	−0.0084	0.01652	−0.02640
	(−0.281)	(−0.475)	(−0.338)	(0.810)	(−1.190)
Mwepc	12.740*	14.238*	3.8368	−1.1477	7.0084*
	(2.473)	(2.976)	(1.436)	(−0.528)	(2.963)
Airwepc	648.80*	601.00*	477.77*	12.318	77.768
	(4.528)	(4.518)	(6.431)	(0.204)	(1.182)
Shwepc	−45.671	−29.339	−110.54	81.599	−35.589
	(−0.291)	(−0.202)	(−1.359)	(1.234)	(−0.494)
Coast	−331.70	−384.28	250.27	383.63*	−450.04*
	(−1.025)	(−1.279)	(−1.492)	(2.810)	(−3.030)
Mil40pc	.79571	15.392	17.354	11.094	−4.6730
	(0.018)	(0.373)	(0.752)	(0.591)	(−0.229)
Constant	1464.6	1374.5	218.31	−47.212	696.68
	(1.045)	(1.05)	(0.301)	(−0.080)	(1.083)
R−squared	0.768	0.789	0.718	0.522	0.594

Notes: T-statistics are in parentheses. For a key to the variables, see the appendix.
* Significant at 5 percent level of confidence for a two-tailed test.

activities such as shipbuilding and, perhaps by happenstance, negatively correlated with the location of automobile production (which converted into ordnance and aircraft production during the war.)

The picture for government-financed facility investment, displayed in table 5.7, is quite different. Here politics mattered. The presidential variables kick in, as investment appears to be greater in larger, more stable states (somewhat contrary to Wright's argument). Congressional tenure, more particularly tenure in

Table 5.7. Locational Determinants of Facility Investments

	Facpc45	Indpc45	Milpc45
Polprod	−312.79	−182.06	−130.73
	(−1.812)	(−1.544)	(−1.621)
Sdev	−434.18*	−270.81*	−163.37
	(−2.323)	(−2.121)	(−1.871)
Ecvpc	76811*	54034*	22778*
	(3.264)	(3.361)	(2.072)
Stenpc	−66.584	−219.20	152.61
	(−0.226)	(−1.088)	(1.107)
Htenpc	640.08	456.71	183.36
	(1.892)	(1.976)	(1.160)
Sleadpc	−87.5E04	−38.3E04	−49.2E04
	(−1.291)	(−0.827)	(−1.553)
Hleadpc	−61.5E04	−39.9E04	−21.6E04
	(−0.375)	(−1.304)	(−1.031)
Scmtpc	210.77	150.47	60.300
	(0.697)	(0.729)	(0.427)
Hcmtpc	−127.13	−78.642	−48.486
	(−0.290)	(−0.263)	(−0.237)
Rural	−0.52679*	−0.29714	−0.22964*
	(−2.253)	(−1.860)	(−2.102)
Unemp	0.007738	0.00109	0.00665
	(0.681)	(0.140)	(1.252)
Mwepc	−1.4973	−0.2219	−1.2754*
	(−1.236)	(−0.268)	(−2.253)
Airwepc	47.807	37.039	10.768
	(1.419)	(1.609)	(0.684)
Shwepc	−16.332	−14.620	−1.7124
	(−0.443)	(−0.580)	(−0.099)
Coast	52.569	−381.123	83.691*
	(0.691)	(−0.599)	(2.354)
Mil40pc	−14.597	−13.618	−0.97863
	(−1.395)	(−1.905)	(−0.200)
Constant	90.136	52.731	37.404
	(0.274)	(0.234)	(0.243)
R−squared	0.833	0.814	0.784

Notes: T-statistics are in parentheses. For a key to the variables, see the appendix.
* Significant at 5 percent level of confidence for a two-tailed test.

the House, also has a significant positive effect. Of the economic and strategic variables, only the rural share of the population affects investment spending (again in a negative direction) at a 95 percent level of statistical significance. The effects are much the same in the regressions separating military and industrial investments, and the variations remain of some interest. There was a tendency for the military investments to flee manufacturing locations and seek the coast and for the industrial investments to locate away from existing military areas.

Although the regression evidence suggests that for defense contracting, and especially for aircraft contracting, productive capacity (rather than political pull) mattered, this does not completely settle the issue of favoritism toward California. The state is consistently an outlier in these regressions, with actual spending exceeding the predicted pattern, typically by about 5 to 10 percent. A more in-depth non-econometric analysis of spending on aircraft and ship-building will help reveal whether this phenomenon was due to unwarranted favoritism toward the region.

Shipbuilding and Aircraft Manufacture in California

During the war, California's shipyards supplied about one-fifth of the value of government ship purchases; they primarily produced Liberty and Victory ships rather than warships. As a result of this pattern of specialization, California accounted for around 34 percent of the Maritime Commission's spending, but only 7 percent of the navy's purchases.[27] Most navy work was concentrated in the Northeast while the western yards of Kaiser and Bechtel's Marinship worked exclusively for the Maritime Commission. Kaiser quickly became the industry's Cinderella story. He had little or no experience in shipbuilding before the war, having concentrated on large-scale construction projects in the West during the 1920s and 1930s; yet the Kaiser group produced more ships for the commission than any other contractor, received higher fees, and "operated entirely in government-owned shipyards." It is small wonder that charges of favoritism circulated widely at congressional hearings in 1946 on wartime shipbuilding contracting.[28]

Addressing this question, Frederic Lane, the commission's respected official historian, observed:

> Against the charge of favoritism must be considered the terms of the contracts negotiated in 1942 and 1943. The Kaiser companies were given terms harder than those given other companies. Kaiser was, as Admiral Vickery said, the lead horse used to set the pace. The only kind of "favoritism" shown Kaiser in these negotiations was the selection of his companies to build new yards which would be paid for by the government and in which the Kaiser Corporation would have a chance to make large fees with very slight investment of the industrialist's capital. It seems to me clear that the reason Kaiser was thus "favored" in the winter and spring of 1942 was because he had at that time much the best record for rapid production.[29]

More generally, Lane noted that the cost of building Liberty ships on the Pacific Coast (at $1.7 million per ship) was consistently lower than in the Lower South (at $2 million) or in other regions (at $1.8 million). The West's higher wage-rates were more than offset by its high productivity levels.[30] Based on these findings, he concluded that the "Commission built many more new ship-ways on the West Coast than in any other region. The high productivity on the West coast proved that this was a wise decision."

Unlike the shipbuilding sector, the California aircraft industry was not a war baby. The industry located in California primarily for economic and techni-cal as opposed to military or strategic reasons. It rode its successes in the com-mercial market into a position of leadership in the late 1930s. As international relations deteriorated, Britain and France placed huge orders with the west-ern producers. By the end of 1939, the region's producers had backlogs total-ling $240 million—more than twice the 1939 sales. But the orders kept com-ing, swelling backlogs to almost $1.5 billion by the end of 1940.[31] In response, the aircraft makers expanded capacity, with the help of federal dollars.

As the aircraft demand continued to soar, the war-production authorities consciously made an effort to locate new production facilities in the nation's interior. The stated reasons were to reduce the possibility of enemy attack and avoid congestion at existing centers. In 1941, the government built four bomber plants in the mid-continent region, to be managed by long-established (typi-cally western-based) aircraft makers coupled with leading automobile firms that supplied the parts.[32] Consolidated ran the government's new Fort Worth, Texas, facility in combination with Ford; Douglas, the Tulsa, Oklahoma, plant, again with Ford supplying parts; North American operated the Kansas City, Kansas, plant with GM's Fisher Body; and Glenn Martin ran the Omaha, Ne-braska, plant teamed up with Chrysler, Hudson, and Goodyear.[33]

As a result, although the aircraft capacity located on the West Coast expanded dramatically during the war, it expanded even more rapidly nationwide. In January 1940, about 44 percent of the nation's aircraft floorspace was located in California, 3,877 square feet of 8.8 million nationally. This fraction fell to 24 percent by January 1944 (25 million out of 106.1 million). While California lost out as a location of production, there was virtually no reduction in the importance of California-based firms. The plants managed by California firms accounted for about one-half of all aircraft output.[34]

As in the case of shipbuilding, Pacific Coast aircraft plants initially had much higher productivity than did those in most other regions. Table 5.8 compares the number of man-hours required at plants in California to those in the na-tion's interior to produce selected aircraft, including the B-24, a heavy bomb-er, the B-25, a medium bomber, and the C-27, a medium transport plane. In all cases, the western plants had a substantial early productivity lead; in 1943, the interior plants required at least one-half more labor per unit of output. This lead is not surprising given the well-documented learning curve in air-craft production and the greater production experience in California. None-

Table 5.8. Labor Productivity in the Aircraft Industry, 1942–45: Direct Man-Hours per Pound of Airframe for Selected Aircraft

Model	Plant	Firm	1942	1943	1944	1945
B-24	San Diego	Consolidated-Vultee	1.37	0.82	0.56	0.58
	Willow Run	Ford	12.38	1.29	0.41	0.31
	Fort Worth	Consolidated-Vultee	1.71	0.69		
	Tulsa	Douglas		4.18	1.04	
	Dallas	North American	6.23	1.36		
B-25	Inglewood	North American	1.37	1.13	0.68	
	Kansas City	North American	3.84	1.70	0.88	0.57
C-47	Long Beach	Douglas	1.84	1.21	0.80	
	Oklahoma City	Douglas		3.96	0.83	0.61

Source: U.S. Army Air Forces, *Source Book of World War II Basic Data Airframe Industry,* vol. 1: *Direct Man-Hours-Progress Curves* (Dayton, Ohio, 1947), 64–68.

theless, it does suggest that the West had a greater capacity to produce planes at the crucial early period of the war and that the aircraft procurement in the region was not due primarily to unwarranted political favoritism.[35]

Conclusions

The empirical analysis of the overall pattern of contract spending, together with the brief case studies of the shipbuilding and aircraft industries, suggests that the primary reason for California's disproportionately large share of defense contracting was its preexisting economic capacity. For aircraft, its prewar leadership position is plainly apparent—over one-third of all the nation's workers in the aircraft and parts industry (and one-half of the airframe workers) were in the state in 1939. For shipbuilding, the region's prewar capacity was less obvious—only about one in twenty shipyard workers was in the state in 1939. But the technical and managerial capabilities developed by Kaiser and others in constructing the West's large-scale infrastructure projects (with New Deal money!) proved readily transferable to building ships for the Maritime Commission. More generally, the highly responsive nature of the region's labor supply circa 1940 allowed the enormous expansion to occur. There were complaints of shortages and overcrowding, but the job got done.

The long-run impacts of the war boom on the state's economic development clearly merit further study. The conversion period holds considerable interest for Americans, and especially Californians, living through the cold war build-down of the 1990s. The Second World War left California with a greatly expanded labor force and an enlarged potential home market, but without a permanent peacetime employment base. (The "permanent war economy" was not yet a reality.) The postwar transition proved easier than most contemporaries thought likely. Better understanding of the contributions of the added production capacity—the West's "war winnings"—and of the state's stronger links to the military establishment, forged during the early 1940s, is a promising subject for future research.

Appendix: Definitions and Sources of Variables

Spending for Contracting and Investment

Sppc45	= total per capita spending for contracts to June 1945 and for facilities to May 1945
Contpc45	= per capita spending for contracts to June 1945
Airpc45	= per capita spending for aircraft contracts
Shippc45	= per capita spending for shipbuilding contracts
Ordpc45	= per capita spending for ordnance contracts
Facpc45	= per capita government spending for facilities to May 1945
Milpc45	= per capita spending for military facilities to May 1945
Indpc45	= per capita spending for industrial facilities to May 1945

Sources: Paul H. Anderson, *State, Regional, and Local Market Indicators, 1939–46,* U.S. Office of Domestic Commerce, Economic Studies No. 67 (Washington, D.C., 1948); Gerald T. White, *Billions for Defense: Government Financing by the Defense Plant Corporation during World War II* (University, Ala., 1980), 81–82.

Presidential Politics

Polprod	= political productivity index for 1940
Sdev	= standard deviation of Democratic share in presidential elections, 1896–1940
Ecvpc	= electoral college votes per capita in 1940

Source: U.S. Bureau of the Census, *Historical Statistics of the United States: Colonial Times to 1970,* pt. 2 (Washington, D.C., 1975), 1075–79.

Congressional Politics

Stenpc	= Senate delegation's tenure per capita as of December 1941
Htenpc	= House delegation's tenure per capita as of December 1941
Scmtpc	= Senate delegation's tenure on the Appropriations, Military Affairs, Naval Affairs, or Truman Committees per capita
Hcmtpc	= House delegation's tenure on the Appropriations, Merchant Marine, Military Affairs, or Naval Affairs Committees per capita
Sleadpc	= Senate delegation's membership as president pro tem per capita
Hleadpc	= House delegation's membership as speaker, majority, or minority leader per capita

Source: U.S. Congress, *Official Congressional Directory,* 2d ed., corrected to 23 Apr. 1941, 77th Cong., 1st Sess. (Washington, D.C., 1941).

Economic Utilization

Rural	=	1940 rural population share
Unemp	=	1940 fraction of the labor force unemployed or on relief

Sources: U.S. Bureau of the Census, *Historical Statistics of the United States: Colonial Times to 1970,* pt. 1 (Washington, D.C., 1975), 24–37; *Sixteenth Census of the United States, 1940: Population,* vol. 3: *Labor Force: Occupation, Industry, Employment, and Income,* pt. 1: *United States Summary* (Washington, D.C., 1943), 27.

Production Capacity

Mwepc	=	total 1939 manufacturing wage-earners per capita
Airwepc	=	1939 aircraft manufacturing wage-earners per capita
Shwepc	=	1939 shipbuilding manufacturing wage-earners per capita

Source: U.S. Bureau of the Census, *Census of Manufactures, 1947,* vol. 3: *Area Statistics* (Washington, D.C., 1950).

Strategy

Mil40pc	=	military employment per capita in 1940
Coast	=	dummy variable reflecting whether the state is on a coastal location

Source: U.S. Bureau of the Census, *Sixteenth Census of the United States, 1940: Population,* vol. 3: *Labor Force: Occupation, Industry, Employment, and Income,* pts. 2–5: *States* (Washington, D.C., 1943), 27.

Notes

1. *San Francisco Chronicle,* 25 Apr. 1943.

2. For the debate over whether World War II was a watershed, see Gerald Nash, *World War II and the West: Reshaping the Economy* (Lincoln, Nebr., 1990); Roger W. Lotchin, *Fortress California, 1910–1961: From Warfare to Welfare* (New York, 1992); Roger W. Lotchin, ed., *Fortress California at War: San Francisco, Los Angeles, Oakland, and San Diego,* special issue of *Pacific Historical Review* 63:3 (Aug. 1994).

3. U.S. Bureau of the Census, *County Data Book, 1947* (Washington, D.C., 1947), 7, 77; "Industry's Leaders Outline West's Industrial Prospects," *Pacific Factory* (Jan. 1946): 48; California State Chamber of Commerce, *Postwar Industrial Growth in California, 1945–1948,* 1948–49 Series Report No. 41.

4. U.S. Congress, House, 77th Cong., 2d Sess., Special Committee Investigating National Defense Migration, *Hearings,* pt. 16 (Washington, D.C., 1941), 6589. In 1939, California had about 33 percent of the nation's aircraft wage-earners and 5.8 percent of its shipbuilding wage-earners.

5. California Division of Labor Statistics and Research, *Labor in California, 1945–1946*

(San Francisco, June 1947); idem, *Handbook of California Labor Statistics, 1951–1952* (San Francisco, April 1953), 81; U.S. Employment Service, *A Short History of the War Manpower Commission* (Washington, D.C., June 1948), 119.

6. Major sectors of the economy such as agriculture, construction, trade, and services grew little in absolute terms during the conflict; the labor force in finance, insurance, and real estate actually declined.

7. U.S. Bureau of Labor Statistics, *Wartime Employment, Production, and Conditions of Work in Shipyards*, Bulletin No. 824 (May 1945), 6–7; "Wartime Expansion in the California Airframe Industry," *Monthly Labor Review* (Oct. 1945): 721–27.

8. Given the high level of unemployment during the Great Depression, it seems highly plausible that labor supply was very elastic and that wages prevailing in the prewar period were not market-clearing.

9. Between 1940 and 1945, the military absorbed about 730,000 California residents, or roughly one-tenth of its population. Over 550,000 entered the military in the first three years of the period. Most of these residents were prime-age males, a group with very high labor-force participation rates.

10. "Prospective Labor Supply on the West Coast," *Monthly Labor Review* (Apr. 1947): 565–66.

11. *California Vital Statistics, 1971* (Sacramento, 1971). How apt are comparisons with the Gold Rush is a difficult question. According to Richard B. Rice, William A. Bullough, and Richard J. Orsi, *Elusive Eden: A New History of California* (New York, 1988), 178, the non-Indian population grew from about 14,000 at the beginning of 1848 to over 200,000 when the state census was taken in 1852. This represents an increase of over 1,400 percent. In relative terms, the Gold Rush clearly dwarfs the Second World War period, but in absolute terms, the roles are reversed.

12. Leisa Bronson, *Industrial Economy of the Pacific Coast States*, Library of Congress, Legislative Reference Service, Public Affairs Bulletin No. 60 (Washington, D.C., Nov. 1947), 16.

13. For a longer discussion of these issues, see Paul Rhode, "The Nash Thesis Revisited: An Economic Historian's View," *Pacific Historical Review* 63:3 (Aug. 1994): 363–92.

14. The links between arguments concerning continuity or discontinuity of change and the allocation of war contracts are not iron-clad. Yet much of the existing literature (such as Nash's *American West Transformed*) reads as the story of how western politicians, with the assistance of favorably inclined Washington administrators, used the war crisis to wrangle more resources for their regions than prewar economic conditions dictated.

15. The best official source on the evolution of procurement policy is R. Elberton Smith, *Army and Economic Mobilization* (Washington, D.C., 1959). Wesley F. Craven and James L. Cate, *Army Air Forces in World War II* (Chicago, 1955), esp. chaps. 8 and 9, and Irving Holley, *Buying Aircraft: Materiel Procurement for the Army Air* (Washington, D.C., 1964), explore the history of aircraft procurement in greater depth. Byron Fairchild and Jonathan Grossman, *Army and Industrial* (Washington, D.C., 1959),

esp. chap. 6, review the role of manpower availability on the location of production and new facilities.

The main work in the economic history field is Robert Higgs, "Private Profit, Public Risk: Institutional Antecedents of the Modern Military Procurement System in the Rearmament Program of 1940–41," in *Sinews of War: Essays on the Economic History of World War II,* ed. Geofrey T. Mills and Hugh Rockoff (Ames, Iowa, 1993), 166–98. A valuable study offering a different perspective is Jacob Vander Meulen, *Politics of Aircraft: Building an American Military Industry* (Lawrence, Kans., 1991). Vander Meulen (esp. pp. 182–224) argues that the arm's-length, competitive bidding practices of the military handicapped the development of the American aircraft industry.

16. The U.S. Maritime Commission, which was required to use competitive bidding under the Merchant Marine Act of 1936, was allowed to employ negotiated contracts and greater discretion by the spring of 1938. Acting on the advice of Joseph P. Kennedy (the commission's chair) to allocate some shipbuilding to the West and South in the interests of national security, the House Committee on the Merchant Marine amended the laws "to take into consideration regional differences in costs, and the need of defense and of relieving unemployment." "The main purpose was to permit the awarding of contracts to West coast yards at higher prices than those bid by East coast yards, but in the Congressional debates and reports it was recognized that the Commission was being given a very free hand 'to trade with shipbuilders.' . . . By [January 1941] Western yards had been drawn by negotiation into the Maritime Commission Program and were able . . . to compete with Eastern yards" (Frederic C. Lane, *Ships for Victory: A History of Shipbuilding under the U.S. Maritime Commission in World War II* [Baltimore, 1951], 102–4).

17. Gerald T. White, *Billions for Defense: Government Financing by the Defense Plant Corporation during World War II* (University, Ala., 1980). As Higgs notes, by 30 June 1945, the DPC owned over 10 percent of the nation's manufacturing capacity "including 96 percent of the capacity in synthetic rubber, 90 percent in magnesium, 71 percent in aircraft, and 58 percent in aluminum" (182).

18. As the war progressed, contracting became somewhat less concentrated. Over the June 1940 to September 1944 period, the top one hundred prime contractors, led by General Motors, Curtiss-Wright, and Ford, accounted for 67 percent of war supply contracts. Among the California-based firms making the list were Consolidated-Vultee (no. 4); Douglas (no. 5); Lockheed (no. 10); North American Aviation (no. 11); Kaiser (no. 20); Todd Shipyards (no. 26); Permanente Metals (no. 42); California Shipbuilding (no. 49); Food Machinery Corp. (no. 64); Standard Oil of California (no. 75); Western Pipe Supply (no. 89); and Northrop (no. 100). See U.S. Congress, Senate, 79th Cong., 2d Sess., Report of the Smaller War Plants Corporation to the Special Committees to Study Problems of American Small Business, *Economic Concentration in World War II,* Senate Document No. 206 (Washington, D.C., 1946), 30–31.

19. U.S. Congress, Senate, 76th Cong., 2d Sess., Special Committee to Investigate the National Defense Programs, *Hearings* (Washington, D.C., 1941–47).

20. Donald M. Nelson, *Arsenal of Democracy: The Story of American War Production*

(New York, 1946), 149–51. According to Nelson's postwar account, the OPM's Plant Site Committee, which reviewed and approved proposals for new defense plants and facilities, was "instructed to decentralize defense industries, in the interest of employment and raw materials. . . . Naturally every section of the country wanted plants, but the tendency of the Army and Navy was to place them in areas where the various materials and products had been created before." Nelson, recognizing that this policy was expedient in the short run, questioned its long-run effects. "We felt that a very serious manpower shortage might develop . . . and we thought it important to select locations for new manufacturing facilities in areas where the nation's resources in manpower, transportation and raw materials could be used to best advantage. For instance, there were some sections of the country, notably in the South and Middle West, where large pools of unemployed men existed because there was no sufficient industry to absorb the available labor supply." See also U.S. Civilian Production Administration, Bureau of Mobilization, *The Facilities and Construction Program of the War Production Board and Predecessor Agencies, May 1940 to May 1945,* Historical Reports on War Administration: War Production Board, Special Study No. 19 (Washington, D.C., 1945), 41–42, 56–62.

21. U.S. Congress, House, 77th Cong., 2d Sess., Select Committee Investigating National Defense Migration, *Hearings,* pt. 27, *Manpower of the Nation in War Production: Book One* (Washington, D.C., 1942), 10258.

22. Ibid.

23. Leonard Arrington, "The New Deal in the West: A Preliminary Statistical Inquiry," *Pacific Historical Review* 38:3 (Aug. 1969): 311–16; idem, "Western Agriculture and the New Deal," *Agricultural History* 49 (1970): 337–51; Don Reading, "New Deal Activity and the States, 1933 to 1939," *Journal of Economic History* 33 (1973): 792–810; Gavin Wright, "Political Economy of New Deal Spending: An Econometric Analysis," *Review of Economics and Statistics* 56 (1974): 262–81; John J. Wallis, "The Birth of Old Federalism: Financing the New Deal," *Journal of Economic History* 47 (1984): 139–60; Gary M. Anderson and Robert D. Tollison, "Congressional Influence and Patterns of New Deal Spending, 1933–1939," *Journal of Law and Economics* 34 (Apr. 1991): 161–75. For an excellent summary of this literature, see Jeremy Atack and Peter Passell, *New Economic View of American History,* 2d ed. (New York, 1994), 642–46.

24. Wright calculated the political productivity index as the product of two factors: (a) the number of electoral votes per capita; and (b) the effect of 1 percent change in the Democratic share of the state's vote on the probability that the state would vote Democratic in the presidential election. The latter factor was calculated based on the experience in elections since 1896.

25. The supply contracts cover the period through June 1945 and the facilities investments through May 1945. The spending data are from Paul H. Anderson, *State, Regional, and Local Market Indicators, 1939–1946,* Office of Domestic Commerce, Economic Studies No. 67 (Washington, D.C., 1948); and White, *Billions for Defense,* 81–82. The demographic and political data are from U.S. Bureau of the Census, *Historical Statistics of the United States, Colonial Times to 1970,* pts. 1 and 2 (Washington, D.C., 1975), 24–37,

1077–79; *Official Congressional Directory,* 2d ed., corrected to 23 Apr. 1941, 77th Cong., 1st Sess. (Washington, D.C., 1941). The manufacturing employment information is from U.S. Bureau of the Census, *Census of Manufactures, 1947,* vol. 3: *Area Statistics* (Washington, D.C., 1950).

26. The full list of variables is quite extensive, taxing the degrees of freedom of the forty-eight state observations and possibly the patience of the reader. The results do not fundamentally change if an abbreviated list of variables is used. Economic variables matter most in the regressions explaining the regional allocation of contracts whereas political and strategic variables enter into the regressions explaining government facilities investments.

27. Gerald T. Fisher, *Statistical Summary of Shipbuilding under the U.S. Maritime Commission during World War II,* Historical Reports of the War Administration, U.S. Maritime Commission, No. 2 (Washington, D.C., 1949), table H-7.

28. Lane, *Ships for Victory,* 808.

29. Ibid., 811.

30. Ibid., 826–28. Building new shipyards in the Deep South actually required a more involved justification: "As expected, labor became scarce on the West Coast. In order to draw on the labor supply of the South the Commission had decided to build new yards there in spite of obvious disadvantages. The Gulf lagged far behind the West, as expected, and was slow in reaching a comparable level of labor productivity. . . . [F]or 1941–1945 as a whole the average cost of Libertys built in the Lower South was $200,000 more per ship than the average cost of those built elsewhere. All things considered, the decision to utilize the labor supply of the Deep South seems to have been well worth this extra cost."

31. Federal Reserve Bank of San Francisco, *Monthly Review of Business Conditions,* 1 Dec. 1941, 63.

32. William Cunningham, *Aircraft Industry: A Study in Industrial Location* (Los Angeles, 1951), 75–108, 116–20, 124–26; John B. Rae, *Climb to Greatness: The American Aircraft Industry, 1920–60* (Cambridge, Mass., 1968), 128–38, 157–61.

33. Ford, now in the leading role, also received Consolidated's help at its new Willow Run, Michigan, plant. North American also operated a plant in Dallas, Texas. See Holley, *Buying Aircraft,* 304–5.

34. U.S. Bureau of Labor Statistics, "Wartime Expansion in the California Airframe Industry," *Monthly Labor Review* (Oct. 1945): 721–27; Cunningham, *Aircraft Industry,* 168–70, 203–15. After "normalcy" returned in 1945, the California-based firms closed their interior branch plants and reconcentrated their operations in Southern California, restoring its former predominance in production.

35. U.S. Army Air Forces, *Source Book of World War II: Basic Data Airframe Industry,* vol. 1: *Direct Man-Hours-Progress Curves* (Dayton, Ohio, 1947), 64–68. At its Willow Run plant, Ford vigorously attempted to apply mass-production practices, derived from its automobile operations, to build B-24s. (Ford's wartime partner, Consolidated, had been the first to use moving assembly lines in the aircraft industry to build B-24s at its San Diego facility.) By late 1944, after demand for B-24s had peaked, Ford

attained labor productivity levels exceeding those achieved anywhere else in the industry. But, as Holley concluded (*Buying Aircraft*, 326–27, 518–29), this "record . . . was not won without cost, for the special tooling that made it possible was extremely expensive (costing between $75,000,000 in total). In short, the Ford triumph in proving that the mass-production methods of the automobile industry could be utilized for aircraft was won at a cost in time lag and tooling costs that went far to offset the subsequent saving in labor costs and the ultimate achievement of mass production." The correlation between per capita spending and income was, in fact, positive, not negative as the "reform" view would suggest.

6

Public Oil, Private Oil:
The Tidelands Oil Controversy, World War II, and Control of the Environment

Sarah S. Elkind

Californians have long regarded powerful corporations with deep ambivalence. From the Gold Rush to World War II, their celebrations of rapid economic growth were tempered only by their consistent criticism of their most success- ful endeavors. Boosters rarely forgot that railroads, water developers, and other utilities made urban, agricultural, and industrial development possible, but these same champions of business proved more than ready to blame any and all disappointments on utility monopolies. Anticorporate rhetoric also became a fixture in California's politics. For decades before Hiram Johnson ran for governor in 1911, Democrats and Republicans competed to label their oppo- nents shills for private utility companies and the railroad. Of course, many other Americans shared this suspicion of big business that became so prom- inent in California politics. Incorporated into the New Deal, this ideology ap- peared in Secretary of the Interior Harold Ickes's efforts to use federal power to promote economic equity and natural preservation as well as growth. In California, however, the unique and long-standing appeal of anticorporate rhetoric made the rejection of this tradition in post–World War II resource policy particularly striking.

During World War II, Californians' exuberant criticism of corporate power all but vanished. For decades afterward, economic policy in California and else- where emphasized extensive use of resources for growth and national defense above all other priorities. Production for the war overshadowed the social en- gineering aspects of federal economic policy. This rollback of preservationist and redistributive programs continued under the Truman and Eisenhower ad- ministrations. By the late 1930s, war production had made economic policies more single-minded and reinforced government-industry cooperation. These changes persisted well after the fighting stopped.[1]

Industry leaders played central roles in wartime planning. This leadership gave them enormous influence over American economic and environmental planning and helped them to return the nation to corporate liberalism during and after the war.[2] The "dollar-a-year men" who left company jobs to run the wartime bureaucracy, but remained dedicated to private enterprise, prevented intransigent institutional expansion.[3] These individuals sought federal assistance for their industries throughout the war years, even as they worked to eliminate burdensome restrictions. They accepted some limits on private enterprise as necessary during the war emergency, but treated these as distinctly short-term arrangements. Pro-business policies during the war and the rapid elimination of federal economic controls afterward reflected the priorities of an industrial sector anxious to ride both the war and its aftermath to greater industrial autonomy.

California's major oil companies took full advantage of the war to concentrate their power and to quiet outside challenges to their control over resources. This control included fighting off federal efforts to establish ownership of underwater oil and silencing public criticism of beachfront drilling. Federal tidelands claims were consistent with New Deal economic manipulation, but quite at odds with the national emphasis on industrial growth during and after the war. Nevertheless, oil companies retained some measure of control over policy in part by direct political activity. Through lobbying, industry-sponsored studies, and participation in government bureaucracies, they made their voices heard in both Sacramento and Washington. Public acceptance of corporate priorities also weakened central control over the economy; ultimately, attempts to increase federal control over California's offshore oil failed because the war reinforced American preferences for limited interference with private enterprise. As a case study, the conflict over California's tidelands reflects national trends in the competition for control of natural resources, the narrowing of the definition of "public interest," and the pivotal role that industry leaders played in determining both.

The revelation that large corporations wielded significant power over natural resource policy in California is not new to environmental history. As Donald Worster, Donald Pisani, Marc Reisner, Norris Hundley, and many others have demonstrated, resources generally flowed to the wealthy and powerful.[4] Robert Gottleib, Margaret Fitzsimmons, and Joseph Sax have explained the ways in which ties between public institutions and commercial interests have constrained natural resource policy options.[5] Still others, such as Robert

Kelley and John T. Cumbler, have demonstrated that the American government deliberately distributed resources to those industries that appeared the most promising or prosperous.[6] These works are critical in identifying industry's influence over resource policy and have explained vital trends in this policy. Yet they have not adequately considered the ways in which the public has embraced industrial priorities. Thus, they have overemphasized direct political power to the exclusion of industry's informal, social influence over policy. Industrial interests ensured that public policy reflected their priorities not merely because they directly influenced the political process; during and after World War II, California's industries defined for the public the terms of the debate over economic and environmental policies.

The Advent of Offshore Drilling

It seems fitting that Southern California, where the automobile so shaped the urban landscape, should emerge as the center of the multifaceted conflicts over oil control and production. In the 1890s, Californians adapted dry-land drilling techniques to recover offshore oil. Beginning in the 1920s, this practice came under fire, as oil exploration interfered with other uses of the beachfront and as competing firms jockeyed for access to valuable resources. Unlike the disputes to come, many conflicts over resources were as much disagreements over how best to foster growth or what constituted the public good as they were disputes over control of the resources themselves.

California's early oil development replicated national patterns. Long collected from natural seeps and used in patent medicines, "rock oil" was first drilled in mid-nineteenth-century Pennsylvania.[7] California's first strikes followed in the 1870s, motivated by the growing market for the petroleum distillate kerosene.[8] Many early California companies appeared to view oil exploration as an excuse to embark on a much wider variety of speculative ventures. They formed not only to "buy . . . and develop oil lands," but also "to locate, acquire . . . and sell water rights and water"[9] and "in any and every way [to] deal in real estate."[10] Even Standard Oil planned to "acquire [and] build . . . pipelines for conveying . . . water" in addition to oil and intended to "improve, develop and cultivate lands whether for mineral or agricultural" purposes.[11] The large number of oil companies formed during these early years and the breadth of their operations capture the "gold rush" mentality of California oil development.

This speculative approach to oil continued for many years. In 1921, following a long hiatus in new discoveries, Shell Oil Company located one of the richest deposits in California, at Signal Hill near Long Beach. Real estate developers had already subdivided and sold much of Signal Hill for suburban housing when the rich oil deposits were found. Within months, the hill bristled with derricks. As Daniel Yergin describes it, "The discovery created a stampede. . . . Money flew all over the hill as oil companies, promoters, and amateurs scrambled to get leases. The parcels were so small and the forest of tall wooden derricks so thick that the legs of many of them actually interlaced." People even received royalties for oil pumped out from under a Signal Hill cemetery.[12]

As the development of Signal Hill proceeded, exploration moved outwards from the original strike and, eventually, into the waters off Long Beach. There, drillers used techniques pioneered off Summerland, California, in 1898.[13] The new rash of pier drilling created a legal quandary. Well-established property laws regulated upland leases; however, these rules did not apply to lands underlying navigable and coastal waters. In 1921, the California legislature passed the Submerged Land Leasing Act to remedy this problem and to permit the state to collect revenue from companies exploiting the tidelands.[14] Nevertheless, tidelands development grew increasingly controversial over the next decade.

Drilling for oil is not a particularly tidy process; in 1920s Los Angeles, the spread of derricks through residential neighborhoods and along crowded beaches made this fact patently obvious. On land, local ordinances required companies to cover the sides of some derricks to protect nearby houses from blowing oil.[15] Containing spills and blowouts, however, proved more difficult in the ocean. Along the waterfront, bathers complained as spills fouled the beaches. Derricks, piers, and other unsightly drilling machinery threatened to reduce tourism and growth in shoreline communities. Although one defender of pier drilling compared the rigs to "New England's rotting fish-wharves, which painters . . . sketch and tourists admire," opposition to the oil piers mounted.

In 1927, California outlawed some pier drilling, but this legislation did not altogether resolve the conflict between recreation and the industrialization of California's beaches.[16] By the mid-1930s, oil companies had found that they could tap underwater fields by drilling diagonally from dry land. This new technique solved the problem of oil spills in the ocean, but still cluttered the shoreline and posed leasing and legal problems. In 1936, Standard Oil began a campaign for a ballot measure to regulate "slant drilling" of offshore reserves. The 1936 act permitted slant drilling only where traditional, upland drilling was depleting oil pressure in the underwater oil pools.[17] The referendum passed, despite strong opposition among independent oil producers. They viewed the measure as an attempt to squeeze them out of the coastal oil business by delivering offshore reserves into the control of the larger oil companies and by decreasing the amount of oil available to the independents. Coastal communities also objected; they still saw oil development as a violation of the public's right to "full enjoyment of the beach, without regard to the plans or desires of private interests."[18]

This debate foreshadowed the shape of resource conflicts to come. Major oil companies exercised strong influence over government policies. Preservationists and local chambers of commerce objected to this arrangement as a violation of public rights. Independent oil producers, meanwhile, accused the majors of manipulating the law to monopolize the industry. As war mobilization began to drive the American economy in the late 1930s, preservationists and public rights advocates would largely fade from the public discussion of oil policy. In retrospect, it seems clear that California's slant-drilling debates provided the last opportunity to discuss the merits of oil development until the Santa Barbara blowout and the Alaska Pipeline controversy of the late 1960s and early 1970s.

Efforts to Assert Federal Control

Until 1937, the federal government appeared content to leave offshore leasing in the hands of the states. But as Europe moved toward war, and as Ickes pursued his dream of creating a Department of Conservation, the federal government abandoned the status quo.[19] In August 1937, Senator Gerald P. Nye of North Dakota proposed that Congress recognize the tidelands in California, Louisiana, and Texas as part of the public domain. This change would have moved responsibility for leasing these lands from the states to the Department of the Interior. Ickes went Nye one better, threatening by turns to declare all undersea oil a naval reserve and to force a suit to determine ownership of the tidelands. Nye's and Ickes's proposals reflected the trend toward greater centralization of resource control that had characterized the Great Depression and the war years.

The attention to proposals for naval oil reserves from dedicated conservationists like Harold Ickes may make the United States Navy look like an environmentalist organization. This is clearly not the case. The American military has historically operated with few of the environmental quality constraints imposed on private companies. Preparedness and wartime emergencies frequently have been used to justify the environmentally dangerous practices that haunt military bases today.[20] Furthermore, Ickes did not see naval oil reserves or military management of oil deposits as a means to preserve the shoreline. He hoped, rather, that federal control over oil deposits would decrease industry influence over drilling policy and reduce wasteful, poorly planned drilling.

Ickes's and Nye's proposals for federal control of offshore leasing proved extremely controversial, in part because they reminded Americans of the Teapot Dome scandal. In the 1910s, the navy had substituted oil for coal as its chief fuel. To ensure sufficient supplies for military needs, in 1911 President Taft created naval petroleum reserves in Elk Hills and Buena Vista Hills, California. In 1914, President Wilson added the more notorious Teapot Dome, Wyoming, deposits. In a separate effort to facilitate general economic development, Congress passed the Federal Mineral Leasing Act in 1920, which authorized the secretary of the interior to lease the public domain for mining or other types of mineral extraction. Under the auspices of this act, Secretary of the Interior Albert Fall leased parts of the Elk Hills and Teapot Dome reserves to close friends. The resulting congressional hearings, called by those who objected to the reestablishment of private control over the reserves, subsequently revealed "loans" that Fall had received from the two leaseholders.[21] Fall was fined and imprisoned.

The Teapot Dome scandal cast a long shadow on federal control of petroleum resources. Even so, the Federal Mineral Leasing Act seemed to offer hope to California oil producers dissatisfied with state administration of the tidelands. They began to submit applications for offshore leases to the Department of the Interior as early as 1924.[22] Some of the applicants for federal leases had held state leases and found their access limited by California's slant- and pier-drilling statutes. Others may have felt that California law permitted too little offshore oil development. Some independents applied because they believed that the majors had manipulated the state legislature to exclude them from the lucrative offshore business.[23] For thirteen years, the Department of the Interior rejected these applications out of hand, not from sympathy for major oil companies, but because the department assumed that proper authority over submerged lands resided with the states.

By the time of the Great Depression, the conflicts between public and private control over oil development, and between small and major companies, seemed decided in favor of large corporations. The Teapot Dome scandal attested to the bankruptcy of federal resource management. The ease with which large corporations acquired prime offshore leases seemed, at least to the outmaneuvered independents, to prove that close ties between state officials and the major companies excluded their smaller competitors. New Deal policies that relaxed antitrust restrictions on American corporations only furthered this impression. From the Depression on, discussions of oil policy would focus on the conflict between small and large companies to the exclusion of more fundamental issues, such as public versus private development or beach preservation versus mineral resource use. These latter questions were to be buried even further by the war emergency beginning in the late 1930s.

In 1937, independent oil producers complained that the majors had set ruinously low prices for their crude. This allegation confirmed many Americans' suspicions that the oil industry was opportunistic and out of control and provoked federal prosecution of key industry leaders for the violation of antitrust laws. The defense claimed that oil companies had only complied with the dictates of the New Deal. One executive complained, "The oil industry feels like a small boy spanked by mamma for doing something papa told him to do." Nevertheless, the federal court convicted eighteen companies and thirty leading executives of conspiring to fix gasoline prices.[24] Naturally, this action did not end attempts to rein in the industry. In 1939, the Senate Committee on the Judiciary considered a bill designed to reduce oil company control of pipelines.[25] That same year, California companies found themselves threatened with new federal antitrust investigations.[26] These attacks on American oil companies reflected the industry's vulnerability to accusations of profiteering from their competitors' and the public's misfortunes.

The revelations brought by these prosecutions made increased federal control of oil resources politically viable. It was in this context that Senator Nye first introduced resolutions to assert federal rights and designate a naval oil reserve.[27] The origins of this idea remain somewhat unclear. Ickes insisted that President Roosevelt first raised the issue, but historians have found little evidence of this. Nye claimed that he acted without prompting from the secretary of the interior. But growing demands from federal lease applicants, including threats of a lawsuit, did precede Nye's actions by only a few months and may have piqued Ickes's interest.[28] Regardless of its genesis, Ickes, the navy, and President Roosevelt all supported Nye's bill and an increased federal role in oil development. They emphasized the importance of oil to the national defense and noted that California's oil resources represented the single most important fuel supply for the Pacific fleet.[29] Broad support for the new naval reserves carried Nye's bill through the Senate, but it could not sustain the proposal in the House of Representatives.

California did not wait for Congress to take away control of its oil or the revenues that drilling generated. In 1938, the state legislature passed the California State Lands Act, which, in addition to establishing a commission to administer mineral leases, claimed for the state unrestricted title to undersea lands, oil, and minerals. In order to secure public support for still-unpopular beachside drilling, the act earmarked a portion of mineral revenues for public parks.[30] Although not sufficient to counter federal claims, the act integrated offshore oil development into California's state government. It did so by creating a bureaucracy, by implementing shared drilling practices sought by major oil companies, and by tying oil development to popular social programs. Jointly, these provisions attracted the broad coalition necessary to sustain state authority.

The failure of Nye's 1937 proposal and the success of California's efforts to consolidate its claims added urgency to questions about oil ownership. In 1939, Nye once again directed the Senate's attention to the tidelands. This time, he narrowed his proposal, recommending only that the federal government establish a naval reserve off the coast of California. He apparently hoped that this action would decrease opposition from other states. The strategy failed. The House Judiciary Committee concluded that, despite the restrictions, the proposal was "the entering wedge" of federal claims to state resources.[31] Meanwhile, the United States Attorney General's Office considered bringing a test case to federal courts challenging state title to submerged lands.[32]

These efforts to assert federal ownership of the tidelands were suspended when representatives from England and France, preparing for war, began negotiating with American oil companies to secure additional petroleum.[33] The prospect of war redirected oil policy from title disputes toward surplus production, a focus that would remain throughout the war years. Edwin Pauley, the treasurer of the Democratic National Committee, an oilman, and a longtime champion of California's oil industry, had a hand in dissuading the administration from pursuing federal ownership for the duration of the war.[34] In 1940, he promised the Roosevelt campaign that he could deliver generous donations from California's independent oil companies if the Departments of Interior and Justice would back off from a vigorous pursuit of the federal title.[35] Later, he argued that continued disputes might reduce petroleum production and thus interfere with the war effort. By 1943, Pauley had convinced members of the administration that wartime production outweighed the importance of establishing federal title to the tidelands.[36]

Even with the tidelands issue shelved, the war presented the Roosevelt administration with ample resource distribution challenges. Petroleum was so essential to military, industrial, and civilian activities that demand for fuel, lubricants, and other petroleum products now seemed insatiable. Similar demands surfaced for a host of other resources as well. The Roosevelt administration responded by diverting resources from nonessential to essential sectors of the economy and by attempting to increase production of critical resources. Despite the obvious complexity of the problem, the public focused more narrowly on the inconvenience of civilian shortages and industry benefits from war-related policies. Significantly, despite occasional accusations of profiteering, most complaints reflected dissatisfaction with federal meddling, not with industrial influence.

In several notable cases, industry clearly took advantage of the war to manipulate the federal government. The erosion of protection for national parks offers some of the clearest examples of this opportunism. In 1942, for example, the National Park Service issued 403 special-use permits to the army and navy. Most of these were more or less consistent with park policies, but some of them proved quite damaging. In California, salt was mined in Death Valley and tungsten was mined in Yosemite, while training in Joshua Tree National Monument left lasting scars on the landscape. The Sierra Club and other park defenders viewed these incursions as signs that mining, timber, and grazing interests had used the war emergency to circumvent preservationist policies.[37] That the War Production Board supported resource harvests in national parks seemed to prove the dangerous potential of industrial influence in federal resource policy.

The War Production Board's position on the national parks may have represented a particularly glaring example of federal-industry cooperation, but industrial leaders influenced many other wartime agencies as well. When appointed as the head of the Petroleum Administration for the War, Ickes himself turned to industry leaders to provide the expertise that he needed to manage national oil resources. He filled three-quarters of the positions in the Petroleum Administration for the War with oil-industry personnel. This number included Ickes's chief assistant, Ralph K. Davies, who was also an executive vice president at Standard Oil of California.[38] In policy terms, these staffing decisions guaranteed a certain level of compliance, but they also ensured that wartime policies would reflect industry priorities.

Where increased production and industry cooperation did not solve resource shortages, the federal government diverted resources to essential military use. This diversion naturally pinched civilians, but also interfered with production of materials of important, though secondary, strategic value. Many federal resource policies starved so-called nonessential sectors of the economy, even when these also contributed to the war effort. For example, increased military consumption of oil hurt military and civilian production in the United States. Similarly, the rush of new employees to airplane plants and shipyards swelled California's population, but the diversion of pipe, steel, pumps, and labor to these factories prevented most communities from expanding their water and sewer systems to serve either the new residents or the expanded industrial facilities.[39] Ultimately, these bottlenecks and shortages contributed to the impression that the federal government created, rather than eliminated, inefficiencies that hindered production.

Resource distribution problems were particularly profound in the case of petroleum. Before even entering the war, the United States sent 20 percent of its tankers to Europe. By 1942, this distribution began to interfere with oil distribution along the Atlantic Coast. In California and the West, the diminished tanker fleet could not deliver crude to refineries fast enough. Ickes took a number of early steps to prevent an oil crisis. For example, he diverted 70,000 rail tankers to increase eastern oil deliveries. He also sponsored the Big Inch and Little Inch pipelines, which would eventually replace railroad transportation of oil between the Gulf and Atlantic Coasts.[40]

In late 1942, Ickes instituted a national gasoline-rationing program. He hoped this program would forestall actual shortages, make more oil available to the war effort, and reduce pressure on overtaxed distribution networks. By encouraging people to drive less, he also hoped to reduce civilian consumption of rubber.[41] Oil shortages, whether real or created by government rationing, were not well tolerated by American drivers. Even a congressional committee concluded that Ickes had panicked too early. The committee concluded that no shortage existed and implied that Ickes had ties with the industry or had created an artificial shortage in order to justify the publicly funded pipelines.[42]

Not satisfied with reducing consumption, Ickes urged American producers to increase their oil output. This request did not lead him to abandon his dedication to Progressive-style conservation, however. Throughout the war, he threatened companies with federal control if they did not "exert sufficient self-control to prevent waste and intemperate exploitation" as they sought to meet growing demand.[43] Regardless of threats and restrictions, oil companies did step up production; in 1942, in a space of two months, California producers opened one hundred new wells and increased the state's oil flow by 6 percent.[44] In 1942, Burnoel Petroleum Company reported to its stockholders that it had so expanded oil exploration that it could not always pay its employees.[45] Some of this new production came from offshore pools, but commentators such as *Business Week* blamed state restrictions on slant and pier drilling for slow development of the California tidelands.[46] As with the national parks, wartime emphasis on production offered new reasons to criticize hard-won restrictions on resource exploitation.

To increase oil production beyond the limits of private enterprise, the Roosevelt administration turned to the United States naval reserves and overseas development. In 1942, Secretary of the Navy Frank Knox signed a contract with Standard Oil to permit the giant firm to drill in the Elk Hills naval oil reserve. In exchange, Standard was to sell refined fuel from the reserves to the navy at a fixed and generous price.[47] Meanwhile, Ickes proposed public construction of a pipeline in Saudi Arabia. This pipeline, he hoped, would preserve domestic supplies for emergencies and limit the power of oil companies over these foreign reserves.[48] Together, these plans produced more controversy than oil. Public outcry over profiteering and references to Teapot Dome forced Roosevelt to revoke the Elk Hills contract. The pipeline proposal never got started, dismissed as another attempt by Ickes to secure federal ownership of the oil industry from "well to service station pump."[49] Every federal proposal to increase oil production seemed to result in accusations of coddling industry or of seeking to smother it.

This peculiar rhetorical stalemate persisted throughout the war years. The National Oil Policy Committee of the Petroleum Industry for the War Council responded to federal investments in synthetic-fuels research with warnings that industry must guard "against governmental domination of research . . . where private research is adequately covering the ground." The oil industry council also asserted that "it is dangerous and impracticable to lock up proven reserves by curtailment or government acquisition of reserves" and demanded the "continuance of domestic operations under state conservation laws."[50] While large corporations painted themselves as the defenders of private enterprise, the independents saw themselves as the last bastion of fair competition. For example, they recognized that Ickes's dedication to foreign oil would starve out independent producers, who depended on domestic drilling operations.[51] It seems the only thing that all members of the oil industry could agree upon was that the federal government could not protect and serve their interests.

These conflicts between small and large oil producers, and between industry and the government, reprised the tidelands debates of the 1930s. Yet the war did not merely continue these discussions. Ickes's attempts to increase federal controls during the war backfired. Gasoline rationing, in particular, weakened public support for federal regulation of the oil industry. By creating artificial shortages and thus driving up prices, Ickes appeared to serve the very industrial interests he had so long criticized. While national pipelines appeared justifiable during the war, the more controversial overseas pipeline seemed to go too far. Furthermore, wartime purchasing plans favoring large corporations in all sectors of the economy appeared to belie Ickes's commitment to fair competition. The war, in many ways, undermined the constituencies that had long supported an increase in federal economic intervention.

After the war ended, advocates of federal ownership attempted to maintain the wartime regulations, but they found their efforts stymied by war-bred impatience with government meddling. Meanwhile, pressure to maintain maximum oil production did not ease, and ownership of the tidelands quickly returned to center stage. In Congress, defenders of private oil development introduced a bill that would have severed federal claims to offshore lands and minerals. The first of several such proposals, the 1945 quitclaim bill, represented a departure from Nye's prewar efforts because it sought to protect California's, Texas's, and Louisiana's existing claims rather than assert federal ownership. The Senate and House quickly passed the bill but could not override Truman's veto.[52] As the presidential veto left tidelands authority ambiguous, Ickes and his allies sought federal ownership through the courts.[53] Congress's new emphasis on returning control of oil to the states reflected both the industry's support for state leasing programs and a shift away from both wartime controls and the goals of New Deal federalism.

In 1945, while Congress considered the quitclaim bill, the United States attorney general sued California, seeking a definitive opinion as to who rightfully owned the tidelands. Many members of Congress had come away from debates on Nye's resolutions believing that such a determination was an essential prerequisite to congressional action. In 1947, the Supreme Court finally issued its ruling in the case, *United States v. California*. In a six-to-two decision, the Court ruled that the federal government had "undisputed title and full dominion over" resources in the submerged lands along the California coast.[54]

Reactions to *United States v. California* revealed the fear of federal authority that supported industrial priorities after the war. The *Los Angeles Times* lamented both the "great blow to California and to all other States" and the Court's so blithely turning its back on "more than a century of precedent" of state ownership of near-shore lands.[55] The *Times* appeared only slightly mollified that the Court did recognize state claims to inland and harbor waters. The specter of ever-expanding federal land appropriations had become a stock feature of state ownership arguments. This side insisted that "no one could foretell the extent to which future Federal administrations may go in asserting the right to expropriate private property . . . on the basis of the vague concept of national power."[56]

Fear of federal expropriation also attracted representatives from non-oil states to back the quitclaim proposals, even though these states would have benefited from national distribution of oil royalties. The city of Boston, for example, noted that the tidelands suit might nullify titles to filled land. This was a serious matter, as three-quarters of the Bay City was built on made land.[57] Ohio's attorney general feared that the Supreme Court's decision might provide a basis for federal appropriation of his state's estimated $500 million worth of harbor and transit improvements, waterworks, and minerals. Pennsylvania's attorney general worried about coal deposits under the Monongahela and Susquehanna Rivers.[58] Nothing, according to representatives from the Rocky Mountain states, would prevent the federal government from claiming upland oil or even refineries in the name of national defense, should the Supreme Court's decision stand.[59]

Of course, increased federal bureaucracy itself could be portrayed as a threat. Defenders of states' rights and industrial privilege used the fear of communist infiltration to discredit the federal government's efforts to consolidate control over oil development. For example, Sheridan Downey, a senator from California, cautioned, "In almost every . . . federal agency there are fellow travelers with little or no loyalty for the American government who are avidly seeking the destruction of our cherished institutions."[60] Critics within the Truman administration also warned of inappropriate favoritism or institutional expansion. In 1945, for instance, U.S. Attorney General Robert Kenny accused Harold Ickes of "unwittingly protecting" speculators more interested in profiting from others' work than in serving national interests. More damning still, Kenny saw the whole tidelands affair as an attempt by Ickes to extend the Department of Interior's authority—and his own—over vast new territories in which oil represented only a minor interest.[61]

Oil companies were more direct, calling federal ownership "inimical to private enterprise."[62] They argued that instead of establishing new naval reserves, the federal government should encourage private drilling of all domestic oil resources as the "speediest and most economical way to achieve the most effective protection of . . . oil resources."[63] There was, perhaps, some merit to this criticism because it would take too long to open new or unused wells for reserves to be of immediate use at the outbreak of a war. These arguments spoke to American fears of international conflict, but also to long-cherished ideals of free enterprise and suspicion of large government. After the war, with its years of antitotalitarian propaganda, unpopular rationing programs, and the diversion of raw materials from consumer to military production, Americans resisted continued federal economic interference.

The transfer of the tidelands from state to federal dominion did not necessarily jeopardize property ownership because the federal government could simply recognize existing titles. But advocates of a federal quitclaim generally ignored this possibility. Proponents of federal ownership emphasized the importance of petroleum conservation in the national defense. Many Americans objected to profiteering from wartime emergencies or from necessary defense measures. It seemed odd, to them, to "turn billions in oil over to the States . . . and then for Uncle Sam to have to buy back a lot of the same oil for the Navy and Army."[64]

Charges of profiteering grew from the perception that in serving their own interests, American corporations did not always serve the public interest. This idea had been a feature of public discourse since at least the late nineteenth century, and it provided proponents of federal ownership with some of their most persuasive arguments.

As the tidelands controversy dragged on, criticisms of self-interest became accusations of corruption. When President Truman justified his veto of the quitclaim bills, he claimed that the oil lobby wanted the people "to turn that vast treasure over to a handful of States, where the powerful private oil interests hope to exploit it to suit themselves."[65] In the same vein, Harold Ickes wondered publicly why "oil seems to have a degenerative effect upon the political morals of men who have served their country honorably."[66] The federal government could protect the public interest, according to Ickes, Truman, and their allies, by ensuring that oil regulation took place in a national arena less susceptible than the states to industry influence and by seeing that all states shared in the revenue and benefits of oil production.[67] Given these messages and mounting public impatience with oil company "profiteering," it is all the more surprising that Americans embraced the California oil industry's pro-growth message after the war.

By the end of World War II, the tidelands controversy had reached a stalemate. The Supreme Court asserted federal ownership; Congress attempted to return the submerged lands to California and the other oil states. Truman vetoed all the quitclaim bills that came before him. The issue was not resolved until 1953, when President Dwight D. Eisenhower ceded to the states all offshore resources within three miles of the coast. For historical reasons and through insistent lobbying, Texas and Louisiana maintained nearly three times as much of the continental shelf; their ownership extended to the three-league mark. Until Eisenhower's quitclaim, public debate on oil and the tidelands wove together a hodgepodge of American political tropes. Celebration of centralized economic planning and attacks on monopolistic corporations reprised Progressive campaigns of the 1910s and 1920s. Redbaiting and homage to private enterprise not only revealed deep suspicions of expanded federal power, but also echoed wartime propaganda. In all of this, however, a critique of tidelands drilling itself was conspicuously absent, eclipsed by the drive for ample production. During the war years, government rationing took the blame for local shortages, which seemed to prove private industry capable of meeting the demand for oil. By supplying both the public and military with adequate service, the oil industry dampened criticism and provided itself with a bulwark against increased federal authority.

Triumph of State and Industry: Conclusions

When the war ended, the crisis mentality that had dominated oil policy since 1939 did not fade. If anything, it increased with surging civilian demand for gasoline and with growing cold war tensions. But unlike earlier national emergencies, postwar oil crises did not prompt increased federal intervention. On the contrary, industry leaders used the new demands as a lever to release themselves from federal controls. The American public, impatient to reconstruct the civilian economy and aware of industry's success in meeting wartime needs, seemed only too willing to ratify industry's vision. Meanwhile, the presence of industry leaders in wartime agencies only furthered the ability of private enterprise to define the terms of the postwar economic policy debate. By the mid-1950s, the transition back to corporate liberalism was complete.

During the 1930s and 1940s, new federal institutions had intervened in oil production, first to stabilize the economy, then to fuel a war machine. After the war, reconstruction of the economy, long-deferred public consumption, and complicated international obligations all ensured the explosion of oil demand. As early as 1944, although the nation had not used up its supplies during the war, the consumption of gas in California outpaced production from local wells and refineries. In 1952, the United States became a net importer of oil for the first time. Many were quick to blame the tidelands conflict rather than growing consumption for the nation's new and unwelcome status as an oil importer.[68] Dependence on imported oil came just as unrest in the Middle East and increased tensions with the Soviet Union threatened American access to foreign resources.[69] In this context, accusations that the tidelands dispute had slowed domestic oil production made federal efforts to gain control appear particularly ill-advised. The very measures intended by Truman and Ickes to bolster American military preparedness seemed to place the nation at risk.

These accusations clearly weakened the federal case, even as they painted California's oil industry as a protector of the national interest. In other arenas, contradictory policies also moved the nation further away from federal ownership. Congressional support for the quitclaim remained strong; but Truman vetoed quitclaim bills in 1946, 1948, and 1952, and created an offshore naval petroleum reserve by executive order on his way out of office in January 1953. Wingate Lucas of Texas decried this as "another attempt on the part of the socialists in the Administration to perpetuate federal control of the tidelands."[70] However, while Truman pursued federal ownership, he consistently named individuals to implement these policies who did not seem to support a broader economic role for the federal government.

After Ickes resigned to protest Truman's nomination of Edwin Pauley for undersecretary of the navy, Truman named Julius A. Krug and then Oscar L. Chapman as secretary of the interior.[71] As secretary of the interior, neither Krug nor Chapman attempted to develop administrative mechanisms to implement a federal leasing program. Instead, they concluded agreements with holders of state-issued leases to permit continued exploration and production of oil along the California coast.[72] Despite Truman's determination to create a naval oil reserve, by tapping Pauley, Krug, and Chapman for these offices, he undermined that very end.

Krug's and Chapman's priorities for the Department of the Interior reflect the shift away from redistribution and toward growth. This transition was closely linked to the wartime emphasis on production, but also to the prominent roles played by industry leaders in developing and implementing federal economic policies during the Depression and World War II. As others have noted, President Roosevelt invited industry leaders to Washington during these two crucial episodes because he needed their expertise and cooperation. Thus, Truman's nomination of Edwin Pauley stood out because of the furor it caused, not because of Pauley's loyalties. The presence of so many industry representatives in federal agencies fostered cooperation, but largely by ensuring that policies met corporate as well as national needs.

The drilling regulations of the Petroleum Administration for the War, intended to conserve petroleum deposits, provide a clear example of the benefits industry received from wartime policies. When confronted with wasteful drilling practices in California fields, for example, the Petroleum Administration for the War introduced a series of rules "designed to assure the production . . . of a continuing supply of California petroleum."[73] Specifically, the Petroleum Administration encouraged repressuring of wells to increase yield, well-spacing standards, and unit plans. All of these reduced oil waste by maintaining the underground pressures necessary to remove oil from the earth. Until limited by these rules, each company operating in a given field benefited from pumping oil out of the pool as fast as possible. Under federal conservation measures, oil companies apportioned crude in each oil field before drilling began.[74]

Despite hand-wringing over the potential burdens of federal conservation measures, these programs made possible the very operating agreements that the industry itself had sought through corporate consolidation and illegal production agreements.[75] This aspect of federal policy drew fire from independent oil producers, who recognized that the new rules limited the amount of oil they could harvest from each of their wells; they complained bitterly that the federal government had sacrificed their interests to those of the major corporations.[76] Clearly, conservation did not reduce either production or consumption of California oil. Rather, these measures allowed increased oil production from each deposit. Federal conservation reflected the priorities of the major oil companies because industries defined efficiency in oil production and generated the strategies to promote it.

While industry influence colored federal conservation policies, it also determined the fate of the War Production Board and other wartime institutions. The large numbers of industry personnel in the federal war agencies created an unusual institutional culture. Many of the "dollar-a-year men" viewed their tenure with the government as temporary and remained committed to private enterprise. Their eagerness to return oil to private control was reinforced by memories of Teapot Dome. If Americans did not trust the large oil companies, they trusted federal administrators even less. Besides, attempts to increase federal control of oil resources seemed only to interfere with postwar petroleum production. As a result, no clear consensus in favor of centralized control emerged out of the war years. Given the opposition within the federal government, without industry support, as developed during the New Deal and the war, or a powerful grassroots demand, as might have evolved had the tidelands issue not been defined as federal trespass on states' rights, no effort to expand federal authority was likely to succeed.

Because industry leaders played such a central role in defining both the terms of the debate and the policy options considered at the state and federal levels, the conflict over California's tidelands was fought over the question of who could administer oil leases to maximize production. This singular focus, well tuned to the wartime emergency and also to the oil crisis that followed, tended to overpower the other two major issues that had dominated discussions of California's oil development before the war. After the mid-1930s, public opposition to offshore drilling on broadly environmental grounds—oil pollution of beaches and the destruction of a recreational shoreline, for example—disappears even from Southern California newspaper coverage. Conflict between small and large producers, one of the key features of the pier- and slant-drilling controversies of the 1920s and early 1930s, shared a similar fate.

In the case of submerged oil lands, public officials intent on the single goal of supplying a war machine redefined the public interest in very narrow terms. This narrow view permitted the California oil industry, relatively efficient in the discovery and development of new oil deposits, to appear quite capable of satisfying the public interest. As this narrow definition became entrenched, energy policy was placed not only in the hands of private enterprise, but increasingly in the hands of major industry players. Although it is tempting to portray these oil representatives as the bad guys of the tidelands story, this narrowing of the definition of the public good should be the focal point here. Although the United States went into the Depression with relatively broad definitions of the public good, it came out of the Second World War nearly obsessed with growth and security. Dissension on either of these two topics became increasingly difficult until the modern environmental movement defined new crises and challenged the hegemony of industrial growth.

Notes

1. Clayton Koppes has discussed the transition from "commonwealth" to "corporate" liberalism in "Environmental Policy and American Liberalism: The Department of the Interior, 1933–1953," *Environmental Review* 7 (1983): 17–41.

2. "Corporate liberalism" describes economic policies that meet industrial needs. Historians contrast this with "commonwealth liberalism," policies dedicated to social needs and more equal distribution of the benefits of modern society. See ibid.

3. Robert Higgs argues in *Crisis and Leviathan: Critical Episodes in the Growth of American Government* (New York, 1987) that once government increased in response to wartime emergency, it could never return to its previous size. Higgs does observe that the federal bureaucracy shrank after World War II. This essay confirms Higgs's conclusions in this regard.

4. Donald Worster, *Rivers of Empire: Water, Aridity, and the Growth of the American West* (New York, 1985); Donald Pisani, *From Family Farm to Agribusiness: The Irrigation Crusade in California and the West, 1850–1931* (Berkeley, Calif., 1984); Marc Reisner, *Cadillac Desert: The American West and Its Disappearing Water* (New York, 1986); and Norris Hundley, *The Great Thirst: Californians and Water, 1770s–1990s* (Berkeley, Calif., 1992). See also Theodore Steinberg, *Nature Incorporated: Industrialization and the Waters of New England* (Cambridge, Eng., 1991), for a treatment of these issues in Eastern water development, and William Kahrl's landmark study of power and urban waterworks, *Water and Power: The Conflict over Los Angeles' Water Supply in the Owens Valley* (Los Angeles, 1982).

5. Robert Gottleib and Margaret Fitzsimmons, *Thirst for Growth: Water Agencies as Hidden Governments in California* (Tucson, 1991). For the legal scholar Joseph Sax's description of the "institutional capture" of government agencies by the parties they are supposed to regulate, see Paul Sabatier, "Interview with Joseph Sax," 25 May 1972, p. 11, Joseph Sax Papers, box 2, Bentley Library, Ann Arbor, Michigan.

6. Robert Kelley, *Battling the Inland Sea: American Political Culture, Public Policy, and the Sacramento Valley, 1850–1986* (Berkeley, Calif., 1989); John T. Cumbler, "The Early Making of an Environmental Consciousness: Fish, Fisheries Commissions, and the Connecticut River," *Environmental History Review* 15 (1991): 73–92; John T. Cumbler, "Whatever Happened to Industrial Waste: Reform, Compromise, and Science in Nineteenth-Century New England," ms., University of Louisville, 1993.

7. Daniel Yergin, *The Prize: The Epic Quest for Oil, Money, and Power* (New York, 1991), 26–27.

8. William R. Freudenberg and Robert Gramling, *Oil in Troubled Waters: Perceptions, Politics, and the Battle over Offshore Drilling* (Albany, N.Y., 1994), 15; Yergin, *Prize*, 25, 28–29.

9. "Abstracts of Articles of Incorporation for California Oil Companies on File in Alameda," Bancroft Library, Berkeley, Calif.

10. Linda Vista Oil, Articles of Incorporation, 1900, in ibid.

11. California Standard Oil Company, Articles of Incorporation, 1899, in ibid.

12. Yergin, *The Prize*, 219–20.

13. Freudenberg and Gramling, *Oil in Troubled Waters*, 17.

14. "Origin and History of Tidelands Case," *Congressional Digest* 27:10 (1948): 233; "Conflicting State and Federal Claims of Title in Submerged Lands of the Continental Shelf," *Yale Law Review* 56 (1947): 356.

15. Kenny A. Franks and Paul F. Lambert, *Early California Oil: A Photographic History, 1865–1940* (College Station, Tex., 1985), 113.

16. Sheridan Downey, *Truth about the Tidelands* (San Francisco, 1948), 6.

17. "Tideland Oil," *Business Week*, 2 Dec. 1944, 32.

18. Glanton Reah, Shoreline Planning Association, to John Anson Ford, 15 Sept. 1936; Guy W. Finney to Ford, 21 Aug. 1936, both in John Anson Ford Papers, box 11/BIII, Huntington Library, San Marino, Calif.

19. Harold Ickes, "A Department of Conservation," *Vital Speeches of the Day* 3:1 (Sept. 1937): 693–95.

20. Since the late 1980s, environmental contamination at United States military facilities has received increasing scrutiny in the press. The military does not have to comply with the same environmental regulations as the private sector, which has permitted careless and otherwise illegal waste-disposal practices to continue at thousands of military installations. More than 120 of these military dumps are at the top of the Environmental Protection Agency's list for Superfund cleanup. Although much of the military's dumping took place before Congress enacted strict environmental regulations, as recently as 1993 the navy requested a five-year exemption from the regulations that prohibit dumping plastics at sea. See, for example, Michael Satchell, "Uncle Sam's Toxic Folly," *U.S. News & World Report* 106 (27 Mar. 1989): 20–22; Seth Shulman, "Operation Restore Earth," *E: The Environmental Magazine* 4 (Mar. 1993): 36–43; Bruce Van Voorst, "A Thousand Points of Blight," *Time* 140 (9 Nov. 1992): 68–69; Tom Alibrani, "Surfer Takes on the Navy," *The Progressive* 57 (Oct. 1993): 17.

21. Gerald D. Nash, *United States Oil Policy, 1890–1964* (Pittsburgh, 1968), 73–75.

22. "Origin and History of Tidelands Case," 233; "Conflicting State and Federal Claims," 356–57.

23. E. J. Preston leased a section of offshore lands near Huntington Beach in the 1930s. A competing company blocked access to his pier. His efforts to seek relief through the California legislature were stymied; he filed for a federal lease and began disputing the state's title to the land in question. See E. J. Preston, "Speech Opposing Senate Joint

Resolution no. 48 as Delivered by E. J. Preston before the Judiciary Committee of the United States Senate," Washington, D.C., 7 Feb. 1946, Arnold Papers, box 124, folder: Pa-Pu, Huntington Library, San Marino, Calif.

24. "Mamma Spank," *Time* 18 (Oct. 1937): 63; "Oil Price-Fixing," *Newsweek*, 31 Jan. 1938, 31.

25. "Light on the Oil Trust," *The Nation*, 3 June 1939, 633–34.

26. "Coast Oil Men Angry," *Business Week*, 2 Sept. 1939, 24.

27. Downey, *Truth about the Tidelands*, 16–18. This resolution, Senate Joint Resolution 208, began life as Senate Bill 2164 in April 1937. The issue was reintroduced as a joint resolution in August of the same year.

28. "Who Owns Offshore Oil Lands," *Business Week*, 11 Sept. 1937, 48–49. According to Ernest R. Bartley, Ickes asked Nye to pursue the naval oil reserve proposal because Nye's home state had no oil resources and therefore no local oil lobby to influence Nye's decision. See Ernest R. Bartley, *The Tidelands Oil Controversy: A Legal and Historical Analysis* (Austin, Tex., 1953), 101.

29. Harold Ickes, *Fightin' Oil* (New York, 1943), 130.

30. Downey, *Truth about the Tidelands*, 19–29.

31. "Tideland Oil Bill Foes Fight House Showdown," *Los Angeles Times*, 23 May 1938.

32. "The Attempted Land Grab," *Southern California Business*, 28 Oct. 1940.

33. "War Stills Oil Turmoil," *Business Week*, 16 Sept. 1939, 18.

34. "Origin and History of Tidelands Case," 234.

35. Ibid.

36. Downey, *Truth about the Tidelands*, 24.

37. Gerald D. Nash, *World War II and the West: Reshaping the Economy* (Lincoln, Nebr., 1990), 158–60; Koppes, "Environmental Policy and American Liberalism," 23, 27.

38. Robert Engler, *The Politics of Oil: A Study of Private Power and Democratic Directions* (New York, 1961), 278.

39. East Bay Municipal Utility District, *East Bay Sewers: Past, Present, and Future* (Oakland, Calif., 1983), 2; John S. Longwell, "Sewage Disposal for Special District No. 1 of the East Bay Municipal Utility District," paper delivered at the California Sewage Works Association Annual Convention, Monterey, 10 June 1946, 3. In 1945, a *Los Angeles Times* editorial urged rapid approval of bonds to finance a project intended to "remedy [an] intolerable sewage situation" that had been delayed too long by "stalling tactics" and "bungling." See "Let's Get On with Sewage Disposal Project," *Los Angeles Times*, 22 June 1945.

40. Ickes, *Fightin' Oil*, 52; Charles C. Scott, *Petroleum Industry Committees in World War II, District V, 1941–1946* (San Francisco, 1947), 10–11, 19. The War Production Board planning committee considered the transportation of critical materials as vital a problem as actual shortages. See War Production Board, Planning Committee, "Analysis of Production Program," 8 Sept. 1942, in Donald Nelson Papers, box 10, Huntington Library, San Marino, Calif.

41. Ickes, *Fightin' Oil*, 50.

42. Ibid.

43. "New Oil Warning," *Business Week,* 15 Nov. 1941, 37.

44. "California Petroleum Situation—December 1942," 8 Feb. 1943, in "Statistics: California Situation," Petroleum Administration for the War Records, box 138, National Archives, Laguna Niguel, Calif. According to this memo, in December 1942 California drillers had 18,500 wells producing 774,000 barrels of oil per day. This was the largest output since November 1929.

45. "Minutes of the Annual Meeting of Shareholders of Burnoel Petroleum Corporation," 31 July 1942, in Burnoel Petroleum Company Papers, Huntington Library, San Marino, Calif.

46. "Tideland Oil," *Business Week,* 2 Dec. 1944, 32.

47. Helen Fuller, "Teapot Dome, 1943 Style," *New Republic,* 21 June 1943, 826–27.

48. Unsigned memo to William F. Humphreys, 16 Mar. 1944, Records of the General Committee, Petroleum Administration for the War Records, box 17, National Archives, Laguna Niguel, Calif.

49. "Oil Hearings Start," *Business Week,* 30 Sept. 1939, 38.

50. Unsigned memo to William F. Humphreys, 16 Mar. 1944, Records of the General Committee, Petroleum Administration for the War Records, box 17, National Archives, Laguna Niguel, Calif. See also "State Oil Control Urged after War, *New York Times,* 8 Oct. 1944, in *National Oil Policy Chronology, 1944: A Current Guide of News, Editorials, and Other Material Appearing in Newspapers, Magazines, Etc.,* prepared by the National Oil Policy Committee of the Petroleum Industry War Council, box 51, Petroleum Administration for the War Records, box 17, National Archives, Laguna Niguel, Calif.

51. Michael Straight, "Double-Cross in Oil," *New Republic,* 20 Oct. 1941, 501.

52. Downey, *Truth about the Tidelands,* 26. The bill was called a "quitclaim" after the legal process by which one person renounces title to property in favor of another's claim. In this case, advocates of state ownership wanted the federal government to renounce its claim in favor of the states.

53. Shortly before his death, Roosevelt authorized U.S. Attorney General Francis Biddle to file a lawsuit intended to settle the still unclear question of tidelands title. Ickes disapproved of this suit, brought against the Pacific Western Oil Company in the U.S. District Court in Southern California, because he felt that the dispute lay between the federal and state governments and, as such, could only be settled if the State of California was the defendant in the case. A few months after the 1945 quitclaim bill was introduced in Congress, the U.S. Attorney General's office, prompted by President Truman and Ickes, dropped the Pacific Western suit in favor of a case against California directly. See Bartley, *Tidelands Oil Controversy,* 137, 161.

54. "The Court: Not California's Oil," *Newsweek,* 30 June 1947, 58.

55. "A Great Blow to California," *Los Angeles Times,* 26 June 1947, sec. 2, p. 4.

56. "Tidelands Justice Up to Congress," *Los Angeles Times,* 15 Oct. 1947, sec. 2, p. 4.

57. Hirsh Freed, Assistant Corporate Counsel of Boston, in Robert Kenny and William W. Clary, *The Facts about the Legislation Quieting State Titles to Lands beneath Tidal and Navigable Waters; Senate Joint Resolution 48, House Joint Resolution 225,* Washington, D.C., 1945, 14.

58. Kenny and Clary, *Facts about the Legislation*, 10–11, 13.

59. E. J. Sullivan, "The Tidelands Question," *Wyoming Law Journal* 3:1 (1948): 19.

60. He did not restrict his concerns to oil, but railed against the Bureau of Reclamation and the Department of the Interior for their "corrupt, insistent effort . . . to dominate California's Central Valley through the control of its agricultural, power and water resources." See Downey, *Truth about the Tidelands*, 2, 4.

61. Kenny and Clary, *Facts about the Legislation*, 24–25, 34.

62. Engler, *Politics of Oil*, 83–85.

63. Fuller, "Teapot Dome," 826–27.

64. J. A. Ford to Estes Kefauver, U.S. Senator, 28 Jan. 1953, John Anson Ford Papers, box 11/BIII, Huntington Library, San Marino, Calif.

65. "Truman: 'It's Robbery in Daylight,'" *San Francisco Chronicle*, 18 May 1952, 5.

66. Harold Ickes, "Generous Texas," *New Republic*, 15 May 1950, 17. This statement targeted Texas senator Sam Rayburn, the sponsor of the 1950 quitclaim bill. Ickes found it particularly frustrating that states that feared federal appropriation of resources seemed so willing to give these same resources away to private industry. He also found it ironic that, although they opposed a federal oil reserve as an unacceptable expansion of federal power, many eastern and western states' rights advocates welcomed federal public works projects with open arms. See Harold Ickes, "Smelly Oil Mendacity," *New Republic*, 10 Sept. 1951, 17.

67. "Truman," 5; "A Premature Death," *New Republic*, 20 Mar. 1954, 3.

68. Gustav Egloff, "Petroleum and National Defense," *Science*, 6 Dec. 1940, 520; "Tideland Oil," *Business Week*, 12 Feb. 1944, 32–33; "Summary of Remarks of Harold L. Ickes before the Petroleum Industry War Council, January 12, 1944, on Some of the Problems of a National Oil Policy," in *National Oil Policy Committee File*, Records of the Petroleum Administration for the War, box 70, division 5, National Archives, Laguna Niguel, Calif.

69. *Congressional Digest*, Senate Report 1143; "Tidelands Impasse," *Business Week*, 21 July 1951, 44–45; "Tidelands Truce," *Business Week*, 10 Feb. 1951, 102–3.

70. "Truman's Legacy to the GOP: Tidelands Oil, Money Worries," *Newsweek*, 26 Jan. 1953, 77.

71. Truman nominated Edwin Pauley for undersecretary of the navy in 1946. Pauley's connections to the oil industry reawakened suspicions that new federal oil reserves would spawn Teapot Dome–style scandals. Pauley eventually withdrew to quiet storms of protest. Krug had worked for four years with the Tennessee Valley Authority but had always regarded government utility ownership with suspicion. As head of the War Production Board, he emphasized cooperation with private enterprise and rapid reduction of economic controls at war's end. Chapman had spent most of the 1930s and 1940s in the Department of the Interior, but embraced the department's role in promoting economic growth over all other aspects of its mission. See Bartley, *Tidelands Oil Controversy*, 26, 27.

72. Harold Ickes, "The Court Proposes, Interior Disposes," *New Republic*, 27 Mar. 1950, 18.

73. Ickes, *Fightin' Oil,* 131.

74. Nash, *United States Oil Policy,* 83, 167–68.

75. See, for example, "Order or Chaos in Oil," *San Francisco Chronicle,* 4 Aug. 1951, 8; "Fight over Undersea Oil," *Business Week,* 1 Jan. 1949, 23.

76. Straight, "Double-Cross in Oil," 501–2.

7

Ethnics at War:
Italian Americans in California during World War II

Gary R. Mormino and George E. Pozzetta

Although historians have long recognized war as an "engine of social change," remarkably little is known about the impact of war on ethnicity and ethnic-group development. Most studies of America during World War II either ignore white ethnic groups altogether or approach the subject from a limited perspective, usually emphasizing the foreign policy and political implications of ethnic loyalties. Those works that engage ethnicity more broadly tend to take the view that World War II was "the fuel of the melting pot" for ethnic Americans. This conception of the war's impact represents white ethnics as succumbing to the inexorable pressures of the war crisis, which placed heavy demands on loyalty, conformity, and patriotism, by abandoning their ethnicity and embracing the dominant culture. Some authors have recognized that, in pursuit of wartime unity, the nation did take steps toward "opening up American society to the ethnics in its midst" by supporting pluralism. However, few studies have looked within white ethnic groups to determine precisely how individuals responded to war conditions and, equally important, how they influenced the larger society by their actions.

On December 6, 1941, several hundred thousand Italian Americans living in California could indulge in individual and collective congratulations. From fisherfolk at San Diego and Black Diamond to artichoke, garlic, and broccoli growers in Gilroy, Stockton, and San Jose, Italians had seized opportunities, carving out economic niches while realizing California's "Mediterranean possibilities." On the eve of war, Italians held endowed chairs at state universities, occupied mayors' offices, and headed local draft boards, symphonies, and garden clubs. Italians owned minor league baseball teams and major league banks. Names such as Ghirardelli, Giannini, Capra, and DiMaggio resonated across America.

While California offers stunning illustrations of Italian pluck and success, a survey of the 1940 landscape reveals also a century of struggle, labor strife, and ethnic conflict. Del Monte may have been founded by an Italian, but thousands of Italian women continued to toil at the canneries on the eve of war. Elsewhere, many Italians continued to work at low-wage occupations.

A blurred group portrait emerges on the threshold of war. One version depicts an extraordinarily successful group bristling with the pride of immigrants upraised. Another version, more unsettling, suggests themes of anxiety, marginality, and uncertainty. Fascism spoke forcefully to immigrants who had succeeded and to those who were frustrated. Cutting across class and regional lines, Fascism offered a new meaning of what it meant to be Italian in America.

The 1940 census recorded 100,911 Italian immigrants in California; Italians comprised California's largest European immigrant group. Ten California cities boasted populations of at least one thousand Italian immigrants: Berkeley, Eureka, Fresno, Los Angeles, Oakland, Sacramento, San Diego, San Francisco, San Jose, and Stockton.[1]

The beckoning economic opportunities of Southern California had attracted large numbers of Italian immigrants: more than 18,000 lived in Los Angeles in 1940. Italians in Los Angeles, like their neighbors, followed the dictates of the automobile. The 1940 census revealed that none of the city's 303 census tracts contained more than 680 Italian immigrants.[2]

On the eve of war, two in five Italians in California lived in the Bay Area. San Francisco's Italian immigrant population numbered 24,036, and this figure doubles when the second and third generation is added. Never again would Italians represent as high a proportion of the city's foreign-born—18.4 percent. North Beach, an Italian neighborhood since the Gold Rush, continued to serve as a hub for capital and culture.[3]

On December 6, 1941, readers of the *San Francisco Examiner* encountered a disturbing story of Fascism in their midst. A fifth column existed in the heart of San Francisco, the *Examiner* contended, relating how the Italian government actively subsidized Italian-run schools and spread Fascist propaganda throughout California.[4]

Complex factors underlay the appeal of Fascism. Benito Mussolini made many Italian immigrants proud to be Italian. Trains now ran on time, while a new militarism and nationalism promised Italy a refurbished image. Mussolini's rapprochement with the Catholic Church in 1929 legitimized his status as a statesman and anti-Communist. Fascism allowed the lowly immigrants to identify themselves with a leader who initially attracted the broad support of corporate and international leaders. Fascism helped Italian Americans relate to an increasingly pluralist society, allowing them to flaunt ethnic successes and claim social recognition. Most Italian Americans viewed Fascism less as a political system than as a renewed Italianità—a vehicle for generating ethnic respectability and acceptance that had much more to do with life in America than events in Italy.

In the 1930s, Rome embarked on an ambitious effort to win the hearts and minds of Italian immigrants and children in the United States. Generously subsidizing Italian-American organizations, the Italian government made important inroads in California during this era. Italian consuls distributed Fascist textbooks and uniforms for students in *Dopo Scuola* (after-school clubs). In 1937, California hosted almost fifty such schools, including six in San Francisco and six in Los Angeles. Before and after classes, students sang "Giovinezza," the Fascist anthem, and saluted a portrait of Il Duce. Honor students won fully paid excursions to Italy. In retrospect, what appears remarkable about the *Dopo Scuola* is how utterly unsuccessful they were in inculcating deep-seated, undivided loyalties.[5]

If children proved to be more American than Italian, many parents found the emotional and ideological tug of Fascism appealing. Adults believed there was nothing contradictory about being a Fascist and an American. The Sons of Italy enthusiastically supported Fascism here and abroad. Brought to California in the 1920s, the Sons of Italy appealed to growing numbers of the Italian middle class, who found the traditional mutual-aid societies irrelevant. During the Ethiopian War, the Sons of Italy rallied to support Italy. Some women even exchanged their gold wedding rings for steel rings fashioned from World War I cannons. After the U.S. embargo on copper shipments, Italian associations in California urged members to show their contempt for such a policy by mailing thousands of copper postcards to the homeland. Italians in San Francisco collected two hundred tons of scrap metal to aid the Italian Red Cross in the Ethiopian campaign.[6]

In San Francisco, Fascism centered around Fugazi Hall, a social and organizational complex in North Beach. By the 1930s, a vibrant Fascist media existed in San Francisco. Three Italian radio programs operated throughout the decade. The most important daily, *L'Italia,* whose editor championed Fascism, boasted a circulation of 15,000 in San Francisco and 4,000 in the rest of California. In addition, pro-Fascist papers were published in Los Angeles (*L'Italo Americano*) and Stockton (*Il Sole*).[7]

Pearl Harbor shattered the insularity of Italian-American life. At the start of the hostilities, the United States classified all noncitizen residents from the Axis nations as "enemy aliens." The war exposed 52,749 California Italians to enemy-alien status. A massive registration of enemy aliens followed; the gov-

ernment quickly imposed travel restrictions and curfews and forced the surrender of radios, cameras, maps, and guns. Officials closed down the state's
controversial Italian *Dopo Scuola*. The *Los Angeles Times* described a "great
manhunt" on the evening of December 8, as local police and federal agents
crisscrossed the region, rounding up suspect Italians. In San Francisco and Los
Angeles, authorities arrested 161 and 82 Italians respectively, whereas in Chicago and New York, much larger cities, only 16 Italians were apprehended.[8]

For some time, various intelligence agencies had been collecting lists of
dangerous civilians, files developed from the rosters of ethnic associations and
newspapers. Within hours following Pearl Harbor, several hundred Germans,
Japanese, and Italians were arrested and interned. Italians living on the West
Coast were eventually transferred to Fort Missoula, Montana, a converted
military fort that the inmates sardonically called *Bella Vista*. Over 1,500 Italians spent time at Fort Missoula, including employees from the Italian pavil-
ion at the New York World's Fair and crew members of Italian ships stranded
in American ports after the government ordered Axis vessels confiscated.[9]

On February 19, 1942, President Roosevelt signed Executive Order 9066, trig-
gering a debate over mass internment and evacuation. Giving the secretary of
war the authority to "designate military areas from which any or all persons
may be excluded," the document's sweeping language permitted the exercise
of wide powers to remove not only aliens, but citizens as well. In short order,
Henry Stimson gave Army Lieutenant-General John L. DeWitt, head of the
Western Defense Command, authority to establish military zones and to exclude designated individuals.[10]

Strong forces inside and outside of the government buffered Italians from
the full force of these measures. The most important legislative voice advocating more selective internment polices came from the congressional Tolan
Committee. Headed by Representative John H. Tolan of Oakland, California,
the committee spoke forcefully against the mass evacuation of Italians and
Germans, arguing that forced relocations would be logistically taxing, economically indefensible, and politically unwise. In late February 1942, the Tolan
Committee listened to the plaintive appeals of German and Italian Americans.
Mayor Rossi of San Francisco implored that Germans and Italians "be con-
sidered separately from . . . the Japanese."[11]

Arrest and confinement rates for Italian aliens were consistently much lower
than for their Axis counterparts under the individual internment initiative,
despite their much greater presence in the population. On December 10, 1941,
FBI Director Hoover announced that 1,291 Japanese, 857 Germans, and 147
Italians had been taken into custody. By June 30, 1942, the FBI had arrested a
total of 9,405 suspect enemy aliens, including 4,764 Japanese, 3,120 Germans,

and 1,521 Italians. After one year of war, internment figures reflected an even more glaring gap. At this juncture, only 210 Italians were interned.[12]

Although Italians escaped the stigmata of mass evacuation and internment, the subsequent relocations and travel restrictions created many difficult, even ludicrous situations. In one instance, officials forced Rose Trovato, a widow living in Del Monte, to move from her home. Her son had died at Pearl Harbor. Vittoria Santo of Castroville had four sons in the army, three of whom had defended Bataan, but officials demanded that she move. A confidential report discovered that in one California district, "nine mothers were given special honors because each had four sons in the U.S. armed forces. All nine were of Italian birth. Seven were not-yet-citizens. None of these seven mothers could visit her boy in camp."[13]

Bewilderment and confusion reigned in Italian neighborhoods. Sixty-five-year-old Martini Bettistessa of Richmond ended his life by hurling himself in front of a train. Milano Rispoli of the Italian Welfare Agency in San Francisco reported an epidemic of grief-stricken Italians, culminating in three suicides in a single week. Police discovered $4,500 in defense bonds at the home of one of the victims.[14]

Industries dependent upon Italian labor suffered. Nowhere was this more evident than in the fishing fleets of San Francisco and Monterey Bays. A student in the 1930s had noted the fierce independence of the Italian fishermen, observing, "It [Fishermen's Wharf] is a community, untouched by the outside world. . . . There is consequently no assimilation to American customs." Such isolation meant that few Italian fishermen had taken out citizenship papers. America's most famous enemy alien, Giuseppe DiMaggio, had arrived in California in 1898 and was now banned from Fisherman's Wharf; he could not even eat at his son's restaurant.[15]

The regulations imposed on noncitizen fishermen lasted eleven months. Soon after San Franciscans endured their first meatless day in the fall of 1942, Italians returned to the fleet. Wartime fish shortages meant high prices and strong demand for seafood. Joe Balestri, for example, made a wartime fortune by popularizing a new fad: shark.[16] Residents of Santa Cruz County expressed concern about the fate of a half-million-dollar crop of brussels sprouts and artichokes awaiting harvest by Italians.[17]

For Pittsburg fisherfolk, Santa Cruz cannery workers, San Francisco scavengers, and Stockton growers, 1942 was *l'anno di ansie,* the year of anxieties. In May 1942 the California legislature's Un-American Activities Committee held public hearings. The *San Francisco Chronicle* welcomed the investigation: "San Francisco's Italian colony . . . is shot through with Fascists who have been propagandizing the philosophy of the dictators with Axis knowledge and Rome's financial aid for 20 years." The Tenney Committee hearings altered the careers and lives of many Italian Americans. The panel subpoenaed scores of prominent California Italian Americans. The hearings allowed Carmelo Zito, the fiery anti-Fascist newspaperman, to indict a long list of enemies. Zito criticized Mayor Rossi and his associates; even the North Beach Catholic Church was attacked for displaying the Fascist flag from the altar. Zito branded Ettore Patrizi, the editor of *L'Italia* and *La Voce del Popolo,* as "the brain" of California's Fascist movement, a "pirate who sails under two flags." Patrizi moved to Reno, joining a small group of Italian excludees.[18]

Sylvester Andriano also faced accusations of disloyalty. Prior to 1942, Andriano, an Italian immigrant and naturalized citizen, had lived the California dream: a graduate of St. Mary's College in 1915, he received his law degree from Berkeley. A confidant of Angelo Rossi, Andriano enjoyed a lucrative law practice—he advised the Italian Consulate—and served on the San Francisco Board of Supervisors. At the time of the hearings, he chaired a local draft board, sat as a director for the Bank of Italy, and served as a police commissioner. Committee members grilled Andriano about his close association with Fascist organizations and his influence with the Italian schools. In October 1942, Lieutenant-General DeWitt forced Andriano and other *prominenti* to leave California.[19]

In the most sensational session of the Tenney hearings, Mayor Angelo Rossi attempted to salvage his political career. Born in Volcano, California, in 1878, the son of Italian immigrants, Rossi moved to San Francisco with his family in 1890. He quickly achieved success as a florist, but his talent as a civic activist and political broker bloomed even more abundantly. In short order, he became president of the Dante Hospital, founder of the Downtown Association, and a foreman of the Grand Jury. In 1931, following successful terms as city supervisor, Rossi was appointed mayor when then-mayor James Rolph was elected governor. Standing for office, Rossi was elected to three consecutive mayoral terms. In 1933 and 1937, Italians overwhelmingly supported Rossi and the Democratic Party.[20]

At the Tenney hearings, Rossi denied all complicity, rejecting the charge that he had ever given the Fascist salute in public. "It's a damnable lie," the mayor protested. He defended himself ineptly, weeping on the stand. Ironically, Rossi could not even speak Italian. In his 1943 re-election bid, Rossi finished a distant third.[21]

In the autumn of 1942 key governmental agencies and individuals lobbied President Roosevelt to lift the Italian enemy-alien classification. Alan Cranston, chief of the Foreign Language Branch of the Office of War Information (OWI), played a pivotal role. Cranston, a native of Palo Alto and future U.S.

Senator from California, was an Italophile who had traveled extensively in Italy and spoke the language fluently.[22]

Cranston argued forcefully for lenient treatment of Italian enemy aliens. He reasoned that previous policies were not only mistaken but harmful in that they injured a loyal people and played into the hands of Axis propaganda without solving the problem of protecting the nation against subversives. Cranston criticized the pro-Fascist Italian-language media. He viewed the removal of the enemy-alien status as part of a larger strategy to win over Italian Americans.[23]

Governmental officials orchestrated the timing and delivery of the enemy-alien declaration for the greatest political gain. Columbus Day 1942, the 450th anniversary of the Italian mariner's first voyage, fit perfectly the needs of politicians and ethnics. Italian Americans scrambled to find in their past the appropriate symbols and heroes to reconnect with their adopted homeland and legitimize themselves in a nation now willing to forgive. U.S. Attorney General Francis Biddle delivered the Columbus Day address at New York City's Madison Square Garden. His dramatic speech peaked with the announcement that "beginning October 19 . . . Italian aliens will no longer be classified as enemy aliens."[24]

In California, the cheers following Biddle's speech were muted by the realization that much of the Pacific Coast remained in the hands of the Western Defense Command. The *San Francisco Chronicle* reported, "U.S. Eases Up on Italians—But Not Here." On October 18, however, Lieutenant-General DeWitt lifted the curfew and travel restrictions on Italian enemy aliens in California. By mid-November 1942, Italian fishing fleets on the West Coast sailed, although new regulations required that either the captain or half of the crew be naturalized.[25]

Attorney General Biddle's 1942 Columbus Day speech concluded one chapter of the homefront war. A compelling question persists: why, given the appearance of widespread Fascist sentiments in California in the 1930s, did Italian Americans receive favorable treatment? U.S. government officials moderated their policies against Italian enemy aliens in part because they had witnessed the draconian treatment of Italians in Canada, Australia, and Great Britain. In each instance, national panic produced hasty and ill-conceived measures that resulted in wholesale roundups.[26]

Moreover, the political importance of the Italian vote undoubtedly swayed Roosevelt, more fox than lion. White ethnics and union members constituted an important constituency in the New Deal coalition. Such political influence convinced Roosevelt to make the decision to dampen moves to arrest and intern prominent pro-Fascists.[27] Ardent pro-Fascists quickly stood in line behind the American Flag. An Office of Strategic Services (OSS) agent in San Francisco thought the transformation "an interesting commentary on the remarkably rapid conversion of the fascist element in the city to democratic principles."

But more subtle reasons help to explain why so few Italians were interned. Although many Americans continued to stereotype Italians with criminal behavior and lower-class lifestyles, they did not connect them with treachery, disloyalty, or authoritarian qualities, which conventional wisdom ascribed to both the Germans and Japanese. The extraordinary success of individual Italians in California uplifted the images of Italians in America. In movies and banking, wine making and baseball, Italians stamped their imprint on American culture. While Frank Capra, Don Ameche, A. P. Giannini, and the Rossi brothers figured prominently in the uplifted image of Italians, few matched the charisma of Joe DiMaggio. In 1941, the "Yankee Clipper" won the Most Valuable Player award in the American League; a fellow Italian American and San Francisco native, Dolph Camili, won the honor in the National League. In that same year, Ernie Lombardi, an Oakland native, led the National League in hitting.[28]

The debate over the relative treatment of Italian enemy aliens obscures the far more important issues on the homefront. The war challenged and shattered the isolation and insularity of Italian-American communities. For California's Italian Americans, World War II was both *Iliad* and *Odyssey*. With so many young men enlisting in the armed forces, residents noted the impact of war upon their neighborhoods. To be sure, military service affected all segments of American society, but it had special ramifications for Italian Americans. By all available evidence, Italian-American men joined the military in numbers out of proportion to their presence in the population. Certainly patriotism guided their behavior, but the demographics of the Italian-American population counted heavily as well. Italian Americans made up a heavier representation of young men than the population at large. California newspapers closely followed the military exploits of its citizens, and the public adopted new heroes. Foreign-language papers trumpeted the accomplishments of Italian Americans in columns entitled "With the Colors" and "Our Honor Roll." In May 1945, an OSS report concluded, "There is hardly one family of Italian extraction on the Pacific Coast that has not given one or more members to the armed forces."[29]

Military service, with its regimentation and standardization, affected all individuals who served, but it especially reshaped the ways of ethnics who had spent their lives in isolated enclaves. The camaraderie of the foxhole and the USO replaced the intimacies of the neighborhood.[30]

World War II permitted Italian Americans to become fully accepted citizens through the crucible of patriotism. Throughout American history, military service has allowed children of marginalized groups the opportunity to prove themselves more American than Americans. Italian Americans eagerly made known their "sacrifices" as a further reinforcement of their claims for greater inclusion in the dominant society. The younger generation in particular pointed with great pride to their numbers in the military, viewing their patriotism as the ultimate indication not only of the loyalty of the group as a whole but of the fact that they had chosen America in the struggle over dual identities.[31]

Yet the war reconnected some ethnics with the ancestral homeland in ways both emotional and experiential. Newspapers reveled in stories of Italian-American soldiers liberating the village of family origin, the GIs often shocking *paesani* with their knowledge of archaic dialects. During the invasion of Pizzo, Italy, a reporter described commandos encountering a well-dressed civilian waving an American flag. The young man identified himself as Amadeo Alessandria, nephew of Amadeo Giannini, the chair of the Bank of America. Alessandria told the troops of his two brothers living in San Francisco.[32]

The case of Andrew Rolle reveals the tangled ambiguity of the war for some young ethnics. The son of Piemontese who had emigrated after World War I, Rolle was born in Providence, Rhode Island, in 1922. His well-educated father loathed Fascism. The family moved to California in the 1920s, settling in Pasadena, a community with few Italian immigrants. Rolle spoke and understood the Piemontese dialect, but had experienced little contact with other Italians in his formative years. When Rolle enlisted in the army, officials discovered that he commanded a knowledge of Piemontese. He parachuted behind enemy lines and worked with partisans in the last months of the war. In a further irony, after the war Rolle became American vice consul in Genoa, conducting official duties until career diplomats arrived.[33] He also spent a fruitful scholarly career attempting to understand the Italian-American experience.

Max Ascoli, an Italian-American intellectual who worked in the State Department, predicted in 1942, "The war has given the final blow to the segregation of the Italian communities in America." The war exerted a powerful integrating force, accelerating the process of acculturation and assimilation.[34] Unlike the oppressive "100% Americanism" campaigns of World War I, government efforts to create wartime unity in the 1940s stressed the contributions of ethnic groups and the theme of cultural pluralism. The national drive to promote greater ethnic inclusion as part of the war effort emphasized the theme of tolerance.

Ethnic inclusion involved costs. In May 1942, thousands of Californians participated in a well-orchestrated "I Am An American Day." In North Beach, many parents forbade children from speaking Italian. A sign in a market read, "Anyone heard talking about the war in the Italian language is subject to arrest." Throughout California, Americanization was winning out. In Stockton, the Italian Gardeners Society postponed their annual picnic during the war. The Stockton Italian Athletic Club pledged themselves to "true Americanism." The Italian Athletic Club in San Francisco became the San Francisco Athletic Club.[35] "The morale of these people is now excellent," observed OSS staff officer Col. Robert S. Hall. He added, "The very great majority of these [Italian Americans] are loyal to the American way of life."[36]

Like their neighbors, Italian Americans enthusiastically supported the war effort in numerous ways. On the most basic levels, such voluntary efforts worked to legitimize the patriotism and loyalty of Italian Americans in the eyes of the wider society. In Stockton, the Sheet Metal Workers nominated Roberta Baldocchi for the "Miss Victory" war bond contest. In Monterey, the cannery workers' union purchased $15,000 in defense bonds. San Francisco Italians raised $8 million to build a hospital ship. The Italian Gardeners Society of Stockton dedicated $6,000 to buy war bonds. Following the removal of the enemy-alien tag, a headline announced, "State Italians to Buy U.S. a Bomber." Dr. Charles Ertola challenged California's 52,000 "friendly Italian aliens" to raise $300,000 to purchase a bomber. The Sons of Italy of Southern California raised funds to buy a station wagon for the Red Cross.[37]

The proliferation of local wartime agencies and committees allowed Italian Americans fresh opportunities to gain community-wide positions and interact with neighbors. Dr. A. H. Giannini chaired the Los Angeles USO Board. In San Diego, Peter Farina demonstrated the intricacies of victory gardening for the city's initiates. In San Jose, a letter to the editor thanked "a Sicilian woman" who had offered her family recipe for sun-dried tomatoes. In San Francisco, residents received sandbags, courtesy of the Italian garbagemen.[38]

The twin pillars of Italian-American life, neighborhood and family, felt the tremors of war. The neighborhood served as the cockpit of the homefront war; it helped raise spirits and funds and buffered the pain of separation and loss. But Italian neighborhoods in California, as elsewhere, were changing, and the war accelerated the transformation. No less dramatic were the transformations in the livelihoods of families. The war meant work, and for many Italian Americans laboring at the bottom rungs, the war meant movement and mobility. Standing in the doorway of a sprawling housing tract built for defense workers, an Italian-born mother explained stoically, "One goes where there is bread."[39]

The massive rush of Italian-American men to join the military brought obvious changes to the old neighborhoods. The first impact was the disappearance of so many familiar faces. Saints Peter and Paul Church in North Beach witnessed the loss of hundreds of parishioners in the first months of the war.[40]

Perhaps no single institution played a more important role during the war than the church. The parish church became a locus for a broad variety of activities both symbolic and mundane. Parishioners, for example, often housed the service flag or honor roll of a neighborhood. San Francisco provides a vivid example of the importance of the wartime church. In 1919 Father Oreste Trinchiere organized the Salesian Boys Club in hopes of controlling the influence of gangs. By 1940, the San Francisco Boys Club claimed 2,000 members; its graduates included luminaries Joe, Vince, and Dom DiMaggio, Hank Luisetti, Frank Crosetti, and Gino Cimoli. With the coming of war, director Angelo Fusco maintained contact with the club's one thousand alumni serving in the armed forces by mailing them the new English-language North Beach paper, *Little City News*.[41]

Italian-American culture has always manifested an intense concern with female behavior, and females typically were highly attentive to cultural mores that mandated chastity, close supervision, and "proper domestic values." Women came under particularly close scrutiny during periods of social change, since the older generation regarded them as the repositories of Italian-American traditions. Commentary on wartime marriages reflects these cultural concerns. During the conflict, marriage rates throughout the nation quickly increased. Older Italians questioned less the frequency of marriages and more the character of these relationships. So-called mixed marriages also generated debate. As young men and women left California hometowns, they encountered more potential partners and enhanced the frequency of outgroup marriages. The endless streams of American servicemen and -women through California intensified these concerns on the homefront.

Italian-American women participated in a dizzying degree of voluntarism during the war. In North Beach, as many as fifty women daily staffed a Red Cross Center. In Stockton, Mrs. Joe Armanino headed the Garden Club, and in San Francisco, Dr. Mariana Bertola chaired the Federation of Women's Clubs. Class largely determined the voluntary associations one joined; some families resisted such activities. In a reminiscence, one Italian American related how she wished to join the Red Cross, but her mother rejected the idea. "Oh, we were *obedient* children," she confessed.[42]

If the war confronted women with confusing options, so too did the conflict create advantages for others. No Italian-American group stood to benefit more from the struggle for democracy than the anti-Fascists. So much of the symbolism and rhetoric of Fascism had been integrated into Italian-American ethnicity in the years leading up to the war that the absolute collapse of Fascist legitimacy after Pearl Harbor left a huge vacuum. In California, as else-where, anti-Fascist forces had attempted to supply adequate substitutions, but they were too weak, diverse, and mutually antagonistic to provide leadership or clearly articulated ethnic symbols.

The eclipse of the Mazzini Society illustrates the feeble state of anti-Fascist affairs in California. In September 1944, membership in the state's two chap-ters included one hundred in Los Angeles and seventy in San Francisco. Na-tionally, the Mazzini Society had disintegrated, the result of fractious leader-ship and the divisive question of whether to support Communist insurgency. By 1944 the Los Angeles chapter, headed by Constantine Panunzio, a sociolo-gy professor at USC, seceded from the national organization. In San Francisco, Professor Gaetano Salvemini bitterly opposed any alliance with pro-Commu-nist elements and constantly fought Carmelo Zito, editor of *Il Corriere del Popolo*, for control of the local movement. An OSS officer noted with sarcasm, "It is remarkable how slightly the local chapter of the Mazzini has touched the life of the solid Italian community of San Francisco or has been able to in-fluence its political orientation."[43]

Organizationally, World War II left a great vacuum in Italian-American communities. If the anti-Fascists and Communists seemed bankrupt, it was unclear what organizations would assume the mantle of leadership in 1945. While the Sons of Italy lodges successfully raised funds for the war, critics questioned whether this organization could succeed after the conflict. "The local branches now seem to have lost their hold on the local Italian colonies," observed the OSS. Returning veterans also exerted a powerful influence in determining the course of Italian-American organizational life. Many older societies died from lack of interest.[44]

Powerful economic forces generated by the war unleashed the greatest sus-tained boom in California history. Italian Americans, through a combination of chance, skill, and a shrewd husbanding of resources, seized the advantages of wartime opportunities. Since the nineteenth century, Italians had dominated the scavenger trades in the Bay Area. Organized tightly around Old World or-igins, members realized the importance of political alliances. In 1935 the Scav-engers Protective Association collected scrap iron for Mussolini; in 1942 it dis-tributed sand bags and donated time for America. Economically, the scavengers' associations had become potent corporations; members wore the union label and owners' hat. In 1920, a share in Oakland's Scavengers Association sold for $500; by the 1950s it fetched $15,000. Yet the war's labor shortages created a crisis for the scavengers, who had always hired from their own ethnic ranks, princi-pally sons from the Genoan village of Lorsica. But grandsons preferred the military or jobs with more glamour. The war years opened the ranks of scavengers to non-Genoans. Mexicans, once employed only as laborers, now entered the business as partners.[45]

On California's farmlands, the value of agricultural products skyrocketed during the war. Many notable Italian-American families skillfully positioned their businesses to benefit handsomely from wartime opportunities. The war dynamized California's diverse agricultural interests and brought significant change in the workforce, marketing strategies, and economic scale. Such combinations were not new. In 1916, Marco Fontana merged four large companies, creating the Cal Packing Corporation, which became Del Monte. Italians organized San Francisco's Colombo Market in 1876 and the Farmer's Market in 1943.[46]

The DiGiorgio family exemplified the successful Italian corporate farmer of the twentieth century. Giuseppe DiGiorgio, a Sicilian emigrant, arrived in California in 1910 after working in eastern fruit commission businesses. Throughout the 1930s and 1940s, DiGiorgio acquired thousands of additional acres in the San Joaquin Valley. Relying upon the Bank of Italy for loans, DiGiorgio purchased one-third interest in the Italian Swiss Colony winery, helping to integrate vertically and diversify his investments. The war allowed DiGiorgio to become the largest shipper of fresh fruit in the world. DiGiorgio and his associates defiantly opposed any effort to unionize the increasingly Mexican workforce.[47]

The D'Arrigo brothers moved to California in the 1920s and began experimenting with Italian crops new to American tastes: broccoli and fennel. Purchasing large amounts of land in the 1930s and 1940s, the D'Arrigos eventually controlled vast tracts of vegetable fields in the Salinas, San Joaquin, and Imperial Valleys. The war years expanded their operations, as the government ordered prodigious amounts of produce.[48]

California's wine industry paralleled the trends toward agribusiness and corporate aggrandizement. Firms that had survived Prohibition and the Great Depression reaped impressive profits during the war. While wine production actually fell between 1942 and 1945, the government purchased enormous amounts of raisins and grapes, the latter used in the production of alcohol. The large wineries—chiefly Gallo, Petri, DiGiorgio, Franzia, Cella, Rossi, Sebastiani, and Italian Swiss Colony—controlled over two-thirds of California's wine industry during the 1940s.[49]

In an irresistible trend, the big companies absorbed smaller vintners. In 1942, Enrico Prati and the Rossi brothers sold their winery and vineyards to the National Distillers Corporation, which in turn sold the Italian Swiss Colony winery in 1953 to the Petri Company. The Cella brothers evolved as an industry giant in the 1940s. Taking over small companies in previous decades, the

Cellas increased their production from eight million gallons of wine in 1935 to thirty million gallons in 1941. The Schenley distillery bought out the Cellas in 1942. In 1943 the Mondavi family purchased the Old Krug winery in the Napa Valley.[50]

The spectacular gains achieved by some Italian-American agribusinesses must be measured against the large numbers of Italian families leaving rural areas since the 1940s. The sheer size and influence of corporate farms meant that many small farmers could not compete in California's high-powered economy. The war opened new doors for Italian cannery workers, tenant farmers, and agricultural operatives.[51] Overall, for rural Italian families and urban residents, California in the 1940s meant flux, migration, and mobility. Newcomers arriving in small towns and metropolitan areas often found few familiar moorings. Organizations groped for new identities, and returning laborers and veterans sought novel institutions.

The war quickened the demise of California's Italian neighborhoods. The shuttle of newcomers drawn to the state's burgeoning war industries and the outmigration of residents drawn to the military or work visibly altered these neighborhoods, such as Oakland's Lake Temescal district. Italian districts, such as the truck-farming communities along San Francisco's East Bay and the peninsula, rapidly disappeared in the postwar years. Everywhere in California there seemed to be a housing shortage in 1945. Large numbers of Italian gardeners and truck farmers once lived in San Pablo, East Oakland, San Lorenzo, and Hayward, but postwar developments created projects with names such as Merced Manor, Westlake, and San Lorenzo Valley. Remarkably, however, the 1950 census documented that after decades of migration, mechanization, and urbanization, 6 percent of foreign-born Italian men over age forty-five were still farm operators or laborers.[52]

The most dramatic change affecting an established ethnic neighborhood occurred in San Francisco. The growth and community development of North Beach as an Italian center effectively ended between 1941 and 1945. North Beach fell victim to a series of short- and long-term developments. Immigration restriction had deprived the enclave of large numbers of newcomers for several decades. Young Italian Americans chose not to remain in North Beach. Many young veterans utilized the GI Bill to attend college, and young families left the old neighborhood for newer suburbs and the booming economies of Santa Clara, San Mateo, and Marin Counties. In spite of efforts on the part of the North Beach Merchants Association to find jobs for all returning veterans, the GI Bill discouraged the purchase of homes in older neighborhoods. The GI Bill and allied government programs subsidized the movement to suburbia.[53]

In 1940, at its peak, one-quarter of San Francisco's Italian population resided in North Beach. Thirty years later, only 10 percent of the city's Italian Americans lived in the historic enclave. Large numbers of Chinese Americans had been encroaching on North Beach since the late 1930s. In 1948, an event augured the demographic future of the area. The president of the Italian Family Club resigned in protest over the sale of the clubhouse to the Chinese War Veterans Association. By the 1970s, the Chinese accounted for half of the population of North Beach.[54]

Fascism had so tainted some Italian institutions that they never recovered; others gradually returned. Italian-language classes, for instance, did not return to San Francisco's Fugazi Hall—closed during the war—until 1955. The Italian Chamber of Commerce, also closed during the war, was not revived until 1954. San Francisco's Italian-language newspapers also died, while several English-language papers took their place. The Italian World War I Veterans Association never met again.[55] Moreover, the conflict within the ethnic group, as well as the fear engendered by the internment and the exclusion of many heads of organizations and numerous other community leaders, led to the disintegration of San Francisco's Italian community after the war.

Conclusion

In 1941, Italian Americans stood at a number of important crossroads. They were California's largest European immigrant group, but were experiencing the effects of a generational transition. During the 1930s, many Italian-American leaders had forcefully espoused pro-Fascist sympathies in their efforts to forge acceptable ethnic identities in California.

Historians continue to grapple with the meaning and consequences of Fascism, ethnicity, and the legacy of democracy during wartime. During the last decade, serious attention has been devoted to the topic by California scholars. Since Stephen Fox's 1990 book *The Unknown Internment: An Oral History of Italian Americans during World War II*, California scholars have actively researched what they call "Una Storia Segreta" (a secret story). Their findings harshly criticize an overzealous U.S. government that trampled individual liberties, so traumatizing subjects and families that few would discuss the shameful episodes until recently. In 1997, the U.S. Congress debated whether the president should formally acknowledge "such injustices."[56]

Pearl Harbor disintegrated the Fascist movement in the United States. The war did resolve the debate over the question of dual loyalties, as Italian Americans overwhelmingly demonstrated their attachments to America. For thousands of California Italians, the first year of war spelled confusion and anxiety. When government officials moved quickly to designate all noncitizen Italians as "enemy aliens," impose various restrictions on their freedoms, and intern some residents, their worst fears appeared confirmed. Government officials moderated their policies against Italian enemy aliens because the Italians posed little threat and because of public pressure to lift the stigmatic ban.

Italian Americans confronted issues of identity and politics, but also powerful structural, material, and cultural realities imposed by the war. Little Italies across California saw their residents leave for work in war industries and service in the military. Such widespread residential mobility had profound effects on ethnic institutions and communities, many already in decline. Immigrant churches, newspapers, and mutual-aid societies witnessed changes in their clientele—both in numbers and character—and searched for ways to respond effectively. Italian-American men appear to have served in the armed services out of proportion to their numbers in California. Thus, military life, with its regimentation, travel, and standardized diet, was also a transforming force in reorganizing ethnic life. In addition, increased economic mobility induced by the state's industrial expansion transformed ethnic lives and rearranged the relationships between families and neighborhoods.

The war exposed untold numbers of Italians to new experiences, unimagined in 1940. Travel, work, and combat opened new vistas and possibilities to men and women. These experiences resulted in flux and change. Large numbers of Italians married non-Italians, a dramatic new trend that only quickened after the war. Large numbers of Italian Americans moved to California, especially the southern regions, during and after the conflict. Typically, they moved to the burgeoning suburbs and joined non-ethnic clubs, if any. Older ethnic institutions, such as mutual-aid societies and recreational clubs, struggled to relate to young Italian Americans and newcomers. North Beach, Lake Temescal, and the other Italian-American communities would never be the same.

Notes

1. *Sixteenth Census of the United States, 1940: Population,* vol. 2: *Characteristics of the Population* (Washington, D.C., 1943), tables 15, 24, F-39, 40.

2. Earl Hanson and Paul Beckett, *Los Angeles: Its People and Its Homes* (Los Angeles, 1944), 118–26.

3. *Sixteenth Census of the United States, 1940,* 524, 533, 564, 639, 660; Rose Scherini, "The Italian-American Community of San Francisco" (Ph.D. diss., University of California at Berkeley, 1976), 18–19; Samuel F. Vitone, "Community, Identity, and Schools: Educational Experiences of Italians in San Francisco from the Gold Rush to the Second World War" (Ph.D. diss., University of California at Berkeley, 1981), 61.

4. *San Francisco Examiner,* 6 Dec. 1941.

5. John P. Diggins, *Mussolini and Fascism: The View from America* (Princeton, N.J., 1972); Gaetano Salvemini, *Italian Fascist Activities in the United States* (rpt., New York, 1977); Dono Cinel, *From Italy to San Francisco: The Immigrant Experience* (Stanford, Calif., 1982), 247–57; Vitone, "Community," 6, 304, 319, 325–26; Stephen Fox, *The Unknown Internment: An Oral History of the Relocation of Italian Americans during World War II* (Boston, 1990), 22–41.

6. Diggins, *Mussolini and Fascism,* 106–7; Vitone, "Community," 299–300, 306; Cinel, *From Italy to San Francisco,* 247–57; Gabriella Gacondo, *Socialismo Italiano Esule Negli USA, 1930–1942* (Rome, 1993); Fox, *Unknown Internment,* 22–41; Salvemini, *Italian Fascist Activities,* 91–106; California State Legislature, 55th Session, *Report of the Joint Fact-Finding Committee on Un-American Activities in California* (Sacramento, 1943), 296–321; *San Francisco Chronicle,* 28 May 1942.

7. Scherini, "Italian-American Community," 23–25, 74–84; Marino DeMedici, "The Italian Language Press in the San Francisco Bay Area from 1930 to 1943" (master's thesis, University of California at Berkeley, 1963); Cinel, *From Italy to San Francisco,* 250–52; Sebastien Fichera, "The Meaning of Community: A History of Italians of San Francisco" (Ph.D. diss., University of California at Los Angeles, 1981), 201–11; Vitone, "Community," 141–42, 299–304; *Un-American Activities in California,* 286, 316–21; "Italian-Americans Here Are Loyal Citizens," *Stockton Record,* 11 June 1940; "Fascist Propoganda in Stockton," *Stockton Record,* 13 June 1940; *L'Italo Americano,* 1 May 1942.

8. "Enemy Aliens," *Time,* 16 Feb. 1942, 15; Presidential Proclamation #2527 (8 Dec. 1941), sec. 21–24, Title 50, U.S. Code of Justice; Fox, *Unknown Internment,* 41–88; FBI, "General Intelligence Survey in the United States," July 1982, RG 359, State Department Records, box 3019, National Archives, Washington, D.C.

9. Fox, *Unknown Internment,* 41–88; *Una Storia Segreta* (San Francisco, 1994); Carol Bulger Van Valkenburg, "An Alien Place: The Fort Missoula, Montana, Detention Camp, 1941–1944" (master's thesis, University of Montana, 1988), 22–24; FBI, "General Intelligence Survey in the United States," July 1942, contained in RG 59, State Department Records, box 3019, National Archives, Washington, D.C.; Jerry Mangione, *An Ethnic at Large* (New York, 1978), 327–52.

10. Rose Scherini, "Executive Order 9066 and Italian Americans: The San Francisco Story," *California History* 70 (1992): 366–77. On 29 January 1942, Biddle announced the creation of two prohibited zones and twelve "restricted areas" in California and required all alien enemies to vacate the former areas by the end of February.

11. Ibid.; U.S. House of Representatives, Select Committee Investigating National Defense Migration, *Hearings on National Defense Migration,* 77th Cong., 2d sess., pt. 29: San Francisco Hearings, 21 and 23 February 1942, 10965–70 (hereafter referred to as Tolan Hearings); *La Voce del Popolo* (San Francisco), 20 May 1942.

12. Fox, *Unknown Internment,* 156; Mangione, *Ethnic at Large,* 320–21; FBI, "General Intelligence Survey."

13. *Il Messagiero* (Kansas City), Feb. and Apr. 1942; Edith Terry Brenner to Edward Corsi, 29 Mar. 1943, American Council for Nationality Services Records, "Aliens File,"

Immigration History Research Center, University of Minnesota; Fox, *Unknown Internment*, 58–87; "Testimony of Milano Rispoli," in Tolan Hearings, 11133, 11175–76; *Il Corriere del Popolo* (San Francisco), 6 Aug. 1942; *Il Sole*, 6 May 1942.

14. "2 Aliens End Own Lives," *San Francisco Examiner*, 17 Feb. 1942; *L'Unione* (San Francisco), 13 and 27 Mar. 1942; *Il Messaggiero* (Kansas City), Feb. 1943; Tolan Hearings, 11132–33.

15. Tolan Hearings, 244–45, 11125–26. Congressional testimony estimated that of the 3,000 janitors in San Francisco, 1,200 of them were aliens. See Scherini, "Italian-American Community," 45; Cinel, *From Italy to San Francisco*, 218–21; Richard Dillon, *North Beach* (Novato, Calif., 1995), 172–73; Paul Radin, *The Italians of San Francisco* (Sacramento, Calif., 1935), 59; Deanna Paoli Gumina, *The Italians of San Francisco, 1850–1930* (New York, 1978), 79–97; Raymond Dondero, "The Italian Settlement of San Francisco" (M.A. thesis, University of California at Berkeley, 1953), 240–41.

16. "Wartime Eating," *San Francisco Chronicle*, 23 Nov. 1942.

17. For examples of Italian prisoners of war in California, see *Stockton Record*, 27 Sept. 1944; *San Francisco Chronicle*, 16 July 1945; *Los Angeles Times*, 2 June 1944; Geoffrey Dunn, "*Male Notte*: The Untold Story of Italian Relocation during World War II," *Santa Cruz Magazine*, Feb. 1992, 16–18; Dunn, "*Male Notte*: Santa Cruz Italian Relocation and Restrictions during World War II," *Santa Cruz County History Journal* 1 (1994): 83–89.

18. "The Tenney Inquiry," *San Francisco Chronicle*, 26 May 1942; Diggins, *Mussolini and Fascism*, 77–83; *San Francisco Examiner*, May 1942; *Un-American Activities in California*, 281–321; *L'Unione* (Pueblo, Colo.), 16 Oct. 1942; Scherini, "Italian-American Community," 62–62, 193; M. L. Patterson to Commander W. H. Vanderbilt, 3 Dec. 1943, Records of the Office of Strategic Services (hereafter referred to as OSS Records), RG 226, files 234, 235, National Archives, Washington, D.C.; FBI, "Ettore Patrizi Dossier," files 65-HG-6287, 65-SR-330.

19. See especially "Andriano Silent," *San Francisco Chronicle*, 10 Oct. 1942; "Selective Service Responsibility Mocks Justice," *San Francisco Chronicle*, 25 May 1942; "Andriano Is Suspended," *San Francisco Chronicle*, 28 May 1942; Fichera, "Meaning of Community," 213, 220–21; Scherini, "Executive Order," 372–73; Cinel, *From Italy to San Francisco*, 196; *Il Corriere del Popolo* (San Francisco), 24 Mar. 1942; OSS Records, file 1092, "Italian National Group in California," 10 Mar. 1944.

20. Vitone, "Community," 240, 291–92; *San Francisco Chronicle*, May and October 1942, esp. 26 Oct. 1942; Frederick M. Wirt, *Power in the City: Decision Making in San Francisco* (Berkeley, Calif., 1974), 227–35; Dillon, *North Beach*, 169–70; Fichera, "Meaning of Community," 219–20.

21. *New York Times*, 27 May 1942; *Los Angeles Times*, 27 May 1942; *San Francisco Chronicle*, 26–28 May 1942, 3 Nov. 1943; *Nazioni Unite* (New York), 11 June 1942; Fichera, "Meaning of Community," 219–26.

22. James Edward Miller, *The United States and Italy, 1940–1950* (Chapel Hill, N.C., 1986), 31, 33; OSS Records, file 138, Memorandum, John Wiley to William Donovan, 15 May 1942; Davis to Cranston, 8 Oct. 1942, Records of the Office of War Information (hereafter referred to as OWI Records), RG 208, National Archives, Washington, D.C.

23. Miller, *United States and Italy;*; Fichera, "Meaning of Community," 217–18; Cranston, "Manifesto to Italian of American Origin," 28 October 1942, OWI Records, box 1080; *The Italian Tribune* (Trenton, N.J.), 9 Oct. 1942.

24. Francis Biddle, *In Brief Authority* (Garden City, N.Y., 1962), 229–30, 279–80; "Intelligence: Oval Room" folder, box 107, Ernest Cuneo Papers, Franklin D. Roosevelt Library, Hyde Park, N.Y. (hereafter referred to as FDR Library); Miller, *United States and Italy,* 31; OSS Records, file 542, "The War This Week," 14 Oct. 1942; D. C. Poole to John C. Wiley, 8 Aug. 1942, OSS Records, file 542; "U.S. Eases Up on Italians, but Not Here," *San Francisco Chronicle,* 13 Oct. 1942.

25. "Fisherman's Wharf Is Caught in the Draft," *San Francisco Chronicle,* 16 Apr. 1942; "Italian Aliens Will Be Able to Put to Sea Again," *San Francisco Chronicle,* 3 Nov. 1942; "San Francisco Italians Will Return to Fishing Fleets," *San Francisco Chronicle,* 5 Nov. 1942; "4,000 Italians in Valley Free of Curfew Soon," *San Jose Mercury Herald,* 17 Oct. 1942; "Schools Welcome Lifting of Ban," *San Jose Mercury Herald,* 22 Oct. 1942; "Ban on Alien Italians," *San Jose Mercury Herald,* 13 Oct. 1942. For press clippings gauging the reaction of Biddle's speech, see "Newspaper Clippings," Ugo Carusi Papers, FDR Library.

26. Terri Colpi, *The Italian Factor: The Italian Community in Great Britain* (Edinburgh, 1992); A. W. Brian Simpson, "Detention without Trial in the Second World War: Comparing the British and American Experiences," *Florida State University Law Review* 16 (1988): 255–67.

27. Ronald Filippelli, *American Labor and Postwar Italy, 1943–1945* (Stanford, Calif., 1989); "Intelligence: Oval Room" folder, box 107, Cuneo Papers, FDR Library. In addition to his position in the Justice Department, Cuneo served as legal adviser and ghostwriter for Walter Winchell.

28. "Vince DiMaggio Carries On for His Brothers in the Service," *San Francisco Chronicle,* 3 June 1943; "Joe DiMaggio Is Athlete of Year," *Stockton Record,* 17 Dec. 1941; Noel F. Busch, "Joe DiMaggio," *Life,* 1 May 1939, 62–69; Jack Moore, *Joe DiMaggio* (New York, 1986). DiMaggio voluntarily entered the army as a private in 1943, trading his $43,750 yearly salary for $600 annual pay, further adding to his luster. See *New York Times,* 18 Feb. 1943; *New York Sun,* 17 Feb. 1942; *Time,* 13 July 1936, cover story.

29. "Il Nostro Album d'Onore," *Il Leone* (San Francisco), front-page section heralding the military exploits of Italians; *Il Progresso Italo-Americano* (New York), 13 Oct. 1942; *Il Crociato* (Brooklyn, N.Y.), 20 Dec. 1941, 24 Oct. 1942; *La Nuova Capitale* (Trenton, N.J.), 24 Aug. 1945.

30. Philip Gleason, "Americans All: World War II and the Shaping of American Identities," *Review of Politics,* 43 (Oct. 1981): 515; William McNeill, *American High: The Years of Confidence* (New York, 1986), 27; Col. Robt. B. Hall to DeWitt Poole, 3 May 1945, OSS Records, file 645.

31. The press contains hundreds of examples dealing with the military exploits of Italian Americans. See, for example, *Stockton Record,* 16 Jan. 1942, *San Francisco Chronicle,* 11 Apr. 1943, 10 Oct. 1942. *Little City News,* 18 June 1942, noted that the first American soldier killed in Alaska was Frank Scansi of Napa.

32. "North Beach Reaction to the Ouster," *San Francisco Chronicle,* 26 July 1943; "Italians Surrender," *San Francisco Chronicle,* 9 Sept. 1943; "How North Beach Feels," 9 Sept. 1943; "Allies in Italy Find Lost Kind of Giannini," *San Francisco Chronicle,* 11 July 1943; "Salvemini Discusses Rome's Fall," *San Francisco Chronicle,* 10 Sept. 1943; "North Beach Is Calm and Very Grateful," *San Francisco Chronicle,* 5 June 1944; "Italians of Valley Jubilant, *San Jose Mercury Herald,* 9 Sept. 1943; "Soldiers Find One-Man Ally on Italy Shore," *San Jose Mercury Herald,* 11 Sept. 1943; "Italian-Americans Here Rejoice in Rome Victory," *San Jose Mercury Herald,* 5 June 1944; "Los Angeles Italians Cheered by Surrender," *Los Angeles Times,* 9 Sept. 1943; Gumina, *Italians of San Francisco,* 201.

33. Andrew Rolle, tape recorded interview by Gary Mormino, 12 Aug. 1994, San Marino, Calif.

34. Max Ascoli quoted in John Morton Blum, *V Was for Victory* (New York, 1976), 154.

35. *Los Angeles Times,* 3 and 18 May 1942; *San Diego Union,* 5 Sept. 1943; *San Francisco Chronicle,* 6 and 18 May 1942.

36. Memo to DeWitt Poole from Lt. Col. Robt. B. Hall, "Italians in California," 5 May 1943, OSS Records, file 645.

37. "Italians Here to Buy Ship," *Oakland Post Enquirer,* 21 Oct. 1942; *L'Italia,* 12 June 1942; *San Francisco Chronicle,* 21 Oct. 1942; *Stockton Record,* 14 Feb. 1942, 2 May 1945; *San Francisco Examiner,* 24 Jan. 1943.

38. "Here's What to Do with Spare Tomatoes," *San Jose Mercury Herald,* 15 Oct. 1943; "Luther Rossi Named to Head San Jose Kiwanis," *San Jose Mercury Herald,* 28 Sept. 1943; *San Diego Union,* 25 Apr. 1943; *Los Angeles Times,* 5 Oct. 1942; *Il Corriere del Popolo* (San Francisco), 24 Mar. 1942.

39. Lowell J. Carr and James Edson Stermer, *Willow Run* (New York, 1952), 61.

40. Scherini, "Italian-American Community," 26.

41. Ibid., 163–64; Clarice Minot, "Father Tink and His Boys," *San Francisco Chronicle,* 3 June 1979; Vitone, "Community," 336–39.

42. Quoted in Micaela Di Leonardo, *The Varieties of Ethnic Experience: Kinship, Class, and Gender among California Italian Americans* (Ithaca, N.Y., 1984), 117; Gumina, *Italians of San Francisco,* 199; *San Francisco Chronicle,* 8 and 29 Nov. 1942; *Stockton Record,* 10 May 1940, 16 Dec. 1941.

43. "The Mazzini Society on the Pacific Coast," San Francisco, 4 Sept. 1944, OSS Records, file 1370; John Norman to DeWitt Poole, 8 Mar. 1945, OSS Records, file 1694; "Conversation with Zito," 28 Feb. 1945, OSS Records, file 1683.

44. "California," 10 Mar. 1944, OSS Records, file 1592.

45. Cinel, *From Italy to San Francisco,* 26–27, 53–57, 151–52; *San Francisco Examiner,* 12 Dec. 1941; Scherini, "Italian-American Community," 26, 56, 195; S. E. Perry, *San Francisco Scavengers* (Berkeley, Calif., 1988), 15–17, 28–30, 218.

46. Dondero, "Italian Settlement," 39–40; Cinel, *From Italy to San Francisco,* 212–18; Gumina, *Italians of San Francisco,* 101; Fichera, "Meaning of Community," 245–49.

47. Hans Christian Palmer, "Italian Immigration and the Development of California Agriculture" (Ph.D. diss., University of California at Berkeley, 1965), 234–45; Andrew F. Rolle, *The Immigrant Upraised* (Norman, Okla., 1968), 273–74.

48. Palmer, "Italian Immigration," 224–26; "Local Grower," *San Jose Mercury Herald*, 6 Sept. 1942.

49. Palmer, "Italian Immigration," 251–90; Gumina, *Italians of San Francisco*, 115–33; Di Leonardo, *Varieties of Ethnic Experience*, 168–69; Rolle, *Immigrant Upraised*, 267–73.

50. Palmer, "Italian Immigration," 251–90; Rolle, *Immigrant Upraised*, 267–73.

51. Di Leonardo, *Varieties of Ethnic Experience*, 62; Palmer, "Italian Immigration," 296–305.

52. Palmer, "Italian Immigration," 123–26; Di Leonardo, *Varieties of Ethnic Experience*, 62.

53. Scherini, "Italian-American Community," 13, 59, 220; Gumina, *Italians of San Francisco*, 207–9; Dondero, "Italian Settlement," 68; Edward Banfield, *The Unheavenly City* (Boston, 1970), 15; Cinel, *Italy to San Francisco*, 197; Paola Schellenbaum, "Stereotypes as Cultural Constructs: A Kaleidoscopic Picture of Italian Americans in Northern California," in *Studies in Italian American Folklore*, ed. Luisa Del Giudice (Logan, Utah, 1993), 190; Palmer, "Italian Immigration," 155–59.

54. Italians quickly grasped the intricacies of inter- and intragroup rivalries. Whereas in the East, nativists branded Italians as unassimilable and unwelcome, in the West Italians conspired to restrict and retard the influx of Asians and Mexicans. See Scherini, "Italian-American Community," 25–28; Brian J. Godfrey, *Neighbors in Transition: The Making of San Francisco's Ethnic and Non-Conformist Communities* (Berkeley, Calif., 1988), 74; Dondero, "Italian Settlement," 68–69, 116–20; Fichera, "Meaning of Community," 26, 184–97; U.S. Bureau of the Census, *U.S. Census of 1970, California: General Social and Economic Characteristics* (Washington, D.C., 1970), table 119.

55. Dillon, *North Beach*, 173; Vitone, "Community," 310–11; Scherini, "Italian-American Community," 78.

56. The exhibition *Una Storia Segreta* toured the nation in 1995, receiving widespread acclaim. See "After Silence, Italians Recall the Internment," *New York Times*, 11 Aug. 1997; "Honoring Forgotten Victims of WWII," *Los Angeles Times*, 10 Feb. 1995.

8

War Comes to Chinatown:
Social Transformation and the Chinese of California

K. Scott Wong

Whether or not World War II should be considered the major watershed in twentieth-century American history continues to be debated, but there is no doubt as to the significance of this period in Asian-American history. The war is perhaps as important as the passage of the 1965 Immigration Act, which finally allowed Asian immigration to the United States to proceed on a level equal to other immigrant streams. It brought about both welcome and terrifying changes in the Asian-American community, but these changes have not been adequately represented in the historiography of Asian-American studies. As the war pulled Asian Americans into factories and offices, the armed forces and internment camps, their tenuous position in American society was brought into bold relief. First-generation Asian immigrants, who by law were ineligible for citizenship, found themselves caught between their loyalties, real and imagined, for their countries of origin and the United States. The second generation, on the other hand, was often put in a position of having to claim their "Americanness" in the face of their parents' and their own relationships with Asia. This dilemma was especially true for Japanese Americans, two-thirds of whom were American citizens by birth, as they were forcibly placed in internment camps simply because of their race.

Because of internment, however, the wartime experience of Japanese Americans has dominated the study of the impact of the war on the Asian-American community, especially in the case of California. Therefore, within Asian-American studies, research on the Second World War has focused almost exclusively on the hardships of internment and the military heroics of the 442nd and 100th Battalions, to the exclusion of other Asian-American groups. In this sense, the subsequent construction of the war has been narrowed into a bipolar discourse of injustice and achievement, ignoring the complex circumstances in which most other Asian Americans found themselves in this important period of American social change.

Using Chinese-American publications of this period and a number of oral history interviews, this essay will demonstrate that the Second World War was instrumental in the formation of an already developing modern Chinese-American identity among the second generation, as Chinese Americans were determined to show their concern for the welfare of China while claiming their place in America. Therefore, it can be said that Chinese Americans viewed the war from three "fronts": the fate of China, the fighting in both major theaters of the war, and the social issues confronting Chinese Americans on the home-front. The social changes engendered by the war made it possible for many Chinese Americans eventually to lead lives that were no longer solely defined by the limits of Chinatown. Thus, like other marginalized sectors of the American public, the war years ushered in a new era for Chinese-American communities, most noticeably in San Francisco.

Chinese-American communities, better known as "Chinatowns," had long been under siege. San Francisco's Chinatown, historically the major settlement of Chinese in the United States, was a key site of the anti-Chinese movement. For example, in 1876 San Francisco hosted federal hearings on Chinese immigration, and by then there was already a history of anti-Chinese activity in the city. Chinatown was often viewed as an immoral vice district and the Chinese as mysterious people who could never become "true Americans." One witness at the federal hearings described the Chinese community in San Francisco as "an indigestible mass in the community, distinct in language, pagan in religion, inferior in mental and moral qualities, and all peculiarities, is an undesirable element in a republic, but become especially so if political power is placed in its hands."[1] Nevertheless, San Francisco continued to be the major port of disembarkation for immigrants from China, eventually leading to the establishment of the Angel Island Immigration Station because of the belief that most Chinese were entering the country illegally as "paper sons." This immigration station, located in San Francisco Bay, operated from 1910 to 1940, detaining thousands of Chinese immigrants, sometimes for more than a year, before they were allowed to enter the country.[2] Due to negative imagery, language and cultural differences, the fear of illegal immigration, and a hostile racism that kept them confined to Chinatown, prewar Chinese Americans lived in near isolation from mainstream American society. Unable to find jobs or homes outside of Chinatown, Chinese Americans were rendered nearly invisible and marginal to the greater American experience. For this reason, in the 1930s and early 1940s, the residents of Chinatown, especially the merchants and the political elite, went to great lengths to transform the image of Chinatown from its old reputation as a mysterious ethnic enclave into a tourist attraction based on a restaurant and curio-shop economy.[3]

Regardless of its image in American society at large, San Francisco's Chinatown was the cultural heartland of Chinese America. It was the national headquarters of the Chinese Consolidated Benevolent Association (CCBA), which oversaw relations between Chinese fraternal associations. The community supported a number of daily and weekly publications in both Chinese and English, and it was generally regarded as the most important Chinese-American community in the nation, followed by that in New York.[4] Due to its proximity to China, despite the rigors of the Chinese exclusion acts and the long-term detentions on Angel Island, Chinese immigrants continued to bring new life into the San Francisco community. By the Second World War, a distinctively Chinese-American culture had developed in San Francisco's Chinatown, a culture that was shaped by the residents' relationship to China and its role in the politics of Asia, their often hostile relationship with white America, and the coming of age of a second generation struggling to define its place in American society.

As a result of various exclusion laws, few Chinese women were allowed to immigrate, and with the passage of anti-miscegenation laws in California and other western states, which specifically prohibited the intermarriage of Chinese and whites, the development of Chinese-American families was severely stunted.[5] Therefore, it was not until the mid-thirties that Chinese America finally had a sizable adult second generation.[6] These men and women, American-born and thus American citizens, often found themselves caught between their loyalty to and identification with Chinese culture and tradition and their desire to be fully accepted in American society. Because of the difficulty in finding jobs outside of Chinatown, many Chinese Americans came to believe that their futures would be more secure in China than in America. For this reason, it was not uncommon for some Chinese families to send their children, especially sons, to China for some of their education so that they would perfect their use of the Chinese language, learn Chinese culture firsthand, cultivate professional contacts, and perhaps meet a future spouse.

This tension between the desire to claim a place in American society and the feeling that one could have a more promising future in China found expression in the famous essay contest of 1936, sponsored by the Ging Hawk Club of New York, "Does My Future Lie in China or America?" The essays that received first and second place were printed in the *Chinese Digest*, a Chinese-American periodical published in San Francisco. The winner, Robert Dunn from Somerville, Massachusetts, a student at Harvard University, placed his future in America, maintaining that one could serve China "by building up a good impression of the Chinese among Americans, by spreading good-will and clearing up misunderstandings, by interesting the Americans in the Chinese thru [sic] personal contacts and otherwise, and, if necessary, by contributing generously to the financing of worthy enterprises in China."[7] He continued by stating that he preferred American social values, criticizing Chinese standards of culture. He asserted, "They [his Chinese relatives] pour contempt upon religion, especially upon Christianity, and fail to see the preciousness and value of the individual life. This culture and attitude is contrary to mine, and I fear that I shall be unhappy in the process of yielding to it." He concluded his essay by saying, "[I] owe America as much allegiance as I do China; . . . it is possible to serve China while living in America; . . . remunerative employment, though scarce, is not impossible to obtain in either China or America; and I would avoid the unhappiness and social enstrangement due to conflicting cultures by staying in America."[8]

The second-place essay took the opposite position. Kaye Hong, a resident of San Francisco, focused much of his essay on the restrictions placed on Chinese Americans due to American racism. He lamented, "I have learned to acknowledge that the better jobs are not available to me and that the advancement of my career is consequently limited in this fair land."[9] Hong rejected the rhetoric on which many Chinese in America relied, which stressed the past accomplishments of Chinese civilization. Instead, he forcefully declared, "The ridicule heaped upon the Chinese race has long fermented in my soul. I have concluded that we, the younger generation, have nothing to be proud of except the time-worn accomplishments of our ancient ancestors, that we have been living in the shadow of these glories, hoping that these arts and literature of the past will justify our present. Sad but true, they do not. To live under such illusions is to lead the life of a parasite."[10] Hong proposed that returning to China would give him the opportunity to serve China by aiding in its modernization, and only a modern China would garner the respect of the world. This sentiment had been prevalent among Chinese since they began immigrating to the United States. They often believed that a stronger Chinese government would be able to improve the position and treatment of Chinese in America. Unfortunately, this was not necessarily the case.

These two essays, and the responses sent in by readers of the *Chinese Digest*, capture some of the cultural conflicts in which the second generation found itself. Unable to find meaningful employment outside of Chinatown, some looked to China for economic opportunity while maintaining a sense of duty to China's salvation. Others were more optimistic about their chances in Amer-

ica and acknowledged a distance from Chinese culture, a distance that would
have made their adjustment to life in China more difficult than they were willing
to endure. In truth, most Chinese Americans in the thirties chose to cast their
lot in America. American bred and educated, most simply became swept up in
Chinese-American lives and tried their best to find employment and lead productive, if restricted, lives. Furthermore, as the political situation in China became increasingly unstable, travel to China and the hope of finding gainful
employment became less feasible. A touch of irony can be seen in the later lives
of both Robert Dunn and Kaye Hong. Dunn actually went to China before the
war and worked there for a number of years before returning to the United
States. He later worked in the Asian Division of the Library of Congress. While
in China, he also began using his full name, Robert Dunn Wu. Kaye Hong, on
the other hand, remained in the United States and did not go to China until it
opened to tourism in the 1980s.[11]

The *Chinese Digest,* in which these two essays were published, was the first
newspaper in English directed toward American-born Chinese. Founded in
San Francisco in 1935 by Thomas Chinn and Chingwah Lee, the *Chinese Digest* was published as a weekly and, later, a monthly, until 1939. It was then
published irregularly until it closed in 1940. Thomas Chinn was born in Oregon in 1909 to immigrant parents, and the family moved to San Francisco's
Chinatown in 1919. When he reached adulthood, Chinn was committed to the
idea that Chinese Americans should leave their ethnic enclave and adapt more
readily to American society. He came to believe that an English-language publication devoted to second-generation Chinese-American concerns would help
facilitate that transition. At the same time, he believed that a knowledge of
Chinese history and culture would benefit the second generation. With these
goals in mind, Chinn sought financial backing for his newspaper.[12]

Chinn acquired his initial financial support from his friend Chingwah Lee.
Lee, eight years Chinn's senior, was also an advocate of Chinese-American
assimilation, and he agreed to help Chinn begin his newspaper. Lee was well
known in the community for his knowledge of Chinese culture and had begun serving as a technical consultant in Hollywood for films that called for
Chinese art objects. When the film version of the Pearl S. Buck novel *The Good
Earth* went into production, Lee was called upon to recruit Chinese actors for
the film. Eventually, he landed an on-screen part for himself as well.[13] Lee used
the money he made from his work on the film to fund the paper, with Chinn
as editor and Lee and William Hoy, another Chinese American who sought
greater access to American society, as associate editors.[14] It now seems ironically fitting that *The Good Earth,* a film later criticized for being one of many
that used Caucasian actors to play the roles of major Chinese characters, would

actually provide the funding for the first newspaper aimed at second-genera-tion Chinese Americans.

During its five-year run, the *Chinese Digest* did indeed try to bridge the gap between the second generation's ties to the culture of their parents and Chi-natown and their own attempts to enter the American mainstream. The pa-per usually carried news of events in China, especially concerning the increasing Japanese aggression in the area. There were also feature articles on traditional Chinese history and art. The majority of the paper, however, was devoted to articles about San Francisco's Chinatown, news of other Chinese-American communities, Chinese-American sports events, fashion tips, and some adver-tisements for Chinese-owned stores or those with a Chinese-American employ-ee. A men's clothing store, Moore's, located on the edge of Chinatown, regu-larly took out ads in the *Chinese Digest,* always mentioning that they employed Edward Leong, their "Chinese representative." Advertisements for fashionable clothes, milk, sports equipment, and beauty shops all speak to an increasingly modern and Americanized audience. As one resident of San Francisco's Chi-natown recalled, "By the time I was in high school, the big thing, if you had money, was to have a car. . . . Then a girl. You would have to dress fairly well, not in dress-up clothing but in sports clothing. My father wouldn't give us any money for working in the store, but we did get an allowance, and I'd use that to try to get the right clothes. Of course, athletics was very important. I guess you could just call us all-American types."[15] In this sense, it is evident that sec-ond-generation Chinese Americans were very much like their counterparts in other racial and ethnic groups. Regardless of the degree of their attachment to Chinese culture, many exhibited an overriding identification with main-stream American youth culture.

It was, however, impossible to ignore the dire situation in China. The first issue of the *Chinese Digest* stated that one of its missions was to report the "truth" about Japanese activity in China.[16] It is important to bear in mind that for Chinese and Chinese Americans, the Second World War was not confined to the years 1941 to 1945, but began when Japan made its first incursions into Manchuria and Inner Mongolia. As a result of the Mukden Incident of 1931, Japanese troops assumed control of Manchuria, and throughout the 1930s the Japanese army put increasing pressure on China and came to control more Chinese territory. By 1937, Japanese aggression in China was unbridled, epit-omized by the infamous "Rape of Nanjing." In fact, in most Chinese histories of the war, the period of 1937 to 1945 is referred to as the War of Resistance as opposed to the Second World War because, for most of this time, the rest of the world was not involved in the Sino-Japanese conflict, and China felt iso-lated in its attempts to ward off the invasion. During this period, therefore, many Chinese and Chinese Americans felt doubly assaulted, abandoned by the international community in its struggle against Japan and victimized by racial discrimination in America.

In addition to Japanese aggression in China and the limited employment possibilities outside of Chinatown, the Chinese in San Francisco were also concerned with Japanese-American economic competition within Chinatown. As early as 1935, Chinese-American merchants were concerned that Japanese Americans were intruding into Chinatown business space. An editorial in the *Chinese Digest* of November 22, 1935, stated, "The Japanese have already taken the southern half of Chinatown—our best bazaar section—and we are reminded what harm is being done our bazaars when cheap imitations and flimsy curios flood Grant Ave. . . . We must post up a warning sign: Keep Chinatown Chinese."[17] As recently as the summer of 1993, while interviewing a number of Chinese-American veterans of World War II in San Francisco, I was informed while walking down Grant Avenue, "All these stores here were owned by Japanese. But after the war started, they all had to close and Chinese were able to move back in. Hell, it's Chinatown."[18]

In this same editorial, the *Chinese Digest* warned against a group of "Eastern capitalists" who were said to be interested in constructing a "Little China" in a corner of Chinatown as a tourist attraction during the 1939 San Francisco Golden Gate International Exposition. The *Digest* declared, "We must make haste to inform our city officials that we do not contemplate having outsiders represent us. These easterner adventurers cannot adequately portray our customs, habits, and culture. Their one aim would be to extract money from tourists at our expense. At best they will arrive at a Hollywood version of long-fingered Mandarins chasing sing-song girls across a chop suey joint. We are tired of comedies."[19] Although many may have wanted the opportunity to leave the confines of Chinatown, second-generation Chinese-American residents of the community also viewed Chinatown as their cultural base. Thus, they realized the importance of self-representation. They sought to protect their community from being stereotyped and exploited by those who had little connection to or concern for the actual residents and cultural integrity of the community.[20] Chinese Americans in San Francisco thus felt besieged on a number of fronts. The ongoing war in China was a constant concern, especially for those who had families in China; the bleak economic and social prospects for the emerging second generation were a persistent worry; and even within Chinatown, competition from Japanese Americans and outside interests was seen as an economic and cultural threat.[21]

With America's entry into the Second World War in late 1941, American Chinatowns underwent an important transformation. By entering the war,

Chinese Americans were able, in a variety of ways, to demonstrate their patriotism for the United States and their heartfelt Chinese nationalism. With so many other American men and, to a lesser extent, women, entering the armed forces, American women and racial minorities entered the workforce in unprecedented numbers. These economic and social changes can be seen as a turning point in modern Chinese-American history. Upon becoming allies in the war against Japan, American images of Chinese and Chinese Americans changed for the better. The sinister mask of Fu Manchu was replaced by the tragic photograph of the lone baby sitting and crying in the bombed-out railroad station in Nanjing, and the image of the weak and ineffectual Chinese was replaced by posters of heroic Chinese men and women fighting to defend their country from Japanese invaders. In 1938, Chiang Kai-shek and his American-educated wife, Song Mei-ling (Madame Chiang Kai-shek), were named *Time* magazine's "Man and Wife of the Year," an image that was in sharp contrast to earlier (and later) impressions of the Chinese.[22]

But more important than imagery were the new social and economic opportunities open to Chinese Americans, who were eager to take advantage of these opportunities in order to claim their place in San Franciscan and American society. This change is most evident in the variety of occupations that Chinese Americans took during the war. The sociologist Rose Hum Lee reported that Chinatowns throughout the United States were experiencing labor shortages, especially in restaurants. For the first time, significant numbers of Chinese Americans were able to leave the restaurants, laundries, and gift shops to join the armed services and other defense-related industries. She referred to one American-born University of Minnesota–trained master in architecture who found work in the war industry—the first technical job he had held since his graduation fifteen years earlier. Before the war, he had managed his father's restaurant. When he found this new job, his American-born, business-trained wife took over his responsibilities at the restaurant.[23] As Diane Mark has pointed out, "The reopening of American industry to Chinese Americans came at a time of labor shortages, just as it had decades earlier, when Chinese were an important part of the working force in the railroads and California industries. By the 1940s there was a generation of United States citizens, educated in American schools, and already trained for the blue and white collar jobs which were opening up to them."[24] Finally able to leave jobs that were dictated by the Chinatown economy or other limited choices such as laundries and restaurants, Chinese Americans joined other Americans, many for the first time, in the shipyards, aircraft factories, offices, and white-collar professions.

While "Rosie the Riveter" is most often portrayed as a Caucasian woman, it is important to remember that she was also African-American, Latina, and

Asian-American. One such woman was An Yoke Gee. Ms. Gee was born on the Monterey Peninsula in 1895 and was thus an American citizen. However, she later married a Chinese immigrant and was thereby stripped of her citizenship due to the Cable Act of 1922, which declared that any woman who married an alien ineligible for citizenship would lose her citizenship. Since all immigrants except Asians were eligible for naturalization, this bill was obviously designed to curtail the formation of Asian-American families. Despite her loss of citizenship, An Yoke Gee went to work in the Kaiser shipyard at the age of forty-six.[25] Eventually, her daughter Maggie followed her into the defense industry. Maggie Gee was a student at the University of California at Berkeley when the war began. She soon quit classes in order to work as an electrical draftsperson at the Mare Island Naval Shipyard in north San Pablo Bay. Her primary duty was to chart the electrical wiring for the repair of damaged submarines. Soon, however, Maggie Gee decided that she wanted to do something more exciting to assist in the war effort. She and two friends decided to enroll in flight school. They went to Minden, Nevada, and learned to fly. At that point, the Women Airforce Service Pilots (WASPs) were recruiting, and Maggie was accepted.[26] One of only two Chinese-American women in the WASPs, she trained at Sweetwater, Texas, and eventually flew a variety of aircraft. The WASPs transported airplanes from one base to another and flew mock missions in order to train men who were being sent overseas for combat. The WASPs were disbanded in December 1944 due to pressure from male pilots, who resented their presence. After the war, Maggie Gee finished her college degree and became a physicist for Lawrence and Livermore laboratories in the San Francisco Bay Area. As Judy Yung has eloquently argued, the role Chinese-American women played in "World War II was not just a temporary response to a national crisis, but a turning point in their lives. Once they entered the public arena, they would not only prove their mettle and win the respect of their community but also gain a new sense of self-confidence and pride as Chinese-American women."[27] Thus the war offered new roles in the public sphere for both men and women of the Chinese-American community, in which many of them would continue after the war ended.

While the immediate impact of the war on occupational opportunities can be seen in individual examples such as these, the long-range effects of the war can also be gleaned from the national censuses for 1940 and 1950. Although the national increase from 36,992 Chinese employed in 1940 to 48,409 in 1950 may not appear significant, when specific areas of occupational mobility are examined, the importance of the 1940s for Chinese Americans becomes more evident.[28] Focusing on San Francisco, census data indicates substantial improvements in the occupational opportunities available to Chinese Americans. (The figures provided in table 8.1 indicate that many of the occupational trends in San Francisco were similar to those of the nation for Chinese Americans.) The most obvious and far-reaching changes occurred in the employment of Chinese in professional and semiprofessional fields and in the total number of Chinese-American women employed. In the professional ranks of San Francisco's Chinese Americans, there was a nearly threefold increase among males (217 in 1940; 640 in 1950) and an almost fourfold increase among females (68 in 1940; 243 in 1950). In other fields, males continued to show incremental increases, but the gains for women in these areas, in terms of proportional advances, were substantial. In the area of managers, officials, and proprietors, the increase for San Francisco males was more than a thousand (744 in 1940; 1,935 in 1950), while the number of women in these positions increased five times (32 in 1940; 174 in 1950). In clerical and sales positions, the increases for women were similar to those in the professional fields. Males increased by eight hundred (1,024 in 1940; 1,827 in 1950), but the women's gains were fourfold (179 in 1940; 1,424 in 1950).

The changes in the service sector are also indicative of an expanded labor market for Chinese Americans. For service workers (not including domestic workers), there was an increase of more than a thousand males (1,800 in 1940; 2,851 in 1950), while the number of women in the service sector almost doubled (151 in 1940; 291 in 1950). The number of Chinese-American males who took domestic work in 1940 (780) was cut almost in half by 1950 (404), while the number of female domestic workers rose by only four (84 in 1940; 88 in 1950). In total, there were 6,398 more Chinese Americans in the San Francisco labor force in 1950 than in 1940, and nearly two-thirds of them were women (4,058). While these figures do not explain the reasons for the increasing number of San Francisco's Chinese Americans finding gainful employment, they do indicate that Chinese Americans made occupational advances during the decade. Males were able to leave domestic service jobs in notable numbers, presumably to find better occupations.

Most noticeable, however, is the dramatic rise in the number of Chinese-American men and women who entered the professional and semiprofessional ranks. The nature of the occupations in which Chinese Americans found employment indicates their participation in the American economy beyond the confines of Chinatown. With these gains for Chinese-American men in professional and managerial positions, and the substantial increase in the employment of Chinese-American women in the public sphere, Chinese Americans were, by midcentury, poised to enter the postwar American middle class. While it is well known that the advances on the part of women and minorities dur-

Table 8.1 Chinese Population, United States and San Francisco

	1940		1950		Total Change		Percent Change	
	Male	Female	Male	Female	Male	Female	Male	Female
Chinese population								
United States	57,389	20,115	76,725	40,415	19,336	20,300	34	101
San Francisco	12,264	5,518	15,595	9,218	3,331	3,370	27	67
Chinese employed								
United States	34,081	2,911	40,131	8,278	6,050	5,367	18	184
San Francisco	5,953	918	10,129	3,140	4,176	2,222	70	242
Professionals								
United States	812	221	2,541	914	1,729	693	212	314
San Francisco	217	68	640	243	423	175	195	257
Managers/officials								
United States	7,250	253	8,920	658	1,670	405	23	160
San Francisco	744	32	1,935	174	1,191	142	160	444
Clerical/sales								
United States	3,422	750	4,512	3,210	1,090	2,460	32	328
San Francisco	1,024	179	1,827	1,424	803	1,242	78	694
Domestic service								
United States	1,954	287	746	514	−1,208	227	−62	79
San Francisco	780	84	404	88	−376	4	−48	5
Other service								
United States	10,515	562	13,000	940	2,485	378	24	67
San Francisco	1,800	151	2,851	291	1,051	136	58	88
Crafts								
United States	448	9	1,348	42	900	33	201	367
San Francisco	175	4	622	15	447	11	255	275
Operatives								
United States	7,502	750	6,564	1,711	−938	961	−13	128
San Francisco	999	384	1,430	851	431	467	43	122
Laborers								
United States	1,520	42	1,394	95	−126	53	−8	126
San Francisco	186	6	316	23	130	17	70	283
Unreported								
United States	200	37	532	176	332	139	166	376
San Francisco	28	6	104	34	76	28	271	467

Sources: U.S. Department of Commerce, Bureau of the Census, *Sixteenth Census of the United States, 1940: Population,* vol. 2: *Characteristics of the Nonwhite Population by Race* (Washington, D.C., 1943), 5, 47, 97; idem, *Seventeenth Census of the United States, 1950,* special report: *Nonwhite Population by Race* (Washington, D.C., 1952), 3B-19, 42, 80.

ing the war were often temporary and that many remained in the service industries, the gains for Chinese Americans were nevertheless significant. For the first time, they entered professions previously closed to them, and they found employment outside of Chinatown. With the aid of the GI Bill, many Chinese-American veterans finished college educations, which further expanded their occupational options. The tenuous political situation in postwar China aside, it was no longer necessary for Chinese Americans to seek employment in China.

The military was another very important avenue by which Chinese Americans, citizens and noncitizens alike, came to find a new position in American society. For noncitizens, service in the armed forces offered the opportunity to become an American citizen, a right that many of them had been denied since childhood. Between twelve and fifteen thousand Chinese Americans wore American service uniforms during the war. While most served in the army or the Army Air Corps, others went into the marines and the Coast Guard. Fewer served in the navy because, until the end of May 1942, Chinese Americans were not allowed to enlist for naval positions other than mess stewards and cabin boys. The lifting of these limitations was considered important enough to make the front-page headline of the May 29, 1942, issue of the *Chinese Press*.[29] A draftee from San Francisco, Edward "Kaye" Chinn, was described in the *Chinese Press* as a "typical example of the American of Chinese descent. [He was] a junior college graduate, majoring in aeronautic mechanics, and was working as a mechanic's helper when his [draft] summons came."[30] Chinese Americans served in all branches of the military during the Second World War and in all types of units: combat infantry, engineering, intelligence, transport, fighter and bomber squadrons, and support units.

While most Chinese Americans served in integrated units with white soldiers, about 1,200 served in all-Chinese-American units stationed in the China-Burma-India (CBI) theater. These units belonged to the Fourteenth Air Service Group (14th ASG) under the umbrella of the Fourteenth Air Force, and were thus part of the famous "Flying Tigers."[31] In addition, there was an all-Chinese-American unit of the army, the 987th Signal Company. The official reasons for the formation of these all-Chinese-American units are uncertain. Many veterans of these units have reported that they were led to believe that they were formed at the request of Madame Chiang Kai-shek for propaganda purposes, but no available documents support this belief. Instead, it seems more likely that these all-Chinese-American units, mostly led by Caucasian commanding officers, were created in early 1944 (the 987th was activated in 1943) in the hopes that they would facilitate better relations with the local population in China.[32] While this ploy may have worked in some cases, most of the Chinese Americans in these units who spoke Chinese used one of the dialects from the Cantonese-speaking region of China. These units were sent to more western and northern regions, where different dialects were employed, meaning that some personnel had to be trained in other dialects; some units depended on interpreters, or, more often, they simply did not establish any relations with the local population. Whatever the reason for the formation and eventual efficacy of these all-Chinese-American units, they represent a middle-ground in army race relations. While the personnel were predominantly Chinese-American, they trained on integrated bases, shared facilities with white personnel, and worked closely with predominantly white units. In other words, they were not like the segregated units into which African Americans were placed, but they were racially defined and organized. To this day, the veterans themselves differ on whether or not they should be considered segregated units.

Regardless of their status, most of these veterans look upon their time in the service with great pride. For those who entered the armed forces as noncitizens, military duty often granted them citizenship. In fact, the army even facilitated the granting of citizenship to those who had originally entered the country illegally. At one point, eighteen men who were training in Venice Beach, Florida, could not satisfy the legal entry requirements for citizenship. They were flown to Detroit and taken to Canada so they could then reenter the country legally and thus qualify for citizenship.[33] For the second generation, service was both an obligation and an opportunity to take their place alongside their fellow Americans in the war effort. For both first- and second-generation Chinese Americans, serving in the military was an experience through which they could articulate their American patriotism and Chinese nationalism. James Jay, who served in the 407th Air Service Squadron, told me, "I think I wanted to fight [the] Japanese because of all that I read in the papers about the rape of Nanking and all these killings of civilians. I said I wanted to go to China and fight Japanese. I was born in China so naturally it's part of my heritage. I live in the United States. I don't want to see those two countries go to the Japanese. So they're sort of interlinked together."[34]

The majority of the American-born veterans I have interviewed, however, tell me that they saw themselves as "Americans first and Chinese second." Wood Moy, who was born in China and came to the United States at the age of three, always "felt more American than Chinese." As a member of the 987th Signal Company, Moy's views on going to China were slightly different from those of James Jay. Moy reported, "Even then I didn't feel that I was really Chinese in the sense of having [a] Chinese heritage and that you had to be proud of being Chinese, although I'd had that connection because my family didn't speak a lot of English. But I didn't have that urgency about defending China. I was an American soldier."[35] Others took a more pragmatic view; they simply viewed their time in the service as their duty. Harry Lim of the 407th, when asked about defending China and identifying as an American soldier, states, "Well, it's both. China will need us anyway and we had no choice where the Army sent us."[36] And Richard Gee, also of the 407th, saw a practical advantage in being sent to China: "At least we knew that with our roots, we wouldn't starve. We wouldn't be left alone. Left alone in the sense that if I'm Cantonese, I can still cope with somebody who can speak Cantonese. I knew that I would be able to survive." But his overriding sentiment was his obligation to the United States. He describes his assignment in China as simply "a sense of duty. Because I am an American in the American service as a citizen, native born; [I had] a sense of duty."[37] Although men who were stationed in China in all-Chinese-American units often had ties to San Francisco's Chinatown or had relatives in China, most of them, especially the American-born, did not feel a strong connection to China, but sought instead to reaffirm their place in America.

Whether serving in all-Chinese-American units or not, many Chinese-American military personnel simply wanted to join the military in order to serve their country and prove their loyalty. One Chinese-American soldier wrote: "The average Chinese GI Joe likes and swears by the army. The most obvious reason, of course, is the fact that every Chinese would like to participate in defeating our common enemy—the Jap. Reason Number Two is perhaps more complex, but equally important. . . . To GI Joe Wong, in the army a 'Chinaman's chance' means a fair chance, one based not on race or creed, but on the stuff of the man who wears the uniform of the U.S. Army."[38] While not all Chinese-American servicemen would report that racial antagonism was absent in the army, most saw their time in the service as worthwhile and important to the postwar social status of Chinese Americans.

Military service opened new career opportunities. Some learned skills in the military that they used after the war, and a few found the military to be their chosen career path. One such person is Thomas Lew, now a retired army colonel. Lew was born in China in 1922 and entered the United States illegally as a "paper son" in the early thirties. He came as the son of his uncle and spent two months on Angel Island before he was admitted into the country. After attending elementary school in San Francisco's Chinatown, Lew worked as a houseboy in various homes in the Bay Area while he attended high school. His aspirations at that time were to join the military and eventually to enroll in the Whampoa Academy, a military academy in China originally established by Soviet advisors to the Chinese, with Chiang Kai-shek as its first commandant and Chou En-lai as director of the political department. When the war began, Lew was eager to join the army. "From the moment the U.S. entered World War Two," he recalls, "I tried to enlist but to no avail. [I] found out later that an alien could not enlist, but could be drafted. For months I hounded the president of the San Rafael draft board [he was working as a houseboy in San Rafael at the time] until the law changed. In late 1942 [it was declared that] an alien could be drafted who was eighteen or older." Lew was drafted in November 1942. Once officially in the army, he became an American citizen; he was allowed to admit to his "paper" status and was then naturalized.

Lew became a member of the all-Chinese-American 987th Signal Company stationed in China. After the war, he was discharged, but he signed up with the Army Reserves. In June 1950, during the Korean War, he was recalled to active duty. After the war, he was offered a career in the army. His military career spanned nearly thirty years, including tours in Europe, Japan, Taiwan, and Vietnam, but perhaps his most poignant assignment came in the late fifties when he was assigned to the Presidio in San Francisco. One of his duties was to oversee the administrative communications operations on Angel Island, which was then under the jurisdiction of the army. Colonel Lew is perhaps the only former inmate of Angel Island to return to the island as an official. Coming full circle from Angel Island and back, Lew is one of those Chinese Americans who credits his time in the military with giving him the opportunity to expand his horizons, serve his country, and attain full American status.[39]

Those on the homefront found other ways to support the war effort. Chinese-American volunteer associations organized parades, dances, and parties known as Rice Bowl Parties to raise funds to send to China to help support their families and aid in relief efforts. In fact, these activities began before America entered the war. In 1940, the *Chinese News,* the successor to the *Chinese Digest,* reported, "Early contributions made by overseas Chinese to China have been in the form of direct relief funds; the purchase of Liberty Bonds; the sending of winter clothing, ambulances, and medical supplies; and support for the 'Warphan' and 'Friends of the Wounded' campaigns. During the last three years of the war, overseas Chinese contributed $180,000,000 [U.S. $54,000,000] for relief, or a monthly average of $5,000,000 [U.S. $1,500,000]. The sale of Liberty Bonds amounted to $51,150,346 [U.S. $15,345,000], while National Defense Bonds aggregated $6,265,138 [U.S. $1,880,000] and Gold Bonds, $2,915,880 [U.S. $870,000]."[40]

The Rice Bowl Parties became famous for continuing a practice that was first seen in a parade in New York on May 9, 1938. On this day, some twelve thousand Chinese Americans, seven hundred of whom came from Newark and Jersey City and hundreds more from as far away as Baltimore, Boston, Philadelphia, Wilmington, and Washington, D.C., marched three and a half miles from Mott Street in Chinatown through lower Manhattan. This parade, perhaps the largest showing of Chinese ever in this country, was held on the twenty-third anniversary of Japan's "Twenty-One Demands" on China.[41] In China, it had long been commemorated as a "day of humiliation," but this parade was organized as a "Solidarity Day," testifying that Chinese Americans from different backgrounds could come together publicly for a common cause. In Manhattan alone, it was reported that 1,500 Chinese laundries, restaurants, and shops all closed until five o'clock so that everyone could attend the event. The marchers were divided into ten divisions of a thousand people each; there were floats, dragon dances, banners, and thousands of flags.

Of pioneering significance was one division that consisted of a hundred Chinese girls in traditional dresses (the "cheong sam") carrying a forty-five-by-seventy-five-foot Chinese Nationalist flag. According to the report in the *Chinese Digest*, "without any appeal being made, spectators showered silver and currency into it, to the tune of about $300."[42] This feature of the New York City parade—large numbers of Chinese-American women in Chinese dress carrying a large Chinese flag onto which money was thrown—appears to be the prototype for a series of fundraising parades that would take place in Chinese-American communities over the next few years. According to accounts, the flag became so heavy that each parade had to be stopped three times for the flag to be emptied, and this scene was repeated across the country each time there was a parade to raise funds for China's resistance against Japan. The presence of these women, young and old, taking part in the parade and carrying the flag (which weighed three hundred pounds without the money!) symbolized "the merging of nationalism with feminism: the move of Chinese American women from the domestic into the public arena on behalf of the war effort."[43]

Aside from raising money for China and supporting the troops abroad, Chinese-American women engaged in a variety of social services that sought to support the Chinese-American community. In 1944, Dorothy Eng of Oakland, California, helped found the Chinese Young Women's Society. One of the society's activities was to provide a welcoming social space for Chinese-American servicemen passing through the area, not unlike the typical USO clubs, in response to the fear that Chinese Americans would not be welcome in the regular USO clubs. As Dorothy Eng tells it, "We were still being discriminated against even though the law [exclusion acts] had already been rescinded. It hadn't filtered down to ordinary people. Our service boys were not— well, we can't say that they weren't well received. Maybe they wouldn't be well received, but they were not going to chance it. You are not going to walk into the USO and be snubbed or be ignored. Why chance it? So unless we provided a center in each community for Chinese boys, they had no place to go, no common place to meet."[44] In addition to the hospitality they extended to Chinese-American servicemen, the Young Chinese Women's Society took the opportunity to improve their own understanding of and participation in mainstream American society. Having established this organization as an avenue for aiding the servicemen, Dorothy Eng continued,

[T]he next thing to do was to develop ourselves because we were just as wet behind the ears as the men in the service, because they were coming out of the laundries and out of grocery stores, out of the farms, out of small towns. Their social skills were just as nonexistent as ours. [We wondered] how do you conduct a tea? What do you put on the table? How do you dress? [So we made contact with] Pacific Gas and Electric [and they used to] have a homemakers division. And they would send out a homemaker to talk to various clubs and groups and tell them "Now these are finger foods and [this is] how you prepare them." They also talked about style and dress and hygiene. The whole works. It was a whole real makeover preparing us for the outside world.[45]

In another area of domestic life, Chinese-American women joined other American women in boycotting silk. Responding to the call to stop wearing silk stockings (silk was one of Japan's leading exports), Chinese-American women took up the cause and appeared in photographs wearing cotton hose with the caption, "Be in style, wear lisle."[46] In another photograph, the message was more direct: two Chinese-American sisters, Catherine and Patricia Joe, posed with one aiming a gun at the other for wanting to wear silk stockings. The Chinese characters in the background (dizhi) mean "to resist" or "to boycott," while the caption below reads "You will, will you?"[47] Realizing that using silk aided Japan the Chinese-American community wholeheartedly joined this boycott (later, when the United States entered the war, silk and nylon would be needed for parachutes, medical supplies, and other wartime necessities). Indeed, the boycott was effective enough to reduce Japan's export of silk by three-fifths in 1938, compared to the two previous years.[48]

Chinese Americans also cooperated with other ethnic Americans to demonstrate their loyalty to the United States and raise funds for the war effort. On May 16, 1943, Chinese Americans in San Francisco joined members of twenty-two other nationality groups at the Civic Center to participate in an "I Am An American Day" pageant. Under the direction of the Department of the Treasury's War Savings staff, each group sponsored a booth, some of which sold "art objects and native trinkets," while others sold coffee and refreshments. All of the proceeds would be converted into war securities. In the evening, there was a show that featured each nationality performing "folk dancing, singing, and a variety of other features that . . . illustrate[d] the cultural contribution of each group to the development and upbuilding of America."[49] By participating in such events, Chinese Americans had the opportunity to parade their ethnic heritage while demonstrating their loyalty to America.

Thus the Chinese-American community supported the war effort on three fronts. They did what they could to help China by sending money and supplies; they served the United States by sending their young to war; and they carried out a variety of activities to support the war effort at home, for both the country as a whole and for Chinese Americans in particular. As Renqiu Yu has brought to light in his research on the Chinese Hand Laundry Alliance of New York (whose wartime motto was "To Save China, To Save Ourselves"), Chinese Americans in San Francisco were participating in the war effort in ways that served to "Defend China and Claim America."[50] Florence Gee, a fifteen-year-old student in Berkeley, captured this spirit in her prize-winning essay for the *Oakland Post-Enquirer*'s fifty-dollar war bond "I Am an American" contest. Parts of her essay read, "I am an American-born Chinese. Like all American girls, I have a heroine. Mine is Madame Chiang Kai-shek who, with her husband, is behind the spirit of New China. The War has hit home. I have an uncle in the army and one in the shipyard. My sisters are members of the civilian defense. My mother is taking first aid. I belong to a club where I learn better citizenship. . . . I help my church collect money [for] the United China war relief. That which helps China helps America."[51] While the participants in the essay contest sponsored by the Ging Hawk Club in 1936 may have shown a degree of ambivalence in their feelings toward either China or America, wartime youth like Florence Gee were firmly imbued with a concern and respect for China while maintaining a clear dedication to the United States.

The politics of the Second World War also brought about important legislation that had a direct impact on Chinese Americans. In 1943, the Chinese Exclusion Acts were repealed, allowing for Chinese immigrants to apply for citizenship, and China's annual immigration quota was set at 105. While the immigration clause of the repeal was a token gesture of good faith, the mere fact that exclusion was finally lifted and that Chinese immigrants could become American citizens signaled a new era for Chinese Americans. Another act of legislation that would have a great impact on Chinese America was the 1947 amendment to the War Brides Act of 1945. The original racial restrictions of the act were removed in 1947, which allowed nearly six thousand Chinese women, accompanied by six hundred babies, to enter the country. These two bills allowed Chinese Americans, at long last, to immigrate, marry, and create families at a rate similar to their fellow Americans.[52]

Chinese Americans were fully aware that the war had changed their status in America. In San Francisco and other Chinese-American communities around the country, these changes were felt and appreciated. As one person put it,

In the 1940s for the first time Chinese were accepted by Americans as being friends because at that time, Chinese and Americans were fighting against the Japanese and the Germans and the Nazis. Therefore, all of a sudden, we became part of an American dream. We had heroes with Chiang Kai-shek and Madame Chiang Kai-shek and so on. It was just a whole different era and in the community we began to feel very good about ourselves. My own brother went into the service. We were so proud that they were in uniform. It was nice. We felt part of the society at that time. Right after the war, that was the big change.[53]

And like other servicemen returning from the war, Chinese Americans were eager to get on with their lives. They saw the chance for social mobility, especially through the use of the GI Bill of Rights. A veteran's wife reported,

During WW II, after the kids went into the service, Uncle Sam gave them the opportunity to go back to college; he paid for the college education. So that's how a lot of us were able to get out of the grocery business. My husband was able to go to college, and to learn the air-conditioning/refrigeration business. So when he got to do that, his brothers took over the store. Most of the families who have stores, their children do not go back to the stores. Now you have doctors, technicians, engineers, draftsmen, architects. So, you find that this younger generation has broken the gap between Mama and Papa stores. They go into professions and some of them have set up their own businesses and some are working for other organizations.[54]

As important as the actual opportunity for social mobility was the newfound confidence of which many of the returning Chinese-American veterans speak. A resident of San Francisco summed it up: "What wearing the uniform did was that it opened up things that gave you the confidence that you weren't going to get kicked around. So with the uniform on you felt that you had as much right as anybody else to go [wherever you wanted] or be whatever you wanted. . . . When I came back after the war I had no problem of going around and trying to get a job anywhere. I walked in as if I owned the place. Even without the uniform."[55] And another put it, "To men of my generation, World War II was the most important historic event of our times. For the first time we felt we could make it in American society."[56] While the war certainly did not bring instant racial and social equality to the Chinese-American community, it did instill a sense of confidence and belonging that would eventually take root for many postwar Chinese Americans.

Although the end of the Second World War eventually brought about a Communist victory in China and, soon after, the Korean War, during which America's relationship with China and Chinese Americans again soured, the Second World War offered Chinese Americans a number of opportunities to move into American mainstream society. These opportunities, however, should be seen as both revolutionary and evolutionary. While the postwar era has certainly not been a period of unhindered success for San Francisco's Chinese, the war did allow Chinese Americans to move slowly beyond Chinatown into the broader range of American life. As employment and residential restrictions gradually loosened during and after the war, Chinese Americans enjoyed a newfound acceptance in American society. The increase of Chinese-American men and women in professional ranks and the numbers of Chinese-American women in the public sphere were indeed significant developments for the community. The repeal of the Chinese Exclusion Act ended sixty-one years of immigration restrictions on the Chinese, but still allowed only 105 Chinese to enter the country per year. It would not be until the passage of the 1965 Immigration Act that Chinese were placed on equal footing with other aspiring immigrants. Rose Hum Lee may have overstated the case when she maintained that the war "emancipated the Chinese in the United States," but the social transformations across the country during and after the war also affected American Chinatowns in very important ways, especially San Francisco's Chinatown because of its centrality to Chinese-American culture.[57]

The war years and the accompanying social changes also contributed to the strengthening of a modern Chinese-American identity, which had emerged in the 1930s with the coming of age of the second generation. Acknowledging their familial and emotional ties to China while claiming their place in America by serving in the military and supporting the war effort at home, Chinese Americans were able to see themselves as Americans. No longer relegated by race and ethnicity to low-paying jobs, the social transformation brought on by World War II marked the opportunity for Chinese Americans to advance into the American middle class. The gradual rise in the social position of Chinese Americans during this period perhaps reveals the roots of the "model minority" image of Chinese Americans, an image that would not fully flower until the 1960s. Through the hindsight of historical inquiry, it is now evident that the war left Chinese Americans at the threshold of social mobility and increased assimilation. But in the years immediately following the war, Chinese Americans were simply happy to emerge from the shadows of exclusion.

Notes

1. *Report of the U.S. Congressisonal Joint Special Committee to Investigate Chinese Immigration,* 44th Cong., 2d Sess. Senate Report 689 (Washington, D.C., 1877), v.

2. For a history of Angel Island, see Him Mark Lai, Genny Lim, and Judy Yung, *Island: Poetry and History of Chinese Immigrants on Angel Island, 1910–1940* (rpt., Seattle, 1991). The term "paper sons" comes from the practice of creating fictional sons in China after the 1906 earthquake which destroyed immigration records in San Francisco. Chinese immigrants would claim to have been born in the United States and to have fathered sons in China. They would then sell documents or papers which would

create the lives and identities of these children. Once purchased, the "paper son" would memorize his "paper life" and then attempt to enter the country posing as a citizen or a child of a citizen. The validity of the "son's" story was determined by a series of tedious interviews, hence the long detentions on Angel Island. Two recent studies of Angel Island and the "paper son" system are Madeline Yuan-yin Hsu, "'Living Abroad and Faring Well': Migration and Transnationalism in Taishan County, Guongdong, 1904–1939" (Ph.D. diss., Yale University, 1996), and Erika Lee, "At America's Gate: Chinese Immigration during the Exclusion Era, 1882–1943" (Ph.D. diss., University of California at Berkeley, 1998).

3. Ivan Light, "From Vice District to Tourist Attraction: The Moral Career of American Chinatowns, 1880–1940," *Pacific Historical Review* 43:3 (Aug. 1974): 367–94.

4. In terms of population, there were 17,782 Chinese living in San Francisco in 1940 and 12,753 living in New York City. In contrast, there were only 4,736 Chinese living in Los Angeles in 1940. See *Sixteenth Census of the United States, 1940*. vol. 2: *Characteristics of the Nonwhite Population by Race* (Washington, D.C., 1943), 91.

5. For studies on the effects of the exclusion of Chinese women on the development of Chinese-American families, see Sucheng Chang, "The Exclusion of Chinese Women, 1870–1943," in *Entry Denied: Exclusion and the Chinese Community, 1882–1943*, ed. Sucheng Chan (Philadelphia, 1991), 94–146; and George Anthony Peffer, "Forbidden Families: Emigration Experiences of Chinese Women under the Page Law, 1875–1882," *Journal of American Ethnic History* 6 (1986): 28–46. For information on anti-miscegenation laws, see Megumi Dick Osumi, "Asians and California's Anti-Miscegenation Laws," in *Asian and Pacific American Experiences: Women's Perspectives*, ed. Nobuya Tsuchida (Minneapolis, 1982), 1–37.

6. The native-born Chinese-American population of the United States in 1900 was 5,621. By 1930 it was 17,320 and by 1940 it had reached 22,880. See *Sixteenth Census of the United States, 1940*, 2:516.

7. Robert Dunn, "Does My Future Lie in China or America?" *Chinese Digest*, 15 May 1936, 3.

8. Ibid., 13.

9. Kaye Hong, "Does My Future Lie in China or America?" *Chinese Digest*, 22 May 1936, 3.

10. Ibid.

11. Brief accounts of these two essayists can be found in Thomas W. Chinn, *Bridging the Pacific: San Francisco Chinatown and Its People* (San Francisco, 1989), 143–44.

12. The history of Chinn's involvement with the *Chinese Digest* can be found in Chinn, *Bridging the Pacific*, 144–47, and "A Historian's Reflections on Chinese-American Life in San Francisco, 1919–1991," Regional Oral History Office, Bancroft Library, University of California at Berkeley, 1993, 98–99. For a brief study of the significance of the *Chinese Digest* in Chinese American history, see Julie Shuk-yee Lam, "The *Chinese Digest*, 1935 to 1940," in *Chinese America: History and Perspectives, 1987* (San Francisco, 1987), 118–135.

13. Chinn, *Bridging the Pacific*, 225–26.

14. Thomas W. Chinn, interview by the author, 6 June 1995.

15. Quoted in Victor G. De Bary Nee and Brett De Bary Nee, *Longtime Californ': A Documentary Study of an American Chinatown* (New York, 1972), 152.

16. *Chinese Digest,* 15 Nov. 1935, 8.

17. Ibid., 22 Nov. 1935, 8.

18. Harvey Wong, interview by the author, 25 Aug. 1993.

19. *Chinese Digest,* 22 Nov. 1935, 8.

20. For a study of how the images of Chinatown are manipulated for a variety of political agendas, see K. Scott Wong, "Chinatown: Conflicting Images, Contested Terrain," *MELUS* 20:1 (Spring 1995): 3–15.

21. Despite the wartime animosities between Chinese and Japanese, and the encroachment of Japanese-American businesses into Chinatown, there was hardly any coverage of the internment of Japanese Americans in the English-language Chinatown periodicals.

22. While there is not yet an in-depth study of these shifts in wartime images of both Chinese and Chinese Americans, two useful studies are Harold R. Isaacs, *Scratches on Our Minds: American Views of China and India* (rpt., Armonk, N.Y., 1980), and Patricia Neils, *China Images in the Life and Times of Henry Luce* (Savage, Md., 1990).

23. Rose Hum Lee, "Chinese in the United States Today: The War Has Changed Their Lives," *Survey Graphic* 31:10 (Oct. 1942): 444.

24. Diana Mei Lin Mark and Ginger Chih, *A Place Called Chinese America* (Dubuque, Iowa, 1982), 97.

25. Xiaojian Zhao, "Chinese American Women Defense Workers in World War II," *California History* 73 (Summer 1996): 139.

26. For information on the WASPs, see Vera S. Williams, *WASPs: Women Airforce Service Pilots of Word War II* (Osceola, Wis., 1994).

27. Judy Yung, *Unbound Feet: A Social History of Chinese Women in San Francisco* (Berkeley, Calif., 1995), 224.

28. All employment statistics in this chapter are taken from the *Sixteenth Census of the United States, 1940,* vol. 2:47, and the *Seventeenth Census of the United States, 1950,* vol. 2: *Nonwhite Population by Race* (Washington, D.C., 1952), 3B-19.

29. Lee, "Chinese in the United States Today," 444; *Chinese Press,* 29 May 1942, 1.

30. *Chinese Press,* 24 Jan. 1941, 3.

31. The Flying Tigers were initially known as the American Volunteer Group. In 1940, President Roosevelt approved their formation as a covert American air force whose mission was to defend China. When the United States entered the war and the Fourteenth Air Force was assigned to the China-Burma-India theater, they took on the general name "Flying Tigers." For a history of the Flying Tigers, see Daniel Ford, *Flying Tigers: Claire Chennault and the American Volunteer Group* (Washington, D.C., 1991). The individual units which made up the 14th ASG were Hqs. and Hqs. Sq., 407th Air Service Sq., 555th Air Service Sq., 1157th Sig. Co., 1544th Ord. Co., 1545th Ord. Co., 1077th QM Co., 2121st QM Trk. Co., and the 2122nd QM Trk. Co.

32. The order to create these all-Chinese-American units can be found in a restrict-

ed letter from the War Department dated 16 February 1944 (AG 322) to the commanding general of the Air Service Command. No reason for this action is stated. The notion that they were created to enhance relations with the local population has been related to me in a number of oral history interviews.

33. *14th Air Service Group History,* 1 Sept. 1944–30 Apr. 1945, microfilm from the Department of the Air Force, Air Force Historical Research Agency, roll B0804, frame 1328, Maxwell Air Force Base, Ala.

34. James Jay, interview by the author, 21 Aug. 1992.

35. Wood Moy, interview by the author, 24 Aug. 1993.

36. Harry Lim, interview by the author, 4 June 1995.

37. Richard Gee, interview by the author, 22 Aug. 1993.

38. Charles Leong in *Buckley Armorer,* 4 Feb. 1944, 1, 4.

39. The information on Thomas Lew is taken from an interview by the author, 21 Aug. 1992, and correspondence with the author, 3 Mar. 1996.

40. *Chinese News,* 1 Oct. 1940, 7.

41. In 1915, Japan made a series of demands on China in an imperialistic grab for control over China's internal affairs. The demands were divided into five groups: recognition of Japan's position in Shandong; a special position for Japan in Manchuria and Inner Mongolia; joint operation of China's iron and steel industries; nonalienation of coastal areas to any third power; and control by Japan of China's several important domestic administrations. Although Chinese President Yuan Shikai accepted these terms, the Chinese people protested, and there was an upsurge of Chinese nationalism. Thereafter, the Twenty-One Demands became a symbol of China's humiliation and the need for resistance against the great powers. For details, see Immanuel Hsu, *The Rise of Modern China* (New York, 1970), 582–83.

42. *Chinese Digest,* June 1938, 9.

43. Yung, *Unbound Feet,* 240.

44. Dorothy Eng, interview by the author, 9 June 1995.

45. Ibid.

46. *Chinese Digest,* Jan. 1938, 9.

47. *Chinese Digest,* Feb. 1939, 7.

48. Yung, *Unbound Feet,* 238.

49. *Chinese News,* 15 May 1942, 3

50. See Renqiu Yu, *To Save China, to Save Ourselves: The Chinese Hand Laundry Alliance of New York* (Philadelphia, 1992).

51. *Chinese News,* 15 May 1942, 3.

52. Rose Hum Lee, *The Chinese in the United States of America* (Hong Kong, 1960), 201.

53. Mark and Chih, *Place Called Chinese America,* 97–98.

54. Ibid., 100.

55. Wood Moy, interview by the author, 24 Aug. 1993.

56. Charlie Leong quoted in De Bary Nee and De Bary Nee, *Longtime Californ',* 154.

57. Lee, "Chinese in the United States Today," 444.

9

"Brothers under the Skin"?
African Americans, Mexican Americans,
and World War II in California

Kevin Allen Leonard

When Carey McWilliams moved from Colorado to Los Angeles in 1922, he probably noticed the sizable Mexican-American, Japanese-American, and African-American communities in the Southern California metropolis. By the late 1930s, the exploitation of Asian and Mexican immigrants in U.S. agriculture had captured his attention.[1] World War II led McWilliams to think that racial and ethnic discrimination was the most pressing problem in the United States. In *Brothers under the Skin*, published eighteen months after the Japanese attack on Pearl Harbor, McWilliams criticizes earlier authors who had written about race relations. These scholars had "failed to correlate the Negro problem . . . with the Chinese problem, the Mexican problem, the Filipino problem. When such a correlation is made, it poses the issues in a more understandable fashion."[2]

Brothers under the Skin does not actually correlate the various "racial problems" that McWilliams had identified. Instead, it juxtaposes descriptions of a number of ethnic groups. Each chapter depicts the history of one American minority group—American Indians, Chinese Americans, Mexican Americans, Japanese Americans, Puerto Ricans "and other Islanders," Filipino Americans, and African Americans. One chapter examines the "ethnic laboratory" known as the Territory of Hawaii. In the conclusion, McWilliams asserts that the sociologist Robert L. Sutherland's argument about the "Negro problem" could apply to all racialized groups. Sutherland had said that "the Negro problem is a race problem not in the sense that a purity of Negroid traits has given the American colored person a unique biological nature which makes him behave differently from white people, but rather in that being all or any part Negroid in appearance (the biological fact) has given him a condition of 'high visibility' which enables others to identify him and place him in a special position in society (the sociological fact)."[3] McWilliams insists that the war had made the "race problem" more acute: "Now is not only the opportune time to liquidate the last vestiges of this system [segregation] in America, but we *must* proceed to do so if the critical tensions already developing are not to explode."[4] The "outline for action" at the end of the book calls for the federal government to take affirmative action to end discrimination based on "race, color, creed, or national origin." This action would include the enforcement of existing laws, the passage of a new civil rights bill, and the elimination of the poll tax.[5]

More than any other widely read author of his time, McWilliams recognized that the United States, and especially California, was a multicultural society. Most authors before and since McWilliams have described ethnic and race relations in California from what can be called a "binary perspective," focusing on only two groups of people within the state, such as African Americans and white people, or Mexican Americans and Anglo Americans. Rarely do scholars or nonacademic authors concede that the identities and experiences of African Americans, for example, were influenced by the presence of large Mexican-American and Asian-American communities in adjacent neighborhoods.

This essay seeks to draw attention to Carey McWilliams's insights into California's multiracial or multicultural character. It also attempts to analyze critically McWilliams's interpretation of the Second World War's impact on race relations in California. This essay will briefly explore the experiences of people from two different communities—African Americans and Mexican Americans—to suggest how historians might move beyond a binary model of race relations. The essay begins with an examination of conditions in California prior to World War II. In this examination, I will try to determine if African Americans and Mexican Americans in California would have agreed with McWilliams. Did members of these communities see themselves as "brothers under the skin"? Did racial or ethnic boundaries separate them from each other? If so, did they interact across these racial or ethnic boundaries? The essay then assesses the war's impact on these communities. Did the war make it easier for African Americans and Mexican Americans to recognize similarities among their experiences? Finally, the essay will weigh evidence suggesting that community leaders did recognize similarities among African Americans and Mexican Americans and tried to use these similarities to gain political power.

Even before Pearl Harbor, conditions in many California communities brought African Americans and Mexican Americans into close contact. A small number of African Americans and Mexican Americans lived in the San Francisco Bay Area in 1940. Census takers in 1940 counted fewer than 5,000 African Americans in San Francisco; this was slightly smaller than the number of Japanese Americans in the city. The greatest concentration of African

Americans lived in the Western Addition, a compact neighborhood west of downtown. Much of the city's small Japanese-American population lived nearby in Japantown.[6] It is difficult to estimate how many Mexican Americans lived in the city in 1940 because census counts of the "Mexican-stock" population have been notoriously unreliable. The fear of anti-Mexican sentiment in the 1930s probably led some Mexican immigrants and Mexican-American citizens to avoid census takers.[7] Census takers did, however, count nearly 5,000 Mexican immigrants in San Francisco in that year. Mexican immigrants often lived among U.S. citizens of Mexican ancestry. More than 8,000 African Americans and about 1,500 Mexican immigrants lived across the bay in Oakland. African Americans, Mexican Americans, and immigrants from a number of European cultures lived together in East Bay neighborhoods such as West Oakland and North Richmond.[8]

The small size of the African-American communities in the Bay Area made it difficult for African Americans to occupy a largely homogeneous, mostly black world. Similarly, the small size of Mexican-American communities in the region made it difficult for Mexican Americans to occupy a homogeneous Mexican-American world. Since African Americans often lived near Asian Americans and Mexican Americans, interaction between them was common. Likewise, Mexican Americans in the Bay Area often had contact with Asian Americans and African Americans. Cultural differences may have led to some misunderstandings and tensions, but residents of West Oakland and North Richmond remember that interaction across ethnic borders sometimes caused such boundaries to blur. In these neighborhoods, for example, young men from a variety of cultural backgrounds played basketball together, and some African Americans learned to speak Spanish.[9]

Because of the size of the African-American, Mexican-American, and Asian-American populations in Los Angeles, the kind of social interaction that occurred in the East Bay was less likely in Southern California. The existence of a large African-American community in Los Angeles made it possible for some African Americans to live in neighborhoods in which most of their neighbors were African Americans, to shop in stores managed by African Americans and frequented by African Americans, and to work in businesses operated by African Americans. The same was true for some Mexican Americans and Japanese Americans.

Nearly 64,000 African Americans lived in the city of Los Angeles in 1940, and another 11,000 African Americans lived outside the city limits in the metropolitan area. About half of the city's black population lived on the "East Side," which straddled Central Avenue for several miles south of downtown. Several thousand African Americans inhabited the semirural area known as Watts, at the southern end of the East Side. Many middle-class African Americans lived on the "Westside," which was bounded, in 1940, by Arlington Avenue on the west, Santa Barbara Boulevard on the south, and Tenth Street on the north. The eastern boundary of this neighborhood was not clearly defined.[10] Other African Americans lived throughout the city.

On its northern end, the East Side abutted Little Tokyo, the business and residential heart of the Japanese-American community. Little Tokyo was bounded by Aliso Street on the north, Los Angeles Street to the west, Sixth Street to the south, and Alameda Street to the east.[11] More than 23,000 Japanese Americans lived in the city of Los Angeles in 1940, but less than a third lived in Little Tokyo. The remainder were scattered throughout the city, often in close proximity to African Americans, as in the Evergreen section of East Los Angeles, or near immigrants from Europe, as in the Exposition Park area near the University of Southern California. Another 15,000 Japanese Americans lived outside the city but within the metropolitan area, often congregating in small fishing communities, such as that on Terminal Island in the Los Angeles Harbor, or in agricultural communities, such as that near Gardena, southwest of downtown Los Angeles.[12]

Census takers counted 219,000 people of Mexican ancestry in the Los Angeles area in 1940. Of these, nearly 65,000 were Mexican immigrants. Some have argued that the Census Bureau seriously undercounted the number of Mexican Americans in Southern California, suggesting that the total of 219,000 should be viewed as a conservative estimate.[13] Though tens of thousands of Mexican Americans were concentrated in Boyle Heights, Belvedere, and East Los Angeles, many did not live in exclusively Mexican-American neighborhoods. As the historian George J. Sánchez has concluded, "In almost every section of Los Angeles where Mexicans lived, they shared neighborhoods with other ethnic groups."[14]

Although the size of these ethnic communities may have allowed people to operate in entirely African-American or Mexican-American worlds, people from different ethnic communities encountered each other every day. Many lived in mixed neighborhoods such as the Evergreen district, Boyle Heights, and "Los Angeles southwest." Japanese Americans, Mexican Americans, and African Americans began moving into "Los Angeles southwest" about 1940, as race restrictions on the property expired.[15] Daily activities, such as shopping, brought people into contact with others from different communities. One Japanese-American couple, Tsuma and Jisakichi Ichimura, for example, had operated the Pioneer Grocery in East Los Angeles since 1924. Their customers included Anglo Americans, African Americans, and Mexican Americans.[16]

Many African Americans and Mexican Americans in California in 1940, then, lived near each other and encountered each other in shops and other businesses. Often, however, they did not work in the same places. This lack of sustained contact outside the neighborhood may have hindered communication across apparent ethnic boundaries. Mexican Americans and African Americans may have worked together in low-wage jobs in some industries. In both the Bay Area and Southern California, however, African Americans and Mexican Americans tended to occupy distinct niches within the economy. Many Mexican Americans, for example, worked as laborers on the truck farms within or near urban areas; many worked in the related field of food processing. The historian Vicki L. Ruiz has concluded that canneries, which hired large numbers of Mexican immigrants and Mexican Americans, did not hire African Americans until World War II.[17] African-American women found themselves excluded from most industrial jobs until the war; they most frequently worked as domestics in the homes of white women. African-American men and women were also denied well-paying jobs in the aircraft and shipbuilding industries. When the President's Committee on Fair Employment Practice held hearings in Los Angeles in October 1941, it uncovered evidence of widespread discrimination against African Americans by military contractors. Douglas Aircraft employed 33,000 people, among them 10 African Americans; Bethlehem Shipbuilding employed 2,880 people, but only 2 African Americans; North American Aviation, 12,500 employees, 8 of them African Americans; Lockheed-Vega, 48,000 employees, 54 of them African Americans. Several corporations did not discriminate against Mexican Americans to the extent that they did against African Americans. The Douglas Aircraft representative, for example, said that his company employed "a large number of Mexicans." Nearly one-tenth of Bethlehem Shipbuilding's employees were Mexican Americans.[18] These figures suggest that African Americans and Mexican Americans rarely worked alongside one another in Los Angeles.

Prior to the war, residential patterns in most California cities allowed African Americans and Mexican Americans to recognize the similarities between their groups, while employment patterns often discouraged African Americans, Mexican Americans, and Asian Americans from recognizing similarities among their experiences. These conditions undoubtedly influenced ethnic identity. To be a "Negro" in Oakland, for example, meant something different from what it meant to be a "Negro" in Philadelphia, Mississippi, or in Philadelphia, Pennsylvania. To be a Mexican American in Los Angeles meant something different from what it meant to be a Mexican American in Trinidad, Colorado, or in San Antonio, Texas.

The Japanese attack on Pearl Harbor and the movement of African Americans and Mexican Americans into California's urban areas reversed patterns of interaction across ethnic boundaries. African Americans benefited from the general labor shortage. Within a year after Pearl Harbor, thousands of African Americans had found jobs in aircraft factories, shipyards, and other war plants. At the height of employment in war industries, more than 15,000 African Americans worked in Bay Area shipyards.[19] According to the War Manpower Commission, by February 1943 Douglas Aircraft had 2,200 black employees, North American employed 2,500, and Lockheed-Vega employed 1,700. Two other aircraft manufacturers, Vultee and Consolidated, accounted for another 800 African-American workers. Among shipbuilders, California Shipbuilding (Calship) reported 1,200 black employees; Western Pipe and Steel, 400; Bethlehem, 300; Consolidated, 300; Los Angeles Drydock, 200; and Haagson, 150.[20] In 1945, one African-American leader estimated that 85 percent of African-American workers in Los Angeles were employed in war industries, primarily aircraft and ship production.[21] Mexican Americans also filled thousands of openings in war industries. By 1944, 10 to 15 percent of Lockheed's employees were Mexican-American; the California Shipbuilding Corporation alone employed nearly 1,300 Mexican Americans.[22] These numbers do not prove that any African Americans and Mexican Americans discussed their experiences during coffee breaks and recognized similarities among those experiences. In fact many employers tried to segregate African Americans into all-black crews.[23] They do suggest, however, that the potential for communication across ethnic boundaries in the workplace increased during the war.[24]

If the labor shortage brought together African Americans and Mexican Americans on the production line, it also attracted tens of thousands of African Americans and Mexican Americans to California. This population growth may have served to divide people. San Francisco's black population grew from under 5,000 in 1940 to 32,000 in 1945.[25] The number of African Americans living in Oakland grew from 8,000 in 1940 to nearly 22,000 in 1944. In Richmond, the black population went from 270 in 1940 to more than 5,000 in 1944.[26] As communities grew, the integrated neighborhoods in places such as West Oakland and North Richmond may have been displaced by communities defined more clearly by race or ethnicity. In larger African-American communities, it may have been easier for people to isolate themselves from outsiders. A similar process may have occurred in Southern California. Not all of the mixed neighborhoods of the prewar years became "ghettoes" or "barrios," however. In October 1944, for example, a white journalist reported, "I have lived for more than two months now in a racially mixed neighborhood which is preponderantly Negro, with many Mexicans and a few Chinese and whites."[27] In general, the war increased the percentages of African Americans or Mexican Americans in previously mixed neighborhoods.

If Mexican Americans and African Americans increasingly worked in the same factories but went home to separate neighborhoods, members of these communities may not have begun to recognize similarities among their experiences. Shared work experiences and contact on a daily basis in integrated neighborhoods, however, were not the only ways in which African Americans and Mexican Americans could come to see that they faced similar struggles. Leaders who encouraged people to notice similarities among groups also promoted changes in patterns of interaction among African Americans and Mexican Americans. Before the United States entered World War II, both Charlotta Bass and Floyd Covington had begun to recognize the potential for political cooperation among African Americans, Mexican Americans, and Asian Americans in Los Angeles.

Bass, born Charlotta Spears in South Carolina, moved to Los Angeles from Rhode Island in 1910. Two years later she assumed operation of the *California Eagle*, the West's oldest black newspaper. Soon afterward, she married Joseph Bass, who edited the *Eagle* until his death in 1934. After her husband's death, Charlotta Bass edited the newspaper. Throughout her career, Bass fought for the civil rights of African Americans and against prejudice and discrimination.[28] In the 1930s, Bass began to compare African Americans in Los Angeles to the city's other ethnic communities. In a 1939 radio broadcast, Bass explained that "the economic advancement of L.A.'s Orientals is made possible only through their remarkable sameness of thought and action and is at this time a rank impossibility for Negroes."[29] Although Bass's radio address perpetuated stereotypes about Japanese Americans, Chinese Americans, Korean Americans, and African Americans, it represents an important effort to compare the experiences of two of Los Angeles's ethnic communities.

Covington was born in Denver in 1901, and he graduated from Washburn University in Topeka in 1927. He began serving as the executive director of the Los Angeles Urban League in 1928. By the late 1930s, Covington began to notice similarities among African Americans and Mexican Americans, and he attempted to serve both communities. He chaired a session at the first meeting of El Congreso de Pueblos que Hablan Español, the Spanish-Speaking People's Congress, in April 1939.[30] In his capacity as executive director of the Urban League, Covington presided over the collection and analysis of information about the city's black community in 1940. This effort to gather information was part of the Carnegie Foundation's study of black-white relations that culminated in the publication of Gunnar Myrdal's *American Dilemma*. After Covington surveyed the data collected for the study, he concluded, "There is the possibility of working toward a tri-minority relationship, comprising Mexicans, Orientals, and Negroes. These groups are very largely shunted together in the twilight zone areas and the problems of each parallel, although they are not identical."[31]

Some leaders and organizers in the Mexican-American community, most notably Josefina Fierro de Bright, also recognized some of the similarities among ethnic communities in Los Angeles. Fierro was born in Mexicali in 1920 and grew up in Los Angeles and Madera, in California's Central Valley. She returned to Los Angeles in 1938 to attend UCLA, but she left school to marry the screenwriter John Bright. Fierro became a tireless organizer for El Congreso. Because she spoke English as well as Spanish, she became the leading liaison between El Congreso and organizations outside the Mexican-American community. "I went speaking at least three times a week . . . to raise money with the League of Women Voters, B'nai B'rith, the Negro places, the Jewish clubs, everywhere I could get in and tell them the position of the Mexican people in California," Fierro recalled.[32]

Pearl Harbor and the subsequent incarceration of Japanese Americans had a dramatic effect on some of these community leaders. Many recognized that if Japanese Americans could be imprisoned solely on the basis of their ancestry, other groups might face similar persecution. "If native-born Americans, of Asiatic descent, can be denied all civil rights and civil liberties, what about Americans of African descent?" asked an editorial in *The Crisis,* the NAACP's national organ.[33] After Pearl Harbor, some ethnic-community leaders worked even more diligently to make their communities aware of the similarities among the different ethnic groups. Some of these leaders formed new organizations to address the concerns of several groups. In early 1942, for example, activists from ethnic communities in a number of cities formed the Bay Area Council against Discrimination. The council hoped to attract leaders from various ethnic communities; most of its members, however, were African-American or white. The council worked to end a number of discriminatory practices.[34] In early 1943, it proposed six pieces of legislation, "aimed at the major problems in the field of racial, religious and nationality discrimination." Three of these bills would have outlawed discrimination by local housing authorities, insurance companies, employers, and unions. The remaining three would have repealed the Alien Land Law, which prevented Asian immigrants from owning or leasing land, strengthened the Civil Rights Act, which prohibited discrimination in public accommodations, and outlawed "restrictive covenants," which prevented members of certain ethnic groups from buying or leasing property in many California neighborhoods. The council negotiated with some employers who were accused of discriminatory practices, and it produced colorful

"United for Victory" posters that were displayed in streetcars in San Francisco and in the East Bay.[35]

Other leaders tried to move existing organizations in new directions. In 1942, Covington, the executive director of the Los Angeles Urban League, suggested that "in the light of world events and changes the League should include in either—or both—its active and advisory board representatives of the Spanish-speaking, Hindu, Chinese, and African people"[36] To some extent, Covington acted on his words. The Urban League, he reported, "championed the cause of Negroes, Mexicans, and Orientals at the seat of our local trade school urging this institution to let them in," and it lobbied the Douglas Aircraft Company "to employ Negro-, Mexican-, and Japanese-Americans."[37]

A series of events in California assisted these community leaders in their efforts to awaken their constituents to the similarity of their problems. In the summer of 1942, the so-called Sleepy Lagoon case captured the attention of many people throughout California. On the morning of August 2, 1942, the body of Jose Díaz was found along a road near a swimming hole known as Sleepy Lagoon. Detectives from the Los Angeles County Sheriff's Department concluded that Díaz had been murdered. They arrested twenty-four young men, all but one of them Mexican Americans, who had been involved in a fight at a party the previous night. The twenty-four men were charged with murder; twenty-two of them were tried in a single trial. Twelve were convicted of murder, five were convicted of assault, and the other five were acquitted. Three of the twelve men convicted of murder received life sentences. The other nine were sentenced to five years to life. The five who were found guilty of assault were sentenced to one year in the county jail.[38]

The conduct of the trial enraged many people around the state, for the judge made a number of prejudicial statements to the jury and committed procedural errors. Shortly after the trial began, La Rue McCormick, a candidate for the state senate, organized a meeting for prominent individuals who were concerned about the prejudices of the judge and the prosecuting attorney. These individuals, including the labor organizer Bert Corona, Phil "Slim" Connelly, president of the state CIO, the actor Anthony Quinn, and Josefina Fierro de Bright, formed the Citizens' Committee for the Defense of Mexican-American Youth.[39] Although most members of the Citizens' Committee were Mexican Americans or Anglo Americans, some African Americans supported the committee and its successor, the Sleepy Lagoon Defense Committee. African-American celebrities Hattie McDaniel and Lena Horne attended a buffet to raise funds for the committee and signed their names to a statement that read, "We are here to help you boys, victims of fascist racial incitement, win justice through an appeal and to register our opposition to all forms of racial prejudice, discrimination and bigotry."[40] Charlotta Bass wrote a letter on behalf of the so-called Sleepy Lagoon boys to the state's parole board.[41] Augustus Hawkins, the African-American member of the California State Assembly from Los Angeles, told the committee that he would cooperate in the effort to exonerate the Sleepy Lagoon defendants and asked "that my name be used in any way to support the Citizens' Committee."[42] In its attempts to finance the appeal and recruit individuals to sign petitions, the committee asserted that there was little difference between Mexican Americans and African Americans. A letter asking for a signature on a petition said, "Your action will help guarantee that terror against Mexicans, Negroes, Jews or other minorities will not be tolerated by the overwhelming majority of the win-the-war people of this country." This letter was signed by Orson Welles, Phil Connelly, and Carey McWilliams.[43] As these examples suggest, some African-American community leaders and activists did not see much difference between discrimination against African Americans and the discrimination against the Mexican-American Sleepy Lagoon defendants.[44]

The Sleepy Lagoon case captured the attention of activists throughout California. The Bay Area Council against Discrimination produced a pamphlet about the Sleepy Lagoon trial. The council distributed a typewritten copy of the pamphlet to its members, and it sent printed copies to more than one thousand individuals and organizations around the Bay Area in March 1944.[45]

Although a number of leaders, including those motivated by the Sleepy Lagoon case, had attempted to inspire cooperation among African Americans and Mexican Americans in both the Bay Area and in Southern California, many African Americans and Mexican Americans did not recognize the urgency of the situation until rioting occurred in Los Angeles in 1943. The reasons for the outbreak of racial violence in Los Angeles were undoubtedly complex, and historians have not agreed about the events that preceded the riots. Gerald D. Nash has argued that Mexican-American "zoot-suiters" insulted soldiers and sailors, threw rocks at them, and engaged in even more violent assaults upon them in the months before the riots. Nash's evidence, however, comes primarily from a single military report produced after the riots.[46] Mauricio Mazón, on the other hand, has pointed out that the few scrapes between zoot-suiters and soldiers or sailors were not serious, whereas confrontations between military personnel and other civilians frequently resulted in serious injuries or deaths. Mazón suggests that the riots represent the response of soldiers and sailors to the psychological stress of military service.[47] When describing the riots, both Nash and Mazón rely on information from the *Los Angeles Times* and from Carey McWilliams's *North from Mexico*. According to this information, over several nights in early June, mobs of sailors, soldiers, and civilians roamed the streets of downtown and East Los Angeles, beating young Mexican-American and African-American men, many of whom wore zoot suits. The violence against zoot-suiters spread throughout the metropolitan area. Once military authorities prohibited sailors and soldiers from leaving their bases, the rioting ceased.[48]

Many Anglo Americans argued that soldiers, sailors, and civilians who attacked zoot-suiters were simply helping to wipe out juvenile delinquency. One Los Angeles County supervisor even said, "[A]ll that is needed to end lawlessness is more of the same kind of action as is being exercised by the servicemen."[49] Many Mexican Americans and African Americans, however, insisted that the violence was racially motivated. Black novelist Chester Himes, for example, told readers of The Crisis that the Zoot-Suit Riots were race riots. "What could make the white people more happy than to see their uniformed sons sapping up some dark-skinned people?" Himes asked rhetorically. "It proved beyond all doubt the bravery of white servicemen, their gallantry. Los Angeles was at last being made safe for white people—to do as they damned well pleased."[50] A number of individuals and organizations, including the Los Angeles branch and the national officers of the NAACP, sent telegrams to elected officials asking for a full investigation of the riots. The leaders of these organizations believed that a recurrence of rioting was likely, and they looked to federal and state officials to prevent new outbreaks of violence.[51]

State and federal officials refused to sponsor an open investigation of the riots, and they moved slowly to prevent the recurrence of rioting. Governor Earl Warren did appoint a committee to investigate the Zoot-Suit Riots.[52] The committee urged Warren to meet with law enforcement officials in Los Angeles to discuss the riots, and it encouraged the governor to use his influence with the press to ensure that "incidents may be properly reported and that no undue emphasis be placed on the part played in such disturbances by minority groups." Finally, the committee recommended that Warren create "an interracial committee composed of community leaders and having representatives from the Chamber of Commerce, A.F.L., C.I.O., Church, Social Agencies, and all minority groups." The interracial committee would attempt to address the housing shortage, restrictive covenants, and racial discrimination. "The situation on the East side, where Los Angeles has the largest concentration of persons of Mexican and Negro ancestry, is a potential powder keg," the governor's appointees concluded, "and the inter-racial committee, if quickly established, could do much to relieve this dangerous situation."[53]

Warren ignored the recommendations of his investigative committee. As a result, Mexican Americans and African Americans in Los Angeles took action. The Los Angeles Urban League insisted that the riots had increased the urgency of its program. Urban League leaders tried to convince the African-American and Mexican-American communities that they should look to the League's Leadership Round Table for advice and guidance. The Round Table brought together leaders from various black organizations to discuss the problems of the community.[54] After the riots, the Round Table expanded its membership to include all minority group leaders. As many as eighty people attended the Round Table's meetings. By 1944, the Round Table had "become a center where problems of an interracial character can be freely discussed by a very representative group of people," according to one observer.[55]

Mexican Americans and African Americans also joined white liberals to create the Council for Civic Unity. According to its chairman, the council "was formed to bring together organizations and leaders from all sections of the community, so that they might solve their problems together, and so achieve the greatest degree of unity behind the war effort."[56] Member organizations included the Hollywood Women's Council, the Commission on Race Relations of the Church Federation of Los Angeles, the Women's Division of the American Jewish Congress, a number of labor unions, the NAACP, the League of United Latin-American Citizens, and several African-American churches.[57]

Civil rights activists also pressed Los Angeles Mayor Fletcher Bowron to appoint an interracial committee. Bowron finally appointed the Committee on Home Front Unity in early 1944. Because this committee was an expanded version of a previously all-African-American committee, it was primarily interested in the problems of African Americans. The committee's original members included six African Americans, two Jewish community leaders, one Mexican American, a representative of business interests, and two Christian religious leaders.[58]

Concerns about the possibility of more riots did not end at the Los Angeles city limits. The Los Angeles County Board of Supervisors, urged on by liberal Supervisor John Anson Ford, created the County Committee for Interracial Progress in January 1944.[59] The supervisors appointed twenty-three people to the committee. Nine of the original members were county employees, and the remaining fourteen represented women's clubs, the Chamber of Commerce, the American Legion, Protestant and Catholic churches, the CIO, the Jewish Community Council, the Mexican-American community, and the NAACP.[60]

The Council for Civic Unity, the mayor's Committee on Home Front Unity, and the County Committee for Interracial Progress did not satisfy all leaders of Los Angeles's ethnic communities. Mexican Americans, for example, feared that their concerns would be overshadowed by problems associated with the influx of African Americans into Southern California. Nor did the committees solve the problems of discrimination and racial tension in Los Angeles. They did, however, create spaces in which people from several different communities could come together, talk with each other, and listen to the concerns of people whom they might otherwise have ignored.

The Zoot-Suit Riots aroused concern in many parts of California. After the riots, the Bay Area Council against Discrimination issued statements that condemned interracial violence and suggested to Bay Area newspaper publishers that they not identify crime suspects by race. The council also convinced the city's Board of Supervisors to investigate the extent of discrimination against San Francisco's minority groups. The supervisors held hearings at the end of June, in early July, and again in August. The Bay Area Council against Discrimination helped the board locate witnesses for these hearings. On September 27, 1943, the Board of Supervisors unanimously approved a plan for the prevention of racial violence in San Francisco.[61] This plan created a number of committees that would work with city departments to alter the ways in which those departments treated minority group members, especially African Americans.[62] Later reports, however, indicate that the Board of Supervisors moved slowly in appointing these committees and in implementing the plan that they had approved.[63] After the riots, the Bay Area Council against Discrimination was joined by a number of other interracial committees similar to those in Los Angeles. In December 1943, for example, the Berkeley Interracial Committee affiliated with the council.[64] A Council for Civic Unity was established in the San Francisco Bay Area in 1944.[65] African Americans and white liberals dominated the Bay Area's Council for Civic Unity. Throughout California, most of the members of interracial committees and councils represented the middle-class stratum of their communities.

As this movement toward interracial cooperation among middle-class African Americans and Mexican Americans accelerated during 1944, some leaders tried to convince working-class members of these communities that they shared common concerns. The Los Angeles Council for Civic Unity, for example, designed "a series of six 'National' evenings intended to sugar-coat the educational pill with a liberal portion of entertainment." Each of these evenings focused on a single "national" group ("Negro, Mexican, Jewish, Middle European, Oakies, Arkies, Americans All") and offered "two hours of motion pictures, singing, dancing and sketches designed to familiarize the audience in [*sic*] the cultural contributions of various sections of our national community." These evening programs were intended to be presented in places such as Wilmington, San Pedro, Boyle Heights, and Belvedere. "It is hoped," the council's executive secretary wrote, "that through these presentations the various minorities living within each community will be given a better understanding of each other."[66] On another occasion, the Council for Civic Unity sponsored a meeting for "1000 teen-aged youths of Mexican, Negro and Jewish extraction" at the Soto-Michigan Community Center. The program included a "round table discussion on the advantages of civic unity" led by Rex Ingram, Anthony Quinn, and Jack Guilford. In addition to the discussion, plans included "exhibition boxing, and jitterbugging in the approved styles of each of the 3 groups represented."[67]

Similar educational activities also occurred in the San Francisco area. Fellowship Church, an interracial congregation, sponsored a summer camp in 1944 that attracted one hundred Anglo-American, African-American, Mexican-American, and Filipino-American children. The church reported that only a small percentage of the children had come from its own Sunday School. "The theme of our camp and its program, was built around what we called 'Adventures in Friendship,'" church officials reported. "Our purpose was to deepen the interest of the children in other peoples and other races, to feed this interest with authentic factual materials, and to give the children the personal experience of appreciating the art, music, and objects of other cultures."[68] In a number of places, then, fairly small groups of people from different cultures assembled and were exposed to each other.

Mass meetings supported these fairly small-scale educational events. The Council for Civic Unity in Los Angeles sponsored a meeting in April 1944 at the Philharmonic Auditorium. The program included appearances by Mayor Fletcher Bowron, Orson Welles, and the writer Dalton Trumbo. A group of Hollywood actors performed a play entitled "Divide and Conquer," and the Nash Singers and the L. A. Victory Chorus sang "We're in the Same Boat, Brother." The program began with "The Star-Spangled Banner" and concluded with the recitation of a "Pledge of Unity" that said:

I PLEDGE myself to refrain from any thought, speech or action based on prejudice or discrimination against a race, a creed or a class;

TO JUDGE every man according to his true individual worth;

TO RESPECT and to further in everyday business, political and social relations the ideal of human brotherhood.

I PLEDGE my best effort to the exposure and defeat of the forces which spread intolerance and hatred;

AND to the enlightened mobilization of this community and this nation toward a common goal—

THAT WE may today make a living truth of the great American principle that all men are created equal.[69]

Although this program did not specifically suggest that the experiences of African Americans were similar to the experiences of Mexican Americans, it did convey the message that all people had to confront similar problems. A variety of organizations sponsored similar mass meetings.

As the war continued through 1944, the impending return of Japanese Americans to the Pacific Coast encouraged further cooperation across ethnic boundaries. In October, more than two months before the Supreme Court forced the army to permit Japanese Americans to return to coastal areas, a Pasadena realtor, William C. Carr, reported that "Friends of the American Way, a local organization, is setting a good example of how 'we of the white majority and Negroes of the largest minority, can cooperate together' in securing justice for returning Japanese Americans." Friends of the American Way had located people who promised to provide jobs and housing for returning Japanese Americans. The organization also developed plans to operate a hostel and entertained Japanese-American soldiers on leave in the Los Angeles area.[70]

In January 1945, a number of organizations sponsored a "Conference on Interracial Cooperation" in San Francisco. The conference's organizers wanted "to draw together persons connected with Government Agencies and voluntary organizations in order to plan jointly for the orderly and harmonious integration into community life of" returning Japanese Americans. The people who attended the conference also wanted to create machinery to coordinate "the activities of organizations concerned with interracial and intercultural relations." At the conference, African-American, Filipino-American, and Korean-American leaders said that they would work to "safeguard the rights and liberties of returning evacuees." These leaders agreed that "any attempt to make capital for their own racial groups at the expense of the Japanese would be sawing off the limb on which they themselves sat." They "recognized that all minorities—and for that matter all citizens—were in the same boat, and that to deny full constitutional rights to any racial or religious group would weaken the rights of all." The representatives from minority groups made specific pledges not to disrupt the process of resettlement. Black representatives said that they would not protest when Japanese-American homeowners legally evicted African-American tenants, and Filipino and Korean Americans said that they would not attack Japanese Americans in retaliation for atrocities committed by the Japanese military.[71]

When Japanese Americans began to return to California in early 1945, some black community leaders urged African Americans not to resent Japanese Americans. In a speech to a black audience in San Diego, for example, Rev. Clayton D. Russell claimed that a "sinister campaign is under way in Los Angeles to incite hostility between members of Negro and Nisei minority groups on the basis of competition for housing." Russell said that "racist groups engaged in baiting Japanese" had launched the campaign. "Such elements have only one purpose. They don't care if returning evacuees dispossess Negroes now living in Little Tokyo. Those same forces which would take property away from Japanese Americans would in turn take your property away from you."[72]

Although African-American and Japanese-American leaders tried to prevent conflict between their groups, tension often threatened to damage these relations. In 1945 a black business owner had "reminded the Japanese business men that they must hire Negroes or face a boycott." Pilgrim House tried to defuse the tension. A settlement house that opened in September 1943, Pilgrim House offered a wide variety of services to the African-American population of Little Tokyo. To encourage good relations between the black residents of the district and the returning Japanese Americans, Pilgrim House Director Harold M. Kingsley asked Samuel Ishikawa to work as a volunteer at the house.

In August and September 1945, Ishikawa organized and Pilgrim House hosted two public meetings "to promote good relations among the people who are to live together in Bronzeville." About 100 people attended the first meeting, closer to 150 attended the second. Pilgrim House also encouraged interracial cooperation by bringing Japanese-American children into its nursery school. The director of Pilgrim House offered Japanese Americans the house's facilities—a toy loan, a library, a gymnasium, and the nursery school.[73] Later in the fall, Pilgrim House hosted three more "get-acquainted" meetings for Little Tokyo residents. By 1947 Pilgrim House had opened a Japanese-language school for Japanese-American children. About fifty attended daily.[74] Meetings at Pilgrim House throughout the second half of the 1940s helped to eliminate conflicts among African Americans and Japanese Americans. "Pilgrim House provides the only common ground in the whole district where the diverse elements of the community can meet and thresh out their mutual problems," the chairman of the house's board of managers concluded.[75]

Although Pilgrim House's efforts undoubtedly reduced conflict between African Americans and Japanese Americans in Little Tokyo, these conflicts may have been further reduced because few Japanese Americans decided to live in Little Tokyo after the war. According to representatives of Pilgrim House, about four hundred Japanese Americans entered Little Tokyo every week in the autumn of 1945. Most of these people stayed in hostels in the district "only long enough to secure employment and residence elsewhere."[76] Many Japanese Americans moved into temporary housing, such as barracks and trailer camps. At the end of 1945, one observer estimated that about half of the 23,000 Japanese Americans who had returned to Los Angeles County had found permanent homes. "Of the other half, some 2,200 were in abandoned army barracks built of boards and tar paper; some 1,500 were in hostels run principally by religious groups; and the rest were 'doubling up' with those who had found accommodations."[77]

Throughout the summer of 1945, people from a number of different ethnic communities continued to promote shared understanding and cooperation. On July 20, 12,000 people turned out for a mass rally at the Olympic Auditorium. The organizers of the rally followed with a one-day conference at Los Angeles City College. The promoters of this "Mobilization for Democracy" convention said that 1,200 people, representing more than a thousand organizations with a combined membership of nearly 500,000, participated in the workshops, which focused on "Community Work," "Combatting Discrimination in Employment and Housing," "Education against Prejudice," and "Techniques of Reaching the Public." A number of prominent African Americans, including Augustus Hawkins of the state assembly, the attorney Loren Miller, H. Claude Hudson of the NAACP, and Leon Washington, editor of the *Los Angeles Sentinel*, took part in the conference. The publicity that appeared after the conference, however, neglected to note whether or not Mexican Americans or Asian Americans had participated.[78]

The Mobilization for Democracy organization reveals some of the difficulties that the architects of "interracial democracy" encountered. Almost all of the members of the planning committee that met in the summer and fall of 1945 were middle-class, Anglo-American liberals. Anglo-American liberals also dominated San Francisco's Council for Civic Unity and the California Council for Civic Unity, which was established in 1946.[79] Although they fought against racism, these liberals set an agenda that sometimes failed to consider the most pressing concerns of African Americans and Mexican Americans, especially those from the working classes. When the war ended, for example, thousands of African Americans and Mexican Americans lost their jobs in the aircraft plants and shipyards. Instead of working to eliminate employment discrimination so that some people could keep their jobs, the middle-class organizations concentrated on the elimination of restrictive covenants and other measures that prevented middle-class African Americans from occupying homes in previously all-white neighborhoods.[80] Housing discrimination was a serious problem in California before, during, and after World War II, but many working-class African Americans and Mexican Americans considered employment discrimination a more serious problem.

In working to convince African Americans and Mexican Americans (not to mention Jewish Americans and Asian Americans) that they had common concerns, organizers and leaders from these communities were not simply trying to reduce conflict across ethnic boundaries. Some believed that cooperation across these boundaries could allow African Americans, Mexican Americans, and Asian Americans to gain political power. Although an African American had represented one district in Los Angeles in the State Assembly since 1919, no African American had ever been elected to the Los Angeles City Council or the Los Angeles County Board of Supervisors. No Mexican American had been elected to one of these bodies since the 1870s. In 1945, Charlotta Bass decided to run for the city council. Bass's campaign did not emphasize the need for African-American representation on the council; instead, her platform can be labeled "progressive," in that she called for more thorough planning for converting war plants to peacetime production, the construction of housing to alleviate the shortage created by the war, increased spending for public health and safety, the reduction of electricity rates, and the construction of recreational facilities, child-care centers, and libraries. Bass, however, did not become the first African American elected to the Los Angeles City Council. Tom Bradley earned that distinction in 1963.[81]

African-American and Mexican-American leaders' forays into electoral politics after World War II were largely unsuccessful. The size of city council and county board of supervisors districts throughout the state worked against minority candidates. Officials drew the boundaries between districts so as to carve up African-American or Mexican-American neighborhoods.[82] In 1946, a coalition of ethnic organizations, labor unions, and white liberals succeeded in placing an initiative on the statewide ballot that would have outlawed employment discrimination. This initiative, like the candidacies of most African-American and Mexican-American leaders, failed. More than two-thirds of California's voters rejected the proposition.

Although community organizers found it difficult to elect African-American and Mexican-American candidates and to pass antidiscrimination propositions after the war, a loosely organized coalition persisted for several years. This coalition experienced its greatest success in the courts. NAACP lawyers filed briefs in cases involving Japanese Americans and Mexican Americans, and Japanese American Citizens League lawyers filed briefs in cases involving Mexican Americans and African Americans. In a 1947 housing discrimination case, for example, a South Pasadena family was represented by ACLU and JACL attorneys A. L. Wirin, Saburo Kido, and Frank Chuman, NAACP attorney Loren Miller, and William Strong, who represented the Commission on Social Action of the American Jewish Congress.[83] These attorneys frequently convinced judges to strike down racially restrictive covenants, and in 1947 a federal court declared the segregation of Mexican Americans from Anglo Americans in an Orange County school district unconstitutional.

The civil rights coalition that emerged during and after the war continued to combat discrimination and to seek political power through the end of the 1940s. In 1949, Edward Roybal became the first Mexican American in more than seventy years to win election to the Los Angeles City Council. Roybal's district had large Mexican-American and African-American populations. Neither group, however, constituted a majority within the district. In his campaign, Roybal received support from several black leaders. As Charlotta Bass recalled, "The spring months of 1949 were election campaign months. Our main efforts in the city election campaign was [sic] to insure the election of Edward Roybal to the City Council for the ninth councilmanic district."[84] By the mid-1950s, however, the African-American and Mexican-American communities had grown so quickly and so large that community leaders found their work more challenging. Interaction and communication across ethnic boundaries never completely ceased, but the wartime emphasis on crosscultural cooperation generally gave way to organizations that were more directly focused on the concerns of a single community.[85]

This essay has discussed impulses toward cooperation among Mexican-American and African-American community leaders in California during World War II. It does not examine carefully instances of conflict such as those analyzed by other scholars who have focused on ethnic groups in eastern cities. John F. Stack Jr., for example, has noted that the war led to increased anti-Semitism among Irish Americans in Boston, New York, and Philadelphia.[86] Racial and ethnic conflict occurred in both the Bay Area and in Southern California during and after World War II. Most of the conflict that was recorded in the sources I have examined resulted from the expansion of African-American neighborhoods. As African Americans moved into previously all-white neighborhoods, Anglo-American residents filed countless protests with elected officials, sometimes using violent means to try to prevent African Americans from moving into their neighborhoods.[87] I have uncovered little evidence of widespread conflict between African Americans and Mexican Americans. This lack of evidence may reflect some people's reluctance to report violence between the two groups. "The minority press should unite, even as minority groups must unite," Charlotta Bass wrote.

> No minority newspaper should ever print anything derogatory of any other group. Intolerant acts should not be permitted to go unchallenged. No covert sneer at Catholics or Jews, or Japanese-Americans, the Americans of Mexican birth, or any other racial and cultural minority.

> Do not become unduly alarmed by rumors of intergroup violence. It is in the interest of the metropolitan press to make those rumors grow. Do not pass them along.
>
> Instead, "Accentuate the positive." Praise acts of understanding and courage. Treat every human being, regardless of race, creed, and social status, with the understanding and courtesy you would want to receive from him.[88]

Even if self-censorship hides a history of conflict among Mexican Americans and African Americans, any conflict would not completely overshadow the significance of the movement toward interracial cooperation that is documented here.

This essay is not intended to be a definitive analysis of World War II's impact on African Americans and Mexican Americans in California. Instead, it tries to suggest an alternative to the "binary perspective" from which most historians and other scholars have approached the experiences of African Americans, Mexican Americans, and Asian Americans in the United States. Most studies of African Americans and Mexican Americans have focused exclusively on one group and on relations between that group and the white or Anglo majority. While this approach recognizes the existence of distinct African-American and Mexican-American cultures, it neglects the fact that African Americans and Mexican Americans in California lived in multicultural environments. This essay has suggested that African-American and Mexican-American cultures in California differed from those cultures in other parts of the country. Many African Americans in Oakland in the 1940s, for example, saw themselves as different from African Americans in eastern cities or in the South. Similarly, many Mexican Americans in Los Angeles recognized differences between themselves and Mexican Americans in other parts of the Southwest. These differences often revolved around the existence of large, racialized communities in close proximity to other large, racialized communities. Many African Americans and Mexican Americans interacted on a daily basis in cities throughout California. Although the war sometimes decreased interaction across ethnic boundaries, it also catalyzed leaders within these communities, who tried to build political alliances based on the similarities that they perceived among the experiences of African Americans and Mexican Americans. These leaders were not always able to forge coalitions that could survive the rapid population growth and the political pitfalls of the cold war. Nonetheless, cooperation across racial boundaries helped to limit some kinds of racial and ethnic discrimination in California. Carey McWilliams may have overstated the extent of wartime changes in race relations in the United States. His observations, however, were not inaccurate. World War II did lead some Americans to realize that all of their nation's "racial problems" were similar. This realization set the stage for the civil rights struggles of the 1950s and 1960s.

Notes

1. See Carey McWilliams, *Factories in the Field: The Story of Migratory Farm Labor in California* (Boston, 1939), esp. 66–151.

2. Carey McWilliams, *Brothers under the Skin* (Boston, 1943), 48–49.

3. Ibid., 296. McWilliams quotes Robert L. Sutherland, *Color, Class, and Personality* (Washington, D.C., 1942), xv.

4. McWilliams, *Brothers under the Skin,* 299.

5. McWilliams reiterated his position after the war. In a 1946 essay he argued that "since the war the various aspects of the race problem, seldom correlated in the past, have been drawn together so that all phases of the matter, involving Negroes, Mexicans, Orientals, Indians, Filipinos, etc., have come to be regarded as a single national problem." Carey McWilliams, "What We Did about Racial Minorities," in *While You Were Gone: A Report on Wartime Life in the United States,* ed. Jack Goodman (New York, 1946), 99.

6. William Issel and Robert W. Cherny, *San Francisco, 1865–1932: Politics, Power, and Urban Development* (Berkeley, Calif., 1986), 66.

7. For a brief discussion of the Mexican immigrant and Mexican-American citizen population of the United States, see Arthur F. Corwin, "*¿Quien Sabe?* Mexican Migration Statistics," in Corwin, ed., *Immigrants—and Immigrants: Perspectives on Mexican Labor Migration to the United States,* ed. Arthur F. Corwin (Westport, Conn., 1978), esp. 114–20.

8. Marilynn S. Johnson, *The Second Gold Rush: Oakland and the East Bay in World War II* (Berkeley, Calif., 1993), 25.

9. Ibid., 26.

10. "Historical Background of Negro Survey" (n.d.), Papers of the Los Angeles Urban League, Department of Special Collections, University Research Library, University of California at Los Angeles.

11. Memorandum from Arthur F. Miley to John Anson Ford, 10 Aug. 1943, box 65, John Anson Ford Papers, Huntington Library, San Marino, Calif. (hereafter John Anson Ford Papers). This memo describes a meeting called by Los Angeles mayor Fletcher Bowron to discuss the housing situation for minority groups.

12. Population data comes from the publications of the U.S. Department of Commerce, Bureau of the Census. Additional information about Japanese Americans in Los Angeles is from John Modell, *The Economics and Politics of Racial Accommodation: The Japanese of Los Angeles, 1900–1942* (Urbana, Ill., 1977), 67–75.

13. Gerald Nash accepts the Census Bureau's count of 219,000 Mexican Americans in Los Angeles. See Nash, *The American West Transformed: The Impact of World War II* (Bloomington, Ind., 1985), 108. Other historians have questioned the accuracy of the

census records. Marilynn Johnson, for example, says, "Because of changing definitions of ethnicity and race (white versus non-white), census statistics on Mexican and Mexican-American populations in California are erratic and have no doubt undercounted the seasonal migratory labor force." See Johnson, *Second Gold Rush*, 243n9. Some scholars have completely avoided these debates. George Sánchez, for example, does not offer an estimate of the number of Mexican Americans in Los Angeles. See Sánchez, *Becoming Mexican American: Ethnicity, Culture, and Identity in Chicano Los Angeles, 1900–1945* (New York, 1993). See also "Some Notes on the Mexican Population in Los Angeles County, December, 1941, Prepared by the Information Division, Los Angeles County Coordinating Councils, WPA Project 11887," box 65, John Anson Ford Papers.

14. Sánchez, *Becoming Mexican American*, 74.

15. "From Restriction to Integration . . . How It Works in One Neighborhood," *NOW* 2:8 (Nov. 1944): 5.

16. War Relocation Authority press release, 13 July 1945, "California, Los Angeles Press Releases" file, box 15, Field Basic Documentation, Records of the War Relocation Authority, RG 210, National Archives, Washington, D.C.

17. Vicki L. Ruiz, *Cannery Women, Cannery Lives: Mexican Women, Unionization, and the California Food Processing Industry, 1930–1950* (Albuquerque, 1987), 26, 94.

18. "A Summary of the Hearings of the President's Committee on Fair Employment Practice Held in Los Angeles, California, October 20 and 21, 1941, with Findings and Recommendations," "Los Angeles Summaries" file, box 464, Office Files of Eugene Davidson, 1941–46, Division of Field Operations, Records of the President's Committee on Fair Employment Practice (FEPC), RG 228, National Archives, Washington, D.C.

19. Albert S. Broussard, *Black San Francisco: The Struggle for Racial Equality in the West, 1900–1954* (Lawrence, Kans., 1993), 145.

20. Floyd C. Covington, "Biennial Report of the Executive Director," 1 Mar. 1943, 10, "Urban League of Los Angeles" folder, series 1, box 104, National Urban League Papers, Library of Congress, Washington, D.C.

21. "Says Bias Deprives Nation of Minority Contribution," *NOW* 2:15 (Feb. 1945): 6.

22. "Digest of Proceedings of Conference on the Vocational Future of Mexican-Americans," Los Angeles, 19 Feb. 1944, 1, 9–10, box 345, Legal Division, Hearings, Case #66: Los Angeles Railway Corp., Records of the FEPC, RG 228, National Archives, Washington, D.C.

23. For a description of segregation in a shipyard, see Chester Himes, *If He Hollers Let Him Go* (New York, 1986). Himes's first novel was originally published in 1945.

24. Several of the white women who were interviewed by Sherna Berger Gluck remembered having some contact with African-American women in the aircraft factories in which they worked. See Gluck, *Rosie the Riveter Revisited: Women, the War, and Social Change* (New York, 1987).

25. Broussard, *Black San Francisco*, 198.

26. Johnson, *Second Gold Rush*, 52.

27. Ted LeBerthon, "The Psychopathic South," *NOW* 2:6 (Oct. 1944): 9.

28. Biographical information about Bass can be found in Darlene Clark Hine, ed.,

Black Women in America: An Historical Encyclopedia, 2 vols. (Brooklyn, N.Y., 1993), 1:93; Barbara Sicherman and Carol Hurd Green, eds., *Notable American Women—The Modern Period: A Biographical Dictionary* (Cambridge, Mass., 1980), 61–63. For a small amount of information, see Gerald R. Gill, "'Win or Lose—We Win': The 1952 Vice Presidential Campaign of Charlotta A. Bass," in *The Afro-American Woman: Struggles and Images,* ed. Sharon Harley and Rosalyn Terborg-Penn, 109–18 (Port Washington, N.Y., 1978).

29. Untitled script for radio broadcast, Nov. 1939, "Bass, C. A.—Speeches, 1930s" folder, box 1, Charlotta Bass Papers, Southern California Library for Social Studies and Research, Los Angeles.

30. Mario T. García, *Mexican Americans: Leadership, Ideology, and Identity, 1930–1960* (New Haven, Conn., 1989), 151.

31. Floyd C. Covington, "Political Activity Schedule," 25 May 1940, Los Angeles Urban League Collection, Department of Special Collections, University Research Library, University of California at Los Angeles.

32. Josefina Fierro de Bright, interviewed by Mario T. García, 25 Aug. 1983, quoted in García, *Mexican Americans,* 158.

33. Quoted in an editorial in *Christian Century,* 16 Sept. 1942, reprinted in *Pacific Citizen,* 24 Sept. 1942, 4. At the same time, a number of African Americans and Mexican Americans thought that the internment might offer them economic opportunities. Less than ten days after the attack on Pearl Harbor, some African-American business owners suggested that African Americans could replace Japanese Americans in farming and fishing. See "Business League Sees Negro Fishermen and Farmers as Result of War with Axis," *California Eagle,* 18 Dec. 1941, 8A.

Charlotta Bass reminded *California Eagle* readers of her late husband's vision for African Americans in the Golden State. "Time and again," she wrote, Joseph Blackburn Bass "thundered against the stupidity of Negro citizens ignoring the vast agricultural opportunities which faced them in the state twenty-five years ago." Only a few African Americans took Joseph Bass's advice and purchased farmland in California. "But, today, Negroes once again are faced with a tremendous agricultural opportunity." Japanese Americans had "become masters of the soil throughout our great state," Bass continued. "With unflagging industry and determination, these people have built here an arian [*sic*] empire that is tremendous. If it must be lost to them, why shouldn't it fall into our hands?" Not only would California's rich soil enrich African Americans, Bass argued, it would save black families. "A large scale farming effort in California would assuredly strike the rising juvenile delinquency problem a healthy blow, for, if nothing else, agricultural enterprise KEEPS FAMILY UNITS TOGETHER. The big city in which black parents are hired out day and nite, to whites is the most potent threat to Negro youth." See "Back to the Farm?" *California Eagle,* 12 Feb. 1942, 8A. For an earlier statement of similar sentiments, see "Wield the Big Stick," *California Eagle,* 15 Jan. 1942, 8A.

Some African Americans did reap economic benefits from the internment. When Japanese Americans were rounded up, many African Americans opened businesses in

Little Tokyo, renamed Bronzeville for most of the war. See, for example, "Race Woman Takes Over Jap Cafe," *California Eagle,* 9 Apr. 1942, 2A. Some Mexican Americans also gained from the losses of Japanese Americans. A 1943 report said that one-third of the land previously farmed by Japanese Americans was being worked by "patriotic Mexican laborers." See the press release from Public Relations, Citizens' Committee for the Defense of Mexican-American Youth, 2 Mar. 1943, folder 1 ("News Releases, Mimeographed copies"), box 1, Records of the Sleepy Lagoon Defense Committee, Department of Special Collections, University Research Library, University of California at Los Angeles (hereafter SLDC Records).

34. See Broussard, *Black San Francisco,* 194.

35. Details of all of these activities and pieces of legislation are contained in *News from the Bay Area Council against Discrimination* 1:2 (Jan. 1943). I am grateful to Professor William Issel of San Francisco State University for providing me with copies of the council's newsletter.

36. Floyd C. Covington, "Report of the Executive Director," December 1942, "Hist. Info., Los Angeles, Cal. U. L. 1942" folder, series 5, box 19, National Urban League Papers, Library of Congress, Washington, D.C.

37. Covington, "Biennial Report of the Executive Director," 8.

38. For details of the case, see Citizens' Committee for the Defense of Mexican-American Youth, *The Sleepy Lagoon Case* (pamphlet), SLDC Records.

39. Press telegram from Tom Cullen to the *Daily People's World,* 22 Oct. 1942, folder 1 ("News Releases, Mimeographed copies]"), box 1, SLDC Records.

40. Press release, n.d., folder 1 ("News Releases, Mimeographed copies"), box 1, SLDC Records.

41. Press release, 1 Mar. (no year), folder 1 ("News Releases, Mimeographed copies"), box 1, SLDC Records.

42. *Appeal News* 1:2 (21 Apr. 1943), folder 1 ("*Appeal News* v.1 n.1 to v.2 n.6"), box 2, SLDC Records.

43. Form letter, n.d., folder 7 ("Correspondence, Form letters"), box 2, SLDC Records.

44. According to Alice Greenfield, who edited *Appeal News,* "INTEREST in the work of the Committee is growing. At the last meeting there were four additional unions represented by delegates, two additional Negro groups and one additional Jewish organization. These people are bringing fresh energy and new ideas. It is very encouraging to those of us who have been working with the Committee to know that we have only begun to gather around us the people who are friendly to our purpose. . and who will do something about it." See *Appeal News* 1:1 (7 Apr. 1943), folder 1 ("*Appeal News* v.1 n.1 to v.2 n.6"), box 2, SLDC Records.

45. See *Appeal News* 2:6 (4 Mar. 1944). Support for the Sleepy Lagoon Defense Committee extended beyond California. In March 1943, Dr. Max Yergan, president of the National Negro Congress and executive director of the Council on African Affairs, urged African Americans around the country to support the appeal in the Sleepy Lagoon case. African Americans should "join with all other decent citizens, including those of Mexican extraction, and carry forward a relentless battle until these Mexican-

American youths have been freed from a cruel and unjust conviction and given a chance to become decent American citizens," Yergan said. "Negro Americans, along with all other Americans, must realize that until there is justice for all, there can be justice for none." See the press release from the Citizens' Committee for the Defense of Mexican-American Youth to the *California Eagle, Los Angeles Sentinel, Los Angeles Tribune* (all African-American newspapers), and *PM*, 5 Mar. 1943, folder 2 ("News Releases Preliminary drafts [etc.]"), box 1, SLDC Records.

46. See Nash, *American West Transformed*, 115–16.

47. Mauricio Mazón, *The Zoot-Suit Riots: The Psychology of Symbolic Annihilation* (Austin, Tex., 1984), 54–77.

48. See Nash, *American West Transformed*, 117–18; Mazón, *Zoot-Suit Riots;* and Carey McWilliams, *North from Mexico: The Spanish-Speaking People of the United States* (Philadelphia, 1949), 244–53.

49. John Anson Ford to Nelson A. Rockefeller, Coordinator of Inter-American Affairs, 9 June 1943, box 65, John Anson Ford Papers.

50. Chester Himes, "Zoot Riots Are Race Riots," *The Crisis,* July 1943, 225.

51. "Translation of Communication by Coordinating Council of Latin-American Youths to Washington Authorities That Appeared in 'La Opinion' dated June 9, 1943," "Administrative Files, Department of Justice—Attorney General, Law Enforcement, 1943" file, F 3640:2624, Earl Warren Papers, California State Archives, Sacramento; Thomas L. Griffith to Walter White, 9 June 1943, and telegram, Walter White to Robert W. Kenny, 11 June 1943, "'Zoot Suit' Riots 1943–44" folder, group 2, box A676, Papers of the National Association for the Advancement of Colored People, Library of Congress, Washington, D.C. (hereafter NAACP Papers); telegram from Harry Braverman to Earl Warren, 11 June 1943, "Administrative Files, Department of Justice—Attorney General, Law Enforcement, 1943" file, F 3640:2625, Earl Warren Papers, California State Archives, Sacramento.

52. Joseph T. McGucken, an auxiliary bishop of the archdiocese of Los Angeles, served as the chair of the committee. He was joined by Walter Gordon, the chair of the Bay Area Council against Discrimination, Willsie Martin, the pastor of the Wilshire Methodist Church, Karl Horton of the Youth Correction Authority, and Leo Carrillo.

53. Joseph T. McGucken to Earl Warren, 21 June 1943, "Administrative Files, Department of Justice—Attorney General, Law Enforcement, 1943" file, F 3640:2624, Earl Warren Papers, California State Archives, Sacramento.

54. Report, Arthur F. Miley to John Anson Ford, 8 July 1945, box 65, John Anson Ford Papers.

55. Untitled typewritten report, Mar. 1944, box 62, John Anson Ford Papers.

56. "Address by Dr. Farnham," in Council for Civic Unity "Bulletin," 27 July 1944, folder 3 ("Council for Civic Unity"), box 5, SLDC Records.

57. Council for Civic Unity "Bulletin," n.d., folder 3 ("Council for Civic Unity"), box 5, SLDC Records.

58. Nash, *American West Transformed*, 120; untitled typewritten report, Mar. 1944. African-American activists enthusiastically welcomed the Committee for Home Front

Unity. One black minister said that the committee "brings community problems directly and officially into the Mayor's office. . . . From now on this committee will be studying the problems and seeking a solution to them in direct cooperation with the Mayor." The president of the local branch of the NAACP praised the mayor for establishing this committee and pledged his "full cooperation in helping the Mayor and this committee to mobilize and unite the people of Los Angeles for victory in this struggle of our nation for survival." See "Mayor Selects Group for Unity at Home," *California Eagle,* 13 Jan. 1944, 1.

59. The County Committee for Interracial Progress was a pet project of John Anson Ford. The Zoot-Suit Riots had troubled Ford. In the aftermath of the riots, he criticized the police for their mass arrests of innocent young people, and he persuaded the Board of Supervisors to pass a carefully worded resolution which expressed concern over the violence. Ford was especially concerned about the international repercussions of the riots. He was afraid that the violence could convince Latin Americans that the United States was not committed to democracy and racial equality. Ford's nephew, who was in Guatemala during the war, told his uncle that the riots had "made a very strong and unfortunate impression" in that country. See Ford to Nelson A. Rockefeller, Coordinator of Inter-American Affairs, 9 June 1943, and Ford to W. S. Rosecrans, head of the Los Angeles Inter-American Center, 2 Aug. 1943, both in box 65, John Anson Ford Papers.

60. List of appointees to the County Committee for Interracial Progress, 23 Feb. 1944, box 62, John Anson Ford Papers.

61. See "Report of the Council," n.d., C. L. Dellums Papers, Bancroft Library, University of California at Berkeley.

62. *News from the Bay Area Council against Discrimination* 2:1 (Dec. 1943).

63. Ibid. 2:3 (Feb. 1944).

64. Ibid. 2:1 (Dec. 1943).

65. See Broussard, *Black San Francisco,* 197–99.

66. Everett V. Wile, "Report of the Executive Secretary to the Membership on Activities of the Council for Civic Unity during the Month of May," 5 June 1944, folder 3 ("Council for Civic Unity"), box 5, SLDC Records.

67. Council for Civic Unity "Bulletin," 27 July 1944, folder 3 ("Council for Civic Unity"), box 5, SLDC Records.

68. "Children Develop Intercultural Understanding in Novel Interracial Church Experiment," *NOW* 2:8 (Nov. 1944): 5.

69. Program, mass meeting at Philharmonic Auditorium, 24 Apr. 1944, folder 3 ("Council for Civic Unity"), box 5, SLDC Records.

70. "Pasadena Prepares for Homecoming Japanese Americans," *NOW* 2:7 (Oct. 1944): 2.

71. "Highlights of Conference on Interracial Cooperation," "Committees on American Principles and Fair Play" file, Washington Office Records, box 9, Records of the War Relocation Authority, RG 210, National Archives, Washington, D.C.

72. "Pastor Warns of Forces Inciting Negro-Nisei," *NOW* 2:14 (Feb. 1945): 13.

73. Samuel Ishikawa, Report on Pilgrim House, 10 Sept. 1945, box 64, John Anson Ford Papers.

74. "Pilgrim House Progress," 18 Oct. 1947, box 65, John Anson Ford Papers.

75. R. Benajah Potter, chairman of the Pilgrim House Board of Managers, to the District Assembly of Rotary District 107, 9 July 1947, box 65, John Anson Ford Papers.

76. Untitled statement attached to 9 Oct. 1945 press release from Michael Brand, publicity chairman for the American Veterans' Committee, box 64, John Anson Ford Papers.

77. Charles B. Spaulding, "Housing Problems of Minority Groups in Los Angeles County," *Annals of the American Academy of Political and Social Science* 248 (1946): 224. The exact number of Japanese Americans living in Little Tokyo after the war is difficult to determine. The War Relocation Authority, which kept track of returning Japanese Americans until 1946, counted 3,188 in the Hollenbeck and Belvedere districts of Los Angeles, east of the Los Angeles River, and 4,725 in "Midtown." I presume that "Midtown" included Little Tokyo, but it probably also included areas outside Little Tokyo. See "After WRA . . . What? A Pre-Liquidation Inventory," a mimeographed booklet published by the War Relocation Authority, box 66, John Anson Ford Papers.

78. "L.A. Democracy Triumphs! Unique Conference of 1200 Delegates Creates Action Programs to Handle Post-War Problems," *Hollywood Independent,* Sept. 1945, 11.

79. See Broussard, *Black San Francisco,* 202–3.

80. In early 1946, for example, David Coleman, the director of the Anti-Defamation League of B'nai B'rith, Daniel G. Marshall, the executive secretary of the Catholic Interracial Council, Charlotta Bass, Thomas Griffith, the president of the NAACP, and Edward G. Robinson formed the Laws Defense Committee. This committee sought to raise funds for the legal defense of Mr. and Mrs. Henry Laws and their daughter, Pauletta Laws Fears. According to the Laws Defense Committee, "This respected Negro family was jailed for the offense of living in their own home which is located in one of the areas in Los Angeles where non-Caucasians are forbidden to live by a private compact of individual property owners." See David Coleman, Daniel G. Marshall, Charlotta Bass, Thomas L. Griffith Jr., and Edward G. Robinson to John Anson Ford, 15 Jan. 1946, box 65, John Anson Ford Papers.

81. Raphael J. Sonenshein, *Politics in Black and White: Race and Power in Los Angeles* (Princeton, N.J., 1993), 45.

82. Ibid., 34.

83. Press release, 8 Oct. 1947, "Restrictive Covenants California 1947–59" folder, box B132, NAACP Papers.

84. Charlotta Bass, "The California Eagle: A Forty Year Record," 1959, typescript, p. 346, Charlotta Bass Papers, Southern California Library, Los Angeles.

85. It is difficult to enumerate all of the reasons for the decline in interaction across ethnic boundaries. An important reason, however, was the effectiveness of red-baiting by opponents of civil rights. See Kevin Allen Leonard, "Crisis in Black and Red: Cold War Politics and the Decline of the NAACP in Los Angeles," paper read at the 35th Western History Association meeting, Denver, 13 Oct. 1995; Chris Friday, "The

Marine Cooks and Stewards Union on the Narrowing Path: Race, Class, and Gender in Cold War America, 1948–1956," paper read at the 89th Organization of American Historians meeting, Chicago, 29 Mar. 1996.

86. John F. Stack Jr., *International Conflict in an American City: Boston's Irish, Italians, and Jews, 1935–1944* (Westport, Conn., 1979), 128–42.

87. See, for example, the letters and reports in F 3640:3656, "Administrative Files, Public Works—Race Relations 1944–45" folder and F 3640:2292, "Administrative Files, Governor's Office—Industrial Relations—Immigration and Housing, January–June 1944" folder, Earl Warren Papers, California State Archives, Sacramento. In early 1944, a number of white residents of Willowbrook, an unincorporated area between Watts and Compton, complained about plans to house African-American war workers in a 300-unit housing project in the district.

88. Untitled article, n.d., Charlotta Bass Papers, Southern California Library, Los Angeles.

10

Partisans in Overalls:
New Perspectives on Women and Politics
in Wartime California

Jacqueline R. Braitman

Women's incorporation into the historical discourse on the waged-labor force has led to the realization that women have always worked, whether for a paycheck of their own, the family wage, or in nonwaged, domestic, or slave labor. War economies provide one of the richest areas of research on women and work; war often gave women major inroads into the "male sphere" of waged labor. The now familiar icon of "Rosie the Riveter" resonates with a multitude of meanings regarding the economic and cultural changes sparked by military necessity. In fact, Rosie's experience, especially during World War II, has dominated analyses of women's wartime activities.

Roger Lotchin has recently challenged this monolithic symbol, noting that "women's roles during World War II were remarkably more complicated and diverse than the 'Rosie the Riveter' paradigm," and that "until we move beyond" it, we will fail to appreciate "the exceptionally precocious contribution of women to the war effort."[1] Lotchin claims that a consideration of politics "would be at least as instructive as the endless reiteration of how wartime women gave way to returning GI's in the reconversion process."[2] He admonishes scholars who are interested in the subject of empowerment for their failure to look at the intriguing impact of women on politics, even though, as he points out, women's role in politics provides the most extreme contrast to their role in the workforce.[3] In the realm of democracy, Lotchin argues, women failed to achieve gains comparable to those made in the economic arena because there was no male shortage in the electoral arena. "Fewer women held office . . . after the war than before" in San Francisco and Los Angeles; thus women "achieved virtually no gains at all."[4]

Separating women's increased visibility in the workforce from their relative invisibility in the political realm, I suggest, is an unfair dichotomy by which to judge the impact of war on women in politics, and thus the picture is not as stark as Lotchin makes it out to be. Wage labor and politics are not entirely exclusive, for in the long run, as Susan Hartmann reminds us, "the critical labor shortage opened doors to women in almost all occupation[s and this] lent a new legitimacy to the woman worker, and made government, employers, and labor unions more willing to consider the [overall] needs of women."[5]

An analysis of women in politics need not revolve around elective office, for women's political activity has historically been rooted in extraparty organizational activities. During World War II, for example, women-defined groups representing hundreds of thousands of members were filled with active, politically conscious women from a broad range of classes, races, and educational backgrounds. According to Hartmann, the behavior of women's organizations during WW II revealed the extent to which feminist consciousness survived more than twenty years after the suffrage victory.[6] But perhaps women identified themselves more easily as partisans, for by war's end, Los Angeles alone saw a tremendous growth in women's-only political groups or groups that encouraged women's participation in the public-political sphere: the Beverly-Westwood Citizen's Committee, the Hollywood Women's Council, the Committee for Democratic Action, the West Pico Democratic Club, the Women's Political Study Club, the Women's Action Committee for Victory and Lasting Peace, the Burbank-Roosevelt Democratic Club, and the Jewish Professional Women's Club, to name a few.

Many of the wartime jobs taken by women encouraged politicization, illustrating the confluence of women's work and politics in this period. Women were more visible behind the scenes on the state level, the "chief training grounds" for women in politics.[7] Women were employed as county officers, such as clerks, tax collectors, assessors, treasurers, recorders, auditors, registers of deeds, clerks of the court, and superintendents of schools, and they sat on juvenile and adult probation commissions, roles that continued to grow in the postwar decades.[8] Many city and county offices became predominantly female, while commissions of education and public welfare became female-oriented in membership. Women also moved into traditionally male bastions, serving as constables and justices of the peace.[9] Political activists did not work only in factories but were likely found in these offices as well, and the lens through which they later saw and acted in the political world reflected their diverse wage-labor and partisan experiences.[10]

Echoing this view is an excerpt from the December 1942 issue of *Independent Woman,* the business and professional women's magazine:

Some day it would be interesting to see a complete compilation of the 'little women in politics,' the women in county and local politics, who keep the wheels of democracy turning. Doubtless they enjoy a modicum of glory within their own communities, but except for the occasional woman sheriff or housecleaning mayor, their conscientious service, year in and year out, maintains the efficiency of the schools, the courts, the county offices, the hospitals and prisons. What a pageant it would be to show the work of all these women the country through—the women mayors, selectmen, the health officers and superintendents of education, the town clerks and treasurers, the recorders of deeds, the trustees of state and county institutions.[11]

With this broadened view of politics, it is clear that the war marks neither a clearly demarcated moment of great change in women's political evolution in California, nor a time of overall continuity. To understand this ambiguity, one must remember that it was not only apolitical, bridge-playing, leisured women or unpaid housewives who were donning overalls and joining previously employed working-class women in jobs that were heretofore exclusively male. Whatever their prior employment status, political activists also picked up wrenches and torches, and they brought their leadership talents and values to their wartime occupations. Their involvement aided other women on both the domestic and political fronts.

Similarly, women's wartime experiences often affected their political sensibilities, which in turn influenced their goals and values in the subsequent decades. In effect, the war provided many women the opportunity to exercise political efficacy while broadening their understanding of gender, class, and race-related issues. This awareness was incorporated into their postwar partisan worldview. What's more, World War II allowed women to take the offensive. The public depiction of the war as a struggle for freedom and democracy, according to Hartmann, afforded symbols that could be turned to women's own advantage.[12] While child care had been a problem throughout the war, California women joined political coalitions after 1945 to work for the continuation and permanent extension of child care, an effort that led to legislation signed by Governor Warren in 1948, when he also signed a measure calling for equal pay for equal work.[13]

I contend that the war did not hinder but rather served to foster activism and further propelled women into new or changing political roles, affecting their overall political perspectives. I come to this conclusion from studying the political participation of California partisans from the 1930s to the 1960s and beyond. My earlier research has focused primarily on Democratic women rooted in the New Deal coalition, whose activism over four decades contributed to the continuity of a liberally infused Democratic ideology and helped

fuel the postwar revival of the state's Democratic Party. Their longevity facilitated the eventual institutionalization of gender-specific, feminist politics.
More recently, I have researched New Deal–era Republican women, revealing
an extensive and highly organized network of women's groups throughout the
state. By the postwar decade, Republican women wielded considerable influence in state party policy and electoral campaigns. Both Democratic and
Republican partisan women have been left out of the story of the state's political past and of World War II in general. The war years serve as an integral
part of the broader picture for understanding the political place of these wom-
en, not only because of their personal experiences, but also because California state politics of the early forties were rife with indigenous inter- and intraparty battles, which subsequently affected the state's political evolution.

For political women in general the war was a turning point. As Cynthia
Harrison explains, in 1945 the old suffrage coalition split into three groups, each
with a different (but not necessarily incompatible) agenda determined by ideology and class identification. One group pursued legislation for working
women, one sought an equal rights amendment to the constitution, and the
third aimed to secure a more prominent place for women in political parties.[14]
It is this third group, prior to, during, and after 1945, that has received the least
attention, and to which I will address the remainder of this essay.

The story of California's female Democratic coalition begins in 1934 with
the End Poverty in California (EPIC) gubernatorial campaign of Upton Sinclair; but the war dramatically altered the lives of continuing or newly emerging activists. Often experiencing considerable hardship themselves, women
activists of the prewar generation emerged from the conflict as dedicated as
they had been before the war. Many younger activists' political commitments
grew out of their wartime experiences.

Women gained political efficacy and confidence throughout the war years,
which helped shape the politics of the next generation. For women as well as
men political efficacy is promoted through involvement in partisan or nonpartisan political clubs, like the Young Democrats and the League of Women
Voters (LWV). Throughout the twentieth century, women, on the local, state,
and national levels, have chosen to work through numerous organizations,
often combining LWV activities with their party service.[15] The league allowed
women to engage in political discussions and activities regardless of their partisan affiliation. One-third of the cohort in a 1960s study of California female
politicos were found to have started as LWV members.[16] Many LWV women
also joined the women's divisions of either the Democratic or Republican
parties. Both the league and women's divisions allowed women to hone their

skills and build their own political and professional careers. During World War II the Los Angeles League of Women Voters (LALWV) thrived.[17]

Many women who migrated to California as part of the general demographic shift during the war years joined the LALWV soon after their arrival. They sought out the league to help them assimilate to their new surroundings and to reconnect with the group to which many of them had belonged in their home states.[18] The self-proclaimed role of the Los Angeles League during the war was a formidable one: a local league leader told members that "it is the duty of the League to be wardens of democracy," and as such the league was obligated to "share knowledge with the general public."[19] All of the California League branches worked hard in this vein to increase the availability of voting information and to assure the accessibility of the ballot for members of the armed forces and newly arrived war workers.[20]

The Los Angeles League maintained an intense investigative and educational program during the 1940s, looking into issues of local and international importance. Throughout the early forties, the LALWV's activities were a combination of prewar concerns and those brought on by the exigencies of mobilization, but they did not lose interest in rights for women. In April 1942, the league took up the study of the reemerging Equal Rights Amendment (ERA) and supported the controversial measure.[21] Other concerns included preserving collective bargaining for war workers, building a sufficient supply of emergency housing, and supporting the United Nations after the Dumbarton Oaks Conference in 1944. Nationally, the league trained more than five thousand speakers and distributed more than one million brochures within six months in hopes of educating the public on the role of America and the United Nations in the international arena.[22] The LALWV also advocated prenatal care and maternity clinics and passed a resolution promoting school-based child care as the duty of the entire community.[23] Most of the women in the Democratic coalition joined the league at some point during the war years. In fact, in May 1943 the Beverly Hills-Wilshire League agreed to work with the local Woman's Democratic group.[24]

The LALWV studied a broad spectrum of problems during the war boom, such as community sewage systems, medical care, health and job insurance, veteran's facilities, and quality control of county and state hospitals. They supported rationing and organized an association of women to encourage enrollment of women workers under Civilian Defense. On a particularly sensitive issue, they opposed the extension of the Alien Land Law of 1920, designed to deny land titles to Japanese immigrants, and they supported full rights and fair treatment of Japanese Americans returning from internment camps. They also dealt with domestic peacetime issues regarding the education of young women, promoting prevocational training for girls in junior high. The league's calendar during the war was filled with hundreds of meetings throughout the city; its reach was far and wide.

In 1943, the LALWV began to explore the problem of crossfiling, which allowed a candidate to register in both parties during the primary while party affiliation remained conspicuously absent from the ballot. Four years later, in October 1947, the league officially undertook a study of the issue, promoted a public education campaign, and in 1952 sponsored an unsuccessful state initiative to ban the practice. After intense opposition from Republican incumbents, the league and other opponents of crossfiling finally succeeded in abolishing it in 1958, helping to revitalize the two-party system in California. The longtime Democratic partisan and league member Elizabeth Snyder was crucial in galvanizing support for the measure, helping the campaign accelerate in the early 1950s.

Another California Democrat, June Sherwood, joined the league at the same time as Snyder in the early 1940s. Snyder and Sherwood's friendship started while they were members of the UCLA debate team and leaders of the local Young Democrats. They engaged in heated discussion, and sometimes literally came to blows over the posturing of the Young Communists infiltrating the group. During the war Sherwood engaged in campaigns for Democratic candidates, pursuing support for the league's promotion of child welfare and child care while continuing her studies of economics, government, and housing. For a period, Sherwood and her husband became fellows at the Brookings Institute in Washington, D.C.[25] Upon war's end, Sherwood became the director of the western unit of the LALWV. While raising her family, she also "held practically every position there was . . . of the Democratic Party [in West Los Angeles] . . . the County Committee, the State Committee, chair of the 16th Congressional district, and chair of the candidate development committee."[26]

As a nonpartisan, or more accurately a bipartisan, organization, the LWV also encouraged Republican Party women to exercise political skills during the war. As a member of the Junior League of the Republican Party, the Young Republican Women, and the Republican Federation of Women in the late 1920s, Hilda Hoover McLean campaigned for her uncle, Herbert Hoover, and other conservative candidates. Highly critical of the quality of precinct-level campaigning, she used her time and abilities to organize as many precincts as possible. She joined the California LWV in the late 1930s, was elected to their state board in 1940, and in 1942 was elected state president of the California League of Women Voters. While nursing her third baby, she managed to attend state LWV board meetings, lobby the legislature for child care, the protection of newsboys, and civil service, and draft proposed state legislation for the LWV.[27]

Along with league activities, California women engaged in political partisanship in unprecedented ways during the Second World War. In terms of rank and file, grassroots activism, one contemporary of the period credits the war for women's added influence in mainstream political parties, noting the "imperative to use women workers in leg work and local and state committee positions."[28] This trend, however, had actually started during the Depression and the Progressive era in California. Since "both the Democratic and Republican national party committees had granted equal representation to women" by 1924, there was increased pressure "to secure equality on the state and local committees" as well. The nationwide push for parity became known as the "fifty-fifty plan," which called for "equal representation of women with men on all party committees." This meant that states could require women members on all or some of state, district, or county committees, and thus ensure a chairperson with a vice chairperson of the opposite sex with equal voting power. The fifty-fifty plan was adopted, in whole or in part, by state law in some places and by party regulation in others.

California's legislature passed a fifty-fifty law in 1937, requiring equal representation on all state central committee seats. The law did not, however, include elected county committees or their chairs.[29] State central committees are appointed by elected officials. The California bill was promoted by Mrs. Mattison Boyd Jones, president of the California Federation of Democratic Women's Study Clubs, but it was strongly supported by Republican women as well.[30] The new elections code required that the membership of state central committees be equally divided between men and women. Each delegate to the convention would be directed, by law, to appoint one voter of the same and two voters of the opposite sex.[31] This law had widespread ramifications, increasing the participation and the integration of a new generation of women who were coming of age and moving into mainstream parties, possibly exercising their franchise for the first time.

During the 1940s, the fifty-fifty plan made considerable progress in bringing women into the nationwide party structures. Women's membership on California state central committees increased greatly in 1938 (one year after the new law), with approximately 50 percent in both parties, up from 1 percent in 1934.[32] Much of the day-to-day hard work of party organization fell on the shoulders of women anyway,[33] but between 1940 and 1944, the number of women who chaired Democratic county committees (which are elected positions) increased from twelve to more than one hundred nationwide.[34] By the end of the decade, all but eight states had women equally represented on state and local committees. In California, the law did not extend to county chairs, and records were not even kept by the secretary of state until 1948. By then, however, there were four Republican women elected as county committee chairs (out of fifty-eight counties) and two Democratic women elected to county central committees, which suggests a filtering up to elective integration.

While the attainment of structural positions, arising out of maneuvers such as the fifty-fifty mandate, did not necessarily translate into power or influence, the fifty-fifty law reflects the considerable progress that women, as political actors, had already made during the 1920s and 1930s. The political arena women were entering was evolving and transforming even for male participants in the early decades of the twentieth century. Women's political progress continued throughout the century, especially accelerating in the 1970s. As Marjorie Lansing explains, "The major shift concerning American women in political behavior has resulted from the general acceptance of the legitimacy of the female vote, that is, of a participant role as appropriate for women." The increased visibility of women in the vanguard of California party leadership perhaps contributed to this change.[35]

One observer of California politics, Marguerite J. Fisher, believed that the fifty-fifty law eased "the path for women party workers. It [was] a first and a necessary step, which would be followed [it was hoped] . . . by actual participation in policy formation." She claimed that the law allowed women to feel they had a secure place in the party. Their presence was not dependent on who was in power, or "the whim of a chief": "the knowledge that [women were] guaranteed places . . . may [have been an] incentive for harder work in the service of the party."[36] In some ways the war accelerated the structural integration of women that had already been underway, which counters the view that women were merely filling a political vacuum while male rank-and-file partisans were overseas. The tremendous increase in party registrants for California Democrats started during the Depression, prior to the 1937 law. A liberal faction, including women leaders who would remain active for several decades, was attracted to Upton Sinclair's EPIC campaign. Despite Sinclair's defeat, EPIC supporters gained control of the Democratic Party in 1934 and orchestrated Culbert Olson's gubernatorial victory in 1938.

The gains, however, were short-lived. The number of registered Democrats continued to increase during the early war years, but more women and more total potential votes did not translate into women's winning elections. After Olson's administration, Democrats were hardly winning state elections at all. The party in California was wracked by personal and ideological divisions, heated primary battles, crossfiling, and alienation from the national party, all of which spelled defeat in the general elections. The few wartime congressional successes of 1944, which included Chet Holifield and Helen Gahagan Douglas, can be attributed in part to the generally unacknowledged campaigning leadership of women such as Elizabeth Snyder, Ruth Lybeck, Rosalind Wyman, Florence Clifton, and scores of others. Furthermore, the continued attraction of voters to both Douglas and Holifield in 1948 pulled votes from a potential third party that could have threatened Truman's slim 18,000-vote margin of victory in California.[37] The state Democratic Party's resurgence in the 1950s was aided by Adlai Stevenson's appeal to both men and women during his 1952 presidential campaign. His second campaign, in 1956, increased women's visibility in the party's club movement, which had emerged in the wake of Stevenson's first defeat. Many clubs were initiated by women themselves.

Republican women also made significant headway within two years of the fifty-fifty law, both in separate women's affiliates and in the traditional party apparatus. Sometimes membership intersected. This was most evident in the California Republican Assembly (CRA), an extraparty body designed to endorse candidates in the primary and build up rank-and-file constituent participation. When a woman held a post in the CRA, she was not expected to curtail her activities with women's affiliates. In fact, men and women of the CRA were considered "one common group" and were only "segregate[d] in this manner, by sex, for the purpose of reaching women as a group of voters."[38]

Republican women were well placed throughout California in time for Earl Warren's election in 1942. Women's groups from Pismo Beach, San Luis Obispo, Santa Cruz, Fresno, Contra Costa, Kern, and Tulare Counties were lauded for their contribution to the Warren campaign. Women canvassed door-to-door, held teas for hundreds of guests, and organized women's Republican clubs in every part of the state.[39]

As with Democrats, party activism by Republican women sometimes created opportunities for advancement in the political hierarchy. Bernice Woodard resigned as secretary of the Fact Finding Committee of the CRA to take a post with the federal government. Women were central participants in the scouting, assessing, and selecting of candidates throughout the 1940s. Republican women were recognized by the CRA; they served on the Resolutions Committee and held posts as regional directors.[40] In April 1942, at the ninth annual CRA convention dinner, the guest speaker was Ethel Gillett Whithorn, with Anna Baker, vice president of the CRA, presiding.[41] Edith Van de Water of Long Beach, the Republican National Committeewoman, spoke at the tenth national convention.[42]

Republican women, as with Democrats, often found their activism curtailed by more traditional wifely duties. One woman complained that she could only get away "as often as [she] can persuade [her] husband to do his own cooking." Nevertheless, she claimed to witness tremendous growth and awareness among women in the local meetings arranged by the Women's Council in an otherwise "horribly disorganized" county.[43]

In the early 1940s Jean Wood Fuller responded to an advertisement announcing a Republican Women's Club meeting in Southern California's San Fernando Valley. She recognized the potential of the group and sought to revitalize it, eventually relocating the headquarters to her home. Most of Fuller's time during the war was spent volunteering for the Red Cross and other local fundraisers, but she also worked with the CRA and joined the California Council of Republican Women (CCRW). The CCRW created the platform for the party's candidates and set up meetings with constituents in addition to canvassing door-to-door and coordinating the mailing drives. Eventually Fuller was elected to her county central committee and was thus appointed to the state central committee.[44] Similarly, in 1944 Barbara S. Whittaker ran against and defeated six men for party chair of the 42nd Assembly District in Los Angeles County. This position automatically made her a member of the Republican County Central Committee, of which she was appointed secretary.[45]

Most Californians are familiar with Helen Gahagan Douglas's loss to Richard Nixon in the 1950 senatorial race, but many are unaware of her prior role parlaying women's influence in the party. Douglas worked with Rosalind Wyman, who served as her driver during the 1944 campaign and, after rapidly moving up the political ladder, was elected to the Los Angeles City Council in 1953, where she remained for eighteen years. Ingrid Winther Scobie describes how Douglas's political activity "took place against the backdrop of America's increasing involvement with the war." She served initially as the head of the California Women's Division, and then as a Democratic national committeewoman. Douglas served with distinction until her congressional election in 1944. What really brought her to the attention of party leaders was the 1942 drive she led to round up pro-Roosevelt congressional candidates and get out the vote for them. In a year when Democrats lost heavily elsewhere in the country and incumbent Governor Culbert Olson was defeated by Earl Warren, Democrats won three of six critical congressional seats, including those of Chet Holifield and Jerry Voorhis, and six other southern California offices. Democrats praised Douglas for her organizing efforts.[46]

After much public debate over the use of atomic weapons, Congressman Holifield eventually chaired the House committee on the Civilian Use of Atomic Power, an issue of great importance to Helen Gahagan Douglas and women throughout the nation. Women's groups were well represented at a Los Angeles conference on atomic power in December 1945, indicating that concerns about nuclear power added another dimension to women's political influence.[47] Among the groups in attendance were the Women's Political Study Club, the Women's Action Committee for Victory and Lasting Peace, the Jewish Professional Women's Club, the Hollywood Women's Council, and the National Council of Negro Women. Among her many appearances, Douglas (along with Ronald Reagan) spoke on the subject of atomic power at a mass meeting sponsored by the Hollywood Independent Citizens Committee for the Arts, Sciences, and Professions. More than any other issue, nuclear power drew an increasing number of women into postwar international affairs.

The political career of Julia Gorman Porter also intersected with that of Helen Gahagan Douglas.[48] In 1942, Douglas asked Porter, then president of the San Francisco League of Women Voters, to act as chair of the Northern Women's Division of the Democratic Party, and she would concentrate on the southern part of the state. While Douglas drew other women into the party, she was a newcomer compared to the cohort of the EPIC days, and she tended to move outside of their network. Along with the divided loyalties of other state Democrats, this split negatively impacted the political activities of women in the party. For example, Douglas's reorganization of the Women's Division in the spring of 1941 worked well until intraparty bickering in the North caused it to dissolve.[49] The problem, known as "Olson's swan-song blunder,"[50] arose from the bitter contest between the incumbent party chair William Malone and his challenger George Reilly over who would become the next vice chair of the state central committee. Olson's administration supported Reilly, who defeated Malone but ultimately failed to deliver the important San Francisco vote. When Porter and her successor, Catherine Bauer, resigned from the Women's Division over the Malone and Reilly controversy, the division became so ineffectual that Porter believed this intraparty fight was the leading factor in preventing Olson's re-election in 1942.[51]

Frances Albrier, an African-American woman from Northern California, became interested in women's programs and organizations when she accompanied her grandmother to a local Mother's Club as a young girl. She combined her interests in labor, race, and gender issues when she started the Department of Women in Industry in the Federation of Colored Women's Clubs. Albrier's political initiation came during Franklin Roosevelt's first administration, which led her, along with millions of African Americans, to register as a Democrat in 1936. Two years later she was the first woman to be elected to the Alameda County Democratic Central Committee.[52]

Albrier's career reflects the convergence of work and politics, along with race, in directing the course of political women during the mid-twentieth century. In order to win legislation for working people, Albrier believed one had to go into politics. Her idea was to get into the community policy-making centers, most important the county central committee, which directed the party's policies for the county. While others minimized the role of the party proper, Albrier took it seriously and did her best to educate herself and others. In doing so, she brought other women into the party, and she was made the manager of the East Bay campaign for Culbert Olson, Edmund (Pat) Brown, and James Roosevelt.[53]

When war came, Albrier became a first-aid instructor. After taking welding classes from 11:00 P.M. until 4:00 A.M. every night, she sought a welding job at the Kaiser Shipyards in Richmond. These night classes were set up for women who had to care for their families and/or work during the day. After participating in a one-woman civil rights brigade, for which she is well known, she broke the color line at the Kaiser factories.[54]

Albrier also became active in the Democratic Party's Women's Division which, during the war years, was interested in organizing more Democratic women's study clubs: "Throughout the state we had our own conference, the Women's Democratic Conference, [where] we elected our own officers, . . . like regular officers at a convention." The discussions focused on the "problems of women and youth and how to improve the chances of women as politicians in the party." Albrier explains that "we knew in the future . . . women . . . would become candidates," so the goal was to "back women, and [to help them to] become candidates, and win in the party. . . . Women had been kept back and [had] no encouragement. [Therefore,] unless women backed women, they would not get any place in the party or in politics."[55] While Albrier gradually withdrew from public life in the late forties, others continued or joined the vanguard.

Elizabeth Snyder, born in Minnesota in 1914 and transplanted to Southern California in her early youth, began her political career as a Young Democrat and a member of the UCLA debate team during the Great Depression. Impressed with her local congressman, Jerry Voorhis, she organized student meetings at her house in East Los Angeles, where Voorhis met his local constituency. Even prior to having influence herself, she immersed herself in local races and the gubernatorial campaigns of Upton Sinclair in 1934 and Culbert Olson in 1938.[56]

As war raged in Europe, Elizabeth Snyder won accolades from Voorhis, her first mentor, for her precinct work, for her "enthusiasm and idealism," and for her "splendid manner in organizing East Los Angeles." She was elected national committeewoman of the Young Democrats, and while attending the 1940 Democratic National Convention as an alternate selected by Voorhis, she seconded the nomination of Helen Gahagan Douglas for national committeewoman of the Democratic Party. Snyder's relationship with the Douglases took hold here. Shortly thereafter, Snyder gave speeches about the primary to the party faithful, sharing the bill with Melvyn Douglas at a pre-primary talk in Baldwin Park.[57]

The routines of daily life were dramatically altered once Snyder's husband, Nathan, enlisted and was sent overseas while she worked intermittently as a substitute teacher. Despite these difficulties, Snyder and her friend Florence Clifton helped launch the congressional career of Los Angeles supervisor Chet Holifield. During the war, Snyder also worked the night shift at the Department of Water and Power, which was in the process of shifting over its wattage for the hookup with Boulder Dam. Here she was able to exercise her leadership skills by promoting better working conditions for women typists, who worked under unhealthy and almost primitive conditions.[58]

Snyder moved to a better position with the Canadian Munitions and Supply Agency in the Department of Controlled Materials while living in Washington, D.C., with June Sherwood, who had just given birth to her first child. Once again Snyder's leadership skills came to the fore when she became a supervisor to a pool of two hundred mostly Canadian women, who were frequently restricted in their activities and work privileges. If they did not like the conditions of their employment, their only alternative was to return to Canada. Military officials were very rigid, so Snyder, acting as the spokesperson and worker's representative, demanded and won improved working conditions and better salaries.[59]

While the war years altered Snyder's plan to attend law school, she rose through the Young Democrats as their national committeewoman and found a new mentor in Congressman Chet Holifield. In 1952 she was elected to head the state Democratic Women's Division, and two years later she was the first woman in the country to be elected without prior appointment as the chair of a state political party. However, the controversy surrounding her election reflected the obstacles women still faced while breaking into the traditional male bastions of power within party ranks.

Florence "Susie" Clifton and her husband, Judge Robert Clifton, lived in Snyder's East Los Angeles neighborhood. Susie Clifton had been instrumental in Holifield's campaigns, organizing all of the Southern California precincts. Holifield appointed Snyder and Clifton to delegations, in compliance with the fifty-fifty rule. They worked closely with Holifield, and in time they became like an extended family.[60] Clifton had also been one of the leading campaigners in the Upton Sinclair and Culbert Olson campaigns, and she would later run Helen Gahagan Douglas's and James Roosevelt's contests as well. Her wide range of experience on the campaign trail led to her eventual appointment as the Southern California coordinator for Pat Brown's successful gubernatorial campaign. Brown then appointed Clifton to chair the Industrial Welfare Commission in 1958.

Until the war, little was made of the fact that she and many of her other political friends were women. Working in the Democratic campaigns was "just something that was necessary" and the issues were not gender specific. World War II opened Clifton's eyes to much of the discrimination against women, especially black women, when she worked the night shift at an aircraft plant in Santa Monica. She was immediately recruited as a union organizer at the plant. Soon after, she was shocked to learn that she had inadvertently pledged to discourage her black co-workers from joining the union; she was so alarmed that she disavowed her oath. Until then, she and others, like the vice chair of the Democratic National Committee, Katie Loucheim, had believed that women's interests fell within the larger program of political and social reform and that "women and men ha[d] the same interests in politics and they ought to voice [them] equally."[61] Like others, Elizabeth Snyder had rejected the notion of a women-centered third party, for she had sought change from within the Democratic Party itself. Their experiences as war workers sensitized them to a more gender-specific set of grievances.

Thus, in time, Snyder, Clifton, and many of their female supporters helped promote institution-building and policy-making roles for women within the party and the state bureaucracy, which was still dominated by men after the war. Just as during the war, women within the party could help promote the needs of working women. A clear indication of women's continued postwar influence and growing empowerment was the passage of a bill setting up the California State Commission on the Status of Women in 1964, a spinoff of John F. Kennedy's Presidential Commission on the Status of Women, established in 1961. It has been suggested that such commissions, by encouraging networks of communication and opportunities for raising consciousness about discrimination, helped spark the formation of a mass women's movement in the 1960s.[62] It is important to remember, however, that these commissions often drew their members from the ranks of women who were already active in state and national voluntary and political organizations, which had frequently eschewed specifically feminist identification in the pre- and immediate postwar era.[63]

California lagged behind other states in its establishment of a commission. The Democratic Women's Forum of Los Angeles, an organization designed to encourage women to run for office,[64] set up a workshop on practical politics in the mid-1960s to spur support for President Kennedy's call for more women in civic activism.[65] Many of the women selected to speak were part of the long-term informal coalition which dated back to the Young Democrats in the 1930s. Some went on to become stalwarts in the pro-ERA and pro-choice movements, embracing many issues on the newly evolving feminist agenda. The workshop included a session on "New Frontiers in Politics for Women" by Madale Watson, vice president of the forum, who had joined the Democratic Party in 1946 and later became a vice chair.[66] Ruth Church Gupta led a panel discussion with Clifton and Snyder. Gupta was president of the California Federation of Business and Professional Women, a major force behind the ERA movement, the state commission, and a group which promoted women's political activism throughout the war. Carmen H. Warschaw, a long-time activist, Fair Employment Practices Commission member, and southern chair of the Women's Division, along with Ruth Lybeck, a key figure in the Helen Gahagan Douglas campaigns, were scheduled to explain party structure on the national, state, and local levels. The Women's Democratic Forum of Los Angeles illustrates the continuity of activism among prewar Democratic partisans into the postwar decades. A 1965 flier for the forum advertised Susie Clifton as a mother of four and grandmother who, after being a party activist for thirty-one years, was "California's #1 woman in position and political savvy."[67] She had been a member of the state Democratic Central Committee since 1938. Along with Elizabeth Snyder, Susie Clifton epitomizes the continuity of women who were integrated party stalwarts and whose wartime experiences contributed to their support for feminist perspectives and organizational change.

After gaining party support, the California Democratic Platform called for the creation of a commission on women in August 1964. Soon after, Assemblyman William Brown presented a "Bill of Rights for Women" resolution to the party.[68] When Governor Brown signed the bill, he appointed Susie Clifton, head of the Industrial Welfare Commission, as the first chair of the Commission on Women.

If we look only at electoral outcomes, it is difficult to make judgments about women's involvement in politics. Clearly women were participating in politics in other important ways, at the center of it all, which at times also meant running for elected office. According to Florence E. Allen, "By 1945 women were pulling their own weight in politics," even though they had been denied their rightful publicity. "In spite of the efforts of politicians to shunt women off into the byways of political activity," Allen writes, "women directed political action and participated in the actual planning and working out of legislation so much so that "the history of the work of women along political lines since 1920 actually represents a sameness."[69] For her, the continuity is more striking than the change in this period.

Regardless of the social and cultural resistance to women in politics and the overall low numbers of women in high positions, it should be remembered that women were still vitally active in party politics at the grassroots, local, state, and federal levels. Analyzing the impact of war on California's female politicians then, means more than counting the numbers of women who were elected or appointed. These legitimate questions should be factored into the overall equation, but progress must be seen in terms of women's evolving place within the party structure and the influence women have had on partisan and feminist politics in subsequent decades.[70] Another passage from *Independent Woman* sums it up:

> Women in Congress dazzle the public eye. They are the dramatic figures, who attract nationwide publicity. It is easy and therefore natural to gauge women's place in the political world by these few picturesque figures. Yet it is probable that women are exercising a greater proportionate influence on the conduct of state and local politics, than in the national arena. In the smaller governmental units party lines are adhered to with less vehemence. It is easier for a well qualified woman to command the confidence of her fellow citizens, regardless of what party is in power.[71]

By using California as a case study, it is possible to challenge the notion that the war years saw little in the way of major women's political achievements. Women political activists contributed to wartime politics in heretofore unappreciated ways and helped to fuel postwar feminism and the women's rights movement. The incipient research on California politics during World War II has only explored the beginnings of what will provide a rich historical understanding of California's modern political culture and the role of women within it. In spite of the disruption of war, McCarthyism, and the chilling effect of the cold war on the social and political climate of the nation, female activists continued to flourish within mainstream political parties over several decades. Addressing this gap in the political history of women during the war years in California brings us one step closer to comprehending fully women's political participation throughout the twentieth century.

Notes

1. Roger W. Lotchin, "California Cities and the Hurricane of Change: World War II in the San Francisco, Los Angeles, and San Diego Metropolitan Areas," in *Fortress California at War: San Francisco, Los Angeles, Oakland, and San Diego,* ed. Roger W. Lotchin, special issue of *Pacific Historical Review* 63:3 (Aug. 1994): 393–420, esp. 414–16; idem, "The Historians' War or the Home Front's War?: Some Thoughts for Western Historians," *Western Historical Quarterly* 26:2 (Summer 1995): 185–96, esp. 190–91.

2. Lotchin, "Historians' War," 191.

3. A similar argument is made by William H. Chafe, in *The Paradox of Change* (New York, 1991), chap. 9.

4. Lotchin writes that women (and blacks and Hispanics) had already gained a tenuous foothold before the war, but they were unable to expand upon it after the conflict. What little breakthroughs there were, he says, came before or after the war. This was partly because there was no labor shortage in politics as there was in the workforce. See Lotchin, "California Cities and the Hurricane of Change," 414–16.

5. Susan Hartmann, "Women's Organizations during World War II: The Interaction of Class, Race, and Feminism," in *Women's Being, Women's Place: Female Identity and Vocation in American History,* ed. Mary Kelley, 314–21 (Boston, 1979), esp. 314.

6. Ibid., 321–22.

7. Robert L. Daniels, *American Women in the Twentieth Century* (New York, 1987), 207–13.

8. Ibid. With only partial data of offices available for analysis and a random sampling of California cities, factoring for overall growth of population and city departments, city employment of women more than doubled from 1937 to 1946. (None of these figures include clerks, who were most often women, and were only counted if they were listed under an additional post as well.)

9. *Independent Woman,* Dec. 1942, 383.

10. Historians of women have undertaken comparatively little research into women's political behavior outside of the factory during the early 1940s. While Susan Ware details the political triumphs of women New Dealers on the national level in the decade prior to the war, William Chafe's recent review of the twentieth century neglects partisan politics altogether, save for a brief discussion of the post–Nineteenth Amendment decade. And his discussion of the "paradox of change" in the 1940s paints a bleak picture of a workforce transformed without the accompanying political, economic, and social equality for women. Social historians have rarely strayed into the realm of women in politics, and this neglect reflects in part a long-held view that women were outside of, or marginal to, the traditionally male world of politics, narrowly defined. Our understanding has now broadened to include what has been a longstanding tradition of female political and extraparty behavior which has been an integral dimension of traditional electoral party politics all along. See Susan Ware, *Beyond Suffrage: Women in the New Deal* (Cambridge, Mass., 1981); Chafe, *Paradox of Change.*

11. Emma Bugbee, "The Winners," *Independent Woman,* Dec. 1942, 383.

12. Hartmann, "Women's Organizations during World War II," 321–22.

13. Joan Jensen and Gloria Ricci Lothrop, *California Women: A History* (San Francisco, 1987), 112.

14. Cynthia Harrison *On Account of Sex: The Politics of Women's Issues, 1945–1968* (Berkeley, Calif., 1989), 11.

15. According to Hartmann, the primary divisions between these groups was that of class, which took two forms. "One strain of WWII feminism focused on elevating women's general status, on gaining popular recognition of women as fully competent and equal participants in all aspects of public life. The other centered on issues of day-

to-day survival and sought to promote opportunities for women that would meet their basic material needs. The first emphasis was that of the elite, predominantly white, women's organizations and was manifested principally in the movement for female participation in policy making. The second focus was that of working-class women and embraced such issues as labor standards, child care, and domestic service." See Hartmann, "Women's Organizations during World War II," 319.

16. The study was conducted by the late UCB graduate student Catherine Schulten. Much thanks to Malca Chall of the Oral History Program at the Bancroft Library for sharing this information with me.

17. Excerpts from Annual Meeting Reports, 1942–45, Los Angeles League of Women Voters, Urban History Archives, California State University at Northridge (hereafter LALWV records).

18. From recollections of LALWV member Paula Menkin. Obtained from the Los Angeles League of Women Voters, 1995.

19. Stated by a Mrs. Griffith, Minutes, Hollywood Area, 1941/1942, box S/F14, LALWV records.

20. "Draft of Birthday . . . Introduction . . . Early History, Some Stories to Be Woven In," 2, obtained from LALWV, 1995.

21. LALWV minutes, Board of Directors, Urban History Archives, California State University at Northridge.

22. "The League of Women Voters, Triumphs and Traditions, 1920–1995," flyer, obtained from LALWV, 1995.

23. Board of Directors, minutes, 1943, LALWV records.

24. Ibid.

25. Miscellaneous papers, LALWV records.

26. Sherwood ended up working in the criminal justice system with Attorney General Evil Younger, a Republican, whom Elizabeth Snyder supported in a nonpartisan race and whose wife, Mildred, worked closely with Liz. Liz had asked Sherwood to head the field operations for his campaign and she continued to work with him for twenty years after years of volunteering (after her divorce, she needed to work). June Sherwood, interview by the author, Los Angeles, 1990, 13–16.

27. "Hilda Hoover McLean: A Conservative Crusade for Good Government," interview by Gabrielle Morris, 1977, pp. 19, 20, 28, Oral History Program, University of California at Berkeley.

28. Marguerite J. Fisher, "Women in the Political Parties," *Annals of the American Academy of Political and Social Science* 251 (May 1947): 87–93, quote on 93.

29. An Act to Amend Section 24 of the Direct Primary Law [1913] Relating to Party Conventions, Membership, and Organization of the State Central Committees and County Central Committees. In Effect August 27, 1937. *Statutes and Amendments to the Codes. California*, 1937, 52nd sess., chap. 407, p. 1363.

30. *Los Angeles Times*, 11 June 1956.

31. It is commonly assumed that because the law also allowed any member to attend as a proxy, women could send their husbands or other men to the convention, and

therefore women were mere figureheads. There is no evidence to support the claim that this was always or even often the case. See Dean R. Cresap, *Party Politics in the Golden State* (Los Angeles, 1954), 41.

32. California, Secretary of State, comp., *Officers and Members, State Central Committees* (Sacramento, 1934–62).

33. Fisher, "Women in Political Parties," 89.

34. Susan Hartmann, *The Home Front and Beyond: American Women in the 1940s* (Boston, 1982), 153.

35. Snyder's position impacted the perception of women as political actors in a number of ways. After her election to state chair, for example, a student newspaper at USC ran an article on the possibility of a woman running for higher office, such as the presidency.

36. Fisher, "Women in Political Parties," 90.

37. Royce D. Delmatier, Clarence F. McIntosh, and Earl G. Waters, *The Rumble of California Politics, 1848–1970* (New York, 1970), 308–13.

38. Mrs. Wyman Graham to Mr. Worth Brown, Worth Brown Correspondence, box 32, folder 1: 1939–40/1943, in Anne Bancroft Graham Correspondence, Special Collections, University of California at Los Angeles.

39. Letter to Earl Warren from Fred Weybret, chair of the Committee on Agriculture, regarding San Luis Obispo campaigning, 20 Oct. 1942, and regarding women's activism in Salinas, California Republican Assembly, #2039, box 32, folder 46, Special Collections, University of California at Los Angeles (hereafter CRA records). Women also organized in Central California. Agnes Jarvis of Fresno was field organizer and director for the area. See box 54, folder 2, CRA records.

40. Minutes of the Final Business Session of the Annual Convention of the California Republican Assembly, 7–9 Mar. 1941, box 2, folder 6, CRA records.

41. Ninth Annual Convention, Santa Barbara, 17–19 Apr. 1942, #2039, box 2, folder 6, CRA records.

42. Information on Tenth Convention, box 2, folder 7, CRA records.

43. Letter from Mrs. Wyman Graham, Brentwood, Calif., to Mr. Worth Brown, 19 Mar. 1939, Worth Brown Correspondence, box 32, folder 1: 1939–40/1943.

44. "Jean Wood Fuller, Organizing Women: Careers in Volunteer Politics and Government Administration," interview by Miriam Feingold Stein, 1977, pp. 26–37, Oral History Program, University of California at Berkeley.

45. Ibid., 53–55.

46. During the 1944 election the Hollywood Democratic Club "emerged as the most sophisticated partisan political organization Hollywood had ever seen. . . . it functioned as a full-fledged political organization . . . emerging as a decisive force. . . . In a state where the Democratic Party was still demoralized, the HDC instantly stood out. . . . Each of the HDC's nine endorsed congressional candidates won their primary contests, among them Helen Gahagan Douglas." Ingrid Winther Scobie, *Center Stage: Helen Gahagan Douglas, a Life* (New York, 1992), 134–35. See also Hope Chamberlain, *A Minority of Members: Women in the U.S. Congress* (New York, 1973), 182.

47. Numerous other non-gender-specific groups sent women as representatives. See "Organizations Present at Conference on Atomic Power," 3 Dec. 1945, California Ephemera, Hollywood Independent Citizen's Committee for Actors, Scientists, and Professionals, Special Collections, University of California at Los Angeles.

48. At the 1944 national convention, the year Douglas was elected to Congress, Porter presided over one of the resolutions committee meetings. "Julia Porter, Dedicated Democrat and City Planner, 1941–1975," interview by Gabrielle Morris, 1977, p. 41, Oral History Program, University of California at Berkeley.

49. Scobie, *Center Stage*, 134–35.

50. Robert E. Burke, *Olson's New Deal for California* (Berkeley, Calif., 1953).

51. Porter is not even sure that the Women's Division functioned as a real unit during the 1942 campaign. "Julia Porter," 41.

52. "Frances Mary Albrier, Determined Advocate for Racial Equality," interview by Malca Chall, 1977–78, pp. 140, 162–65, Oral History Program, University of California at Berkeley.

53. Ibid., 165.

54. Ibid., 140.

55. The interviewer, Malca Chall, was impressed: "As long ago as before World War II, then—and after—in the mid-forties, you were talking about this inside the women's clubs, the party clubs?" Ibid., 169.

56. It was around this time that women's ties to the major political parties began to take on more importance. Although the Democrats had established women's clubs as early as 1914, according to Jensen and Lothrop, women were not a significant force until the 1930s, and even then they were not necessarily encouraged to engage in party structure and policy making, except in token ways (*California Women*, 113).

57. "Elizabeth Snyder, California's First Woman State Party Chairman," interview by Malca Chall, 1977, pp. 40, 35a, Oral History Program, University of California at Berkeley.

58. Here the LALWV's interests coincided with Snyder's, for the LALWV also conducted a study of the working conditions at the plant.

59. Elizabeth Snyder, interview by the author, Los Angeles, 1990, 43.

60. Florence Clifton and Judge Clifton, interview by the author, Los Angeles, 1990, 10.

61. Loucheim quoted in *Los Angeles Times,* 12 Aug. 1956, sec. 4.

62. Other important factors were Betty Friedan's *Feminine Mystique,* published in 1963, and Title VII of the Civil Rights Act of 1964. See Leila J. Rupp and Verta Taylor, *Survival in the Doldrums* (New York, 1963); Jo Freeman, *The Politics of Women's Liberation* (New York, 1975), 52–53. It would be useful to profile women on all of the state commissions, trace their previous and subsequent activism, and discern if and where political party activism and gender and/or feminist consciousness combined or departed or were integrally linked. By analyzing California mainstream political party members, it is clear that a continuity exists between political participants of the 1930s through the 1960s and 1970s, and even into the present.

63. By the time many state organizations on the status of women were set up, a number of California female activists had overlapping memberships in several state and national voluntary associations while they were also in the vanguard of "professional volunteers" in mainstream party politics. Members and supporters of the commissions had been active for, in some cases, three or four decades. These groups provided continuity, advocating women's rights, and, later, the Equal Rights Amendment, over several generations.

64. Elizabeth Snyder and many of her cohort were leaders of the organization; Helen Gahagan Douglas was the honorary chairperson.

65. Democratic Women's Forum, flier, California State Democratic Party, Women's Division, California State University at Northridge.

66. Susan Ditz Robbins, *The California Democratic Party: A Twenty-Year Retrospective* (Sacramento, 1989).

67. Democratic Women's Forum, flier.

68. California Democratic Party, Women's Division, California State University at Northridge.

69. Florence E. Allen, "Participation of Women in Government," *Annals of the American Academy of Political and Social Science* 251 (May 1947): 94–103, quotes on 95 and 98.

70. The problem is complex because of the diversity of the participants. As Jensen and Lothrop write, "World War Two drew women to public life in a greater degree than ever before, but the variety of the experiences remained profound" (*California Women*, 160–61).

71. Bugbee, "Winners," 383.

Contributors

JACQUELINE R. BRAITMAN is affiliated with the Department of History and the Center for the Study of Women, University of California at Los Angeles. She publishes on women in California politics and is finishing a manuscript on the progressive reformer Katherine Philips Edson.

RONALD D. COHEN, a professor of history at Indiana University Northwest, is the author of *Children of the Mill: Schooling and Society in Gary, Indiana, 1906–1960* (1990) and the forthcoming *Rainbow Quest: Folk Music and American Society, 1940–1970*.

SARAH S. ELKIND is an assistant professor at the University of Wisconsin at Stevens Point. She is the author of *Cities and Water Politics: The Battle for Resources in Boston and Oakland* (1998) and is writing a book on the role of industry in twentieth-century resource policy.

WILLIAM ISSEL is a professor of history at San Francisco State University. He has published a number of essays, including "Business Power and Political Culture in San Francisco, 1900–1940," "Liberalism and Urban Policy in San Francisco from the Thirties to the Sixties," and "The Catholic Church and Organized Labor in San Francisco, 1932–1958."

KEVIN ALLEN LEONARD, an assistant professor of history at Western Washington University, has published essays in the *Western Historical Quarterly* and several anthologies. He is working on a book about the impact of World War II on race relations in Los Angeles.

ROGER W. LOTCHIN, a professor of history at the University of North Carolina at Chapel Hill, is the author of *San Francisco, 1846–1856: From Hamlet to*

City (1974; rpt., 1997) and *Fortress California, 1910–1961: From Warfare to Welfare* (1992).

LINDA HARRIS MEHR, director of the Margaret Herrick Library of the Academy of Motion Picture Arts and Sciences, received a Ph.D. in history from the University of California at Los Angeles in 1973 and has taught history and film courses at the University of Southern California and the University of California at San Diego. She is the author of *Motion Pictures, Television, and Radio: A Union Catalog of Manuscript and Special Collections in the United States* (1978), which she is currently updating, and numerous articles on archive holdings and library reference.

GARY R. MORMINO is Duckwall Professor of History at the University of South Florida. He is the author of *Immigrants on the Hill: Italian Americans in St. Louis, 1882–1982* (1986) and coauthor (with George E. Pozzetta) of *The Immigrant World of Ybor City: Italians and Their Latin Neighbors in Tampa, 1885–1985* (1987).

GEORGE E. POZZETTA was, until his death in 1994, a professor of history at the University of Florida at Gainesville. He is the coeditor (with David R. Colburn) of *America and the New Ethnicity* (1979), the editor of *Pane e Lavoro: The Italian American Working Class* (1980), the coauthor (with Gary R. Mormino) of *The Immigrant World of Ybor City: Italians and Their Latin Neighbors in Tampa, 1885–1985* (1987), and the author of numerous books in Garland Publishing's Immigration and Ethnicity Series.

PAUL RHODE, a professor of economics at the University of North Carolina at Chapel Hill, is the author of numerous essays on economics and economic history.

ARTHUR VERGE, a professor of history at El Camino College in Torrance, California, is the author of *Paradise Transformed: Los Angeles during the Second World War* (1993). He is working on a book about the popular culture of Southern California.

K. SCOTT WONG, an associate professor of history at Williams College, is coeditor (with Sucheng Chan) of *Claiming America: Constructing Chinese American Identities during the Exclusion Era* (1998) and has published essays in a number of journals and edited collections. He is working on a book about the impact of World War II on Chinese Americans.

Index

Typeset in 10.5/13 Minion
with Minion display
Designed by Dennis Roberts
Composed by Celia Shapland
for the University of Illinois Press
Manufactured by Thomson-Shore, Inc.

University of Illinois Press
1325 South Oak Street
Champaign, IL 61820-6903
www.press.uillinois.edu